GUY STANDING

The Politics of Time

Gaining Control in the Age of Uncertainty

A PELICAN BOOK

PELICAN
an imprint of
PENGUIN BOOKS

PELICAN BOOKS

UK | USA | Canada | Ireland | Australia
India | New Zealand | South Africa

Pelican Books is part of the Penguin Random
House group of companies whose addresses can
be found at global.penguinrandomhouse.com

Penguin
Random House
UK

First published 2023
001

Text copyright © Guy Standing, 2023

The moral right of the author has been asserted

Book design by Matthew Young
Set in 11/16.13pt FreightText Pro
Typeset by Jouve (UK), Milton Keynes
Printed and bound in Great Britain by
Clays Ltd, Elcograf S.p.A.

The authorized representative in the EEA is
Penguin Random House Ireland, Morrison
Chambers, 32 Nassau Street, Dublin D02 YH68

A CIP catalogue record for this book is available
from the British Library

ISBN: 978-0-241-47591-1

MIX
Paper | Supporting
responsible forestry
FSC® C018179

Penguin Random House is committed to a
sustainable future for our business, our readers
and our planet. This book is made from Forest
Stewardship Council® certified paper.

www.greenpenguin.co.uk

Contents

Preface

To linger over a drink, to lie in bed next to one's love, to strum a guitar or tinkle on the keyboard, to read or even scribble lines of poetry, to kick a ball a thousand times with one's son or daughter, to run around the boundary hoping to stop a ball – each of us has a long list of activities with which we would like to fill the unforgiving minutes.

Time is precious. As we go through life, we surely come to appreciate that, whatever we do, we should aim to create good memories of how we use our time. Using time wisely is a skill sometimes learned, too often not. Sadly, in our modern hedonistic and materialistic market-driven society, too few people have enough control over their time to be able to develop or exercise that skill. But how can we change that? Through a new politics of time.

Three time regimes have defined human history over the past two millennia: agrarian time, when the seasons and weather shaped how people used their time; industrial time, when the clock was in the ascendant and life was defined in blocks of time; and tertiary time, characteristic of today's economies based on services rather than manufacturing or agriculture, when time-use boundaries have become blurred.

All mainstream political agendas have had implicit positions on time. Many manifestos have included a commitment to reducing labour hours, for example. But an explicit politics of time has not figured in the narratives of political parties, and they have failed to give time freedom – freedom to direct one's own uses of time – the priority it deserves.

I began work on *The Politics of Time* just before the coronavirus pandemic struck the world, and it features prominently in this book. While many commentators have said it changed everything, it is more accurate to say that it accelerated changes that were already under way. But from early on it was clear that lockdowns and wage-subsidy schemes were producing new forms of inequality and new forms of social and economic insecurity, once again providing evidence that the politics of time must be understood within an explicit class-based perspective.

Many people work much more today than throughout most of human history, if you look at both paid and unpaid work. This is generating stress and illness on an epic scale. Revisiting John Maynard Keynes's essay 'Economic Possibilities for Our Grandchildren', written in the midst of the Great Depression, in which he predicted that one hundred years hence or by 2030 people would be working on average only fifteen hours a week, some commentators have identified the present malaise as the 'painfulness of readjustment between one economic period and another', to use Keynes's words. Journalist Suzanne Moore, in a perceptive article, suggests that culture and the arts should be guiding that readjustment, but implies that today they have largely lost the capacity to do so.[1] This, in my view, reflects the erosion of the 'cultural commons' in the recent era of rentier capitalism and the ideological knavery of austerity.

Nevertheless, the fact is that, nearly a century after Keynes made his prediction, it is nowhere near coming to pass, and we are most unlikely to achieve it. Indeed, my guess is that Keynes himself would never have considered reducing his work to fifteen hours a week. He liked work too much.

How then should we think about time in relation to the politics of time? Even the most authoritative philosopher of time, Gerald Whitrow (1912–2000), acknowledged that it was difficult to define. In Chapter 1 of his book *What is Time?* (1972), he recalls the quandary of a medieval priest, who said that so long as nobody posed the question 'What is time?', he felt he knew the answer, but if he had to explain it to someone, he had to admit that he did not know.[2]

The idea of time must have crystallized as humans learned of their own mortality and the cycle of reproduction. It is the human condition to recognize life's parting ways, as we come to appreciate and value time's seasons and passages and the moods of time passing. In 'All the world's a stage', the speech from Shakespeare's play *As You Like It*, we learn of the seven ages of man, and reading Shakespeare's lines on the subject at any age, we surely feel a tug on the emotions. This is not sentimentality. Most of us rush through time – our lives – with a lack of respect for what is passing.

Someone who lives to the age of eighty has a mere 4,000 weeks of life, according to the snappy title of a 'time management' book that came out in 2021.[3] That figure reminds us how precious every week is. And if a high proportion of those weeks is taken up by activities over which we have no control, we should be concerned, if not angry. And we should also be angry if government policies subject some groups in society to controls that we would not accept for ourselves.

I have long struggled with the subject of time, largely arising from discontent with the ideological capture of the concept of 'work'. I recall being invited many years ago to New York to participate in a conference of specialists on time-use surveys. As a young economist, I was no doubt expected to listen and learn. But after seeing table after table of detailed statistics on the time spent on numerous activities by people across the world, I asked the impertinent question, 'Have any of these surveys found anybody having an affair?' Of course, none of them had done so. No doubt the specialists were not amused. But the point is serious. When answering questions on time use, most of us will tend to report what we believe is the norm or what would be regarded as decent, responsible uses of our time. The plethora of statistics on how people allocate their time should be regarded as merely opening gambits. Indeed, even if we keep a diary, we probably rarely use time in the way we later recollect.

A famous debate was held in 1922 between the great physicist Albert Einstein (1879–1955) and the philosopher Henry Bergson (1859–1941), in which Einstein differentiated between 'psychological time' and 'physicist's time'. Thirty years later, he returned to this theme in an essay:

> But what about the psychological origin of the concept of time? This concept is undoubtedly associated with the fact of 'calling to mind', as well as with the differentiation between sense experiences and the recollection of these . . .

An experience is associated with a 'recollection', and it is considered as being 'earlier' in comparison with 'present experiences'. This . . . gives rise to the subjective concept of time, i.e., that concept of time which refers to the arrangement of the experiences of the individual.[4]

This brilliantly reminds us that our perception of time is always jumbled by experience itself and by cultural and social reinforcement. Nothing in time is linear psychologically, except possibly what we are doing in the present. Even then, emotionally and physically, we rarely use time solely on one activity.

This book considers these issues in terms of demands on time and the need for emancipatory policies to obtain more control over our own time or, more correctly, to reduce the control of time by unwanted outside forces. Put more fancifully, it is about the ontological pursuit of what the German philosopher Hegel (1770–1831) called 'the negation of the negation'. Thus, in the three regimes that have shaped time over the last two thousand years, the political struggle has been – or should have been – against the institutions and policies used to control the time of the mass of people in that period. Today, we need to understand what mechanisms are controlling our time, and we need a political strategy to overcome them.

The book also aims to revive the distinctions, established in ancient Greece, between work and labour and between recreation and leisure, and to encourage appreciation of the wonderful use of time in 'commoning' – shared and collaborative activity for the common good. As such, it is the concluding volume in a cycle of books that began in 2009 with *Work After Globalization: Building Occupational Citizenship*. Fortunately, the future has arrived, or at least it has in my imagination, as sketched in the final chapter of this book. It is for others to define the future after that. Freedom is never fully achieved, but that is no excuse for giving up hope.

We need a progressive politics of time as an emancipatory agenda. I hope that this book will contribute to its development. It remains to thank friends, colleagues and relations. In particular, I want to thank Maria Bedford, Isabel Blake, David Bollier, Sarath Davala, Bela Hatvany, Renana Jhabvala, Nic Lane, Peter Linebaugh, Kate Parker, Lord (Robert) Skidelsky, Danae Stratou, Martin Thörnkvist, Yanis Varoufakis, Alan Wheatley and Frances Williams, as well as Michael Hudson and the late David Graeber for sharing a lively podcast on rentier capitalism.

Time in Ancient Times

> It is not that we have a short time to live, but that we waste a lot of it.
>
> — Seneca, *On the Shortness of Life*, c. AD 49

Words, and the images associated with them, both shape and reflect the political imagination. They are rarely neutral. Time has been depicted in various ways throughout history, by representatives of interests that stood to gain by depicting it in a particular way. Roughly speaking, the distribution and the allocation of time to various activities have changed according to the dominant forms of production and have varied systematically by social class.

Homo sapiens must have understood from early in human evolution that time is precious. There is only a certain amount of daylight in a day, only a certain amount of time for seasonal weather conditions, and only a limited amount of time for men and women to grow, adapt, breed and age before they die, even if they are fortunate. Every culture has had some system to track the passing of time, and records of how time has been measured date back thousands of years.

The ancient Egyptians based their calendar on the cycles of the moon and the agricultural seasons. As far back as 2450 BC they followed a twenty-four-hour day and a civil calendar of twelve months, each with thirty days. A calendar year consisted of three four-month seasons, with an extra five days outside the regular months added at the end of the year.[1] Although that model of time measurement has been modified in various parts of the world, it has been broadly adhered to for over five thousand years.

Meanwhile, notions about days and weeks also evolved. The idea of a seven-day week, ending with a day of rest (Sabbath), is part of the creation myth that appears in the biblical Old Testament and was adopted by early Jewish society, which set the Sabbath on what we now call Saturday. However, the seven-day week did not become widespread until the fourth century AD after the late Roman Empire moved to the Jewish system from its eight-day cycle. The Romans named the days of the week after heavenly bodies – the sun, moon and known planets, which were called after Roman gods.

In English, the Roman names of days of the week persist in Saturn-day, Sun-day and Moon-day, though the subsequent Viking occupation of much of Britain accounts for other days being called after Norse gods – Tuesday (Tyr's day), Wednesday (Woden's day), Thursday (Thor's day) and Friday (Frigg's day).

The earliest law to make Sunday a day of rest was an edict issued by the Roman emperor Constantine the Great in AD 321, which stated that 'magistrates, citizens and artisans' were to rest from their labour 'on the venerable day of the Sun'. So, from early in human civilization, a day was set aside for doing no labour, although even then entitlement to rest was determined by class. Later, holy days became mixed with religious celebrations.² But it was not until the evolution of industrial capitalism many centuries later that the days of the week became firmly linked to the performance (or non-performance) of labour.

Time in Ancient Greece

We begin with ancient Greece, or rather with the Athenians. Their notion of the Good Life depended on how people used their time, and their idea of time was quite different from to-day's. We are the worse for that: despite the class and gender stratifications of Athenian society, their concepts of time and its uses deserve to be resurrected.

They essentially had three distinct concepts of time, each represented by a different god. Chronos was the god of linear time – past, present and future – and personified time's destructiveness, the ravages of time. Centuries later, he was depicted as Father Time, a harvesting scythe in hand, and this perspective can be found in numerous works of art and poetry. Think of Shakespeare's *Rape of Lucrece* (stanza 133):

> Misshapen Time, copesmate of ugly Night,
> Swift subtle post, carrier of grisly care,
> Eater of youth, false slave to false delight,
> Base watch of woes, sin's pack-horse, virtue's snare,
> Thou nursest all and murder'st all that are;
> O, hear me then, injurious, shifting Time!
> Be guilty of my death, since of my crime.

Yes, time, as personified by Chronos, is cruel. However, a second, kindlier god, Aion, embodied eternal time; eternity was associated with the afterlife as well as the reproductive cycles of time, such as the seasons. Centuries later, with their hubristic belief in permanent domination of the world, the Romans made Aion a symbol of the Roman Empire, though he eventually let them down when the empire crumbled.

The third god of time was Kairos, who represented opportunism, the moments when decisive action must be taken to achieve an objective. *Carpe diem!* Seize the day! This is an exhortation to be ready, to prepare, to allow enough time to be able to respond to chance. Kairos is the personification of opportunity, fleeting moments, which is why he has so often been depicted with wings on his feet. Again, Shakespeare caught the sense perfectly:

> There is a tide in the affairs of men,
> Which, taken at the flood, leads on to fortune;
> Omitted, all the voyage of their life
> Is bound in shallows and in miseries.[3]

In what some call the Anthropocene, a modern term for our current era in which humanity's quest to dominate nature has come to pose an existential threat to both humanity and nature, we may be in a new moment of Kairos. This has been defined as 'a passing instant when an opening appears which must be driven through with force if success is to be achieved'.[4] Writing today, it seems all too possible that the window of opportunity to halt runaway climate change and environmental destruction will close without the necessary and decisive action being taken.

Guided by the three gods of time, the citizenry of ancient Greece divided the use of time into five types of activity:

labour, work, leisure, play and *aergia* (contemplation). One type of activity they eschewed as beneath them. Labour was what was done by the *banausoi* (labourers and artisans), 'metics' (resident aliens) and slaves, in exchange for subsistence. In this carefully structured society, slaves did labour for their owners, while the *banausoi* produced goods and services for society. The manual labour done by the *banausoi* was thought by Plato and Aristotle to deform both body and mind, rendering such individuals useless for military or political duties.

To be a citizen one had to possess *arete* – that is, excellence or 'moral virtue'. Manual labour not only deformed the mind but those labouring spent too much time in labour, leaving no time for self-education. Labour, in this view, accustomed a man's mind to low-level ideas and absorbed him in producing the mere means of living. And since those who did labour did not have time to learn or know enough to have a say on political affairs, they were denied citizenship and the rights that went with it.

The origin of the word 'labour' indicates that it was something to be avoided. The ancient Greek word for labour, *ponos*, signified pain and effort, and had a similar etymological root to the word for poverty, *penia*. So, labour meant painful, onerous activity done in conditions of poverty. It was hardly something to be idealized. Indeed, as revealed in one of Socrates' exchanges, a poor free man would prefer casual insecure labour to long-term labour security, which was seen as restricting freedom and being close to *douleia* (servitude). So, better to be out of labour altogether but, if it was necessary, it was better to be in insecure labour.

This understanding of labour was to go deep into history. The English word 'labour' is derived from the Latin *labor*, signifying toil, distress and trouble. The verb *laborare* meant to do heavy, onerous tasks. The origin of the French word *travailler* has similar connotations, being derived from the Latin *tripaliare*, meaning to torture with a nasty three-pronged instrument.

Although Greek citizens did not do labour, they did do 'work' (*ergon*), which was activity in or around the home, among relatives and friends, and in the civic space. Work included care for family members, study and education, military training, creative activities (poetry, drama, music), jury service and participation in religious rituals. Its essence was captured in the idea of *praxis*, putting principles into practice, which included 'reproductive' work in maintaining and developing social structures and community ties as well as the physical, intellectual and emotional qualities of the individual. Work among relatives and friends was essential to strengthen civic friendship, or *philia*. It was a reproductive, regenerative and civilizing activity.

The distinction between work and labour was to shape the politics of time throughout our history. Every age has had its peculiarities about what does or does not count as work. The ultimate folly came in the twentieth century, when all work that was not paid labour became non-work. But the distinction between labour and work matters a great deal.

Not all languages have separate words, but many do. In English, the word 'work' shares the same root as the Greek *ergon*, meaning deed, action or occupation, which is decidedly different from 'labour'. In German, a similar distinction is made between *Werk* and *Arbeit*, and in Dutch between *werk* and *arbeid*. Russian has *trud* and *rabota*. In French, the nearest equivalent is between *activité* and *travail*. In Mandarin, the distinction is roughly between *gongzuo* (work) and *laodong* (labour). Yet most commentators ignore the distinction. We should insist on making it.

Leisure as *Schole*

As the political theorist Hannah Arendt (1906–75) elaborated in her inspirational book *The Human Condition* (1958), the ancient Greeks made another crucial distinction that modern economics has done so much to erase – between recreation, or play, and leisure. The Greeks recognized the need for all citizens to have ample time for recreation, including activities needed to restore the capacity for work: to recuperate, to be entertained, to eat, drink and shop, to exercise, and so on. The summit of recreation was embodied in the Olympics.

However, the Greeks kept recreation and consumption distinct from leisure as *schole*, a term that conveyed a combination of education and public participation (and from which the words 'school' and 'scholar' are derived). *Schole* also included attending public dramatic performances, as a way of learning and reinforcing the values of empathy and compassion. The great Greek tragedies and comedies were not just entertainment; they were a socially productive activity. The ideal of *schole* was time used to display what were regarded as the superior virtues – goodness and respect for truth and knowledge. The primary objective of the citizen was to maximize time for *schole*.

For the Athenians, this included maximizing the space, time and ability to participate in the life of the *polis*, in the *agora*, the public space or square, through the idea of *thorubus*, boisterous engagement in public discussion and debate. Socrates distrusted the written word because he believed words had to be explained, through discussion, to avoid or prevent misinterpretation. According to the philosopher Onora O'Neill, 'Plato tells us that Socrates was so worried by the written word's disruption of communication that he relied entirely on the spoken word . . . Socrates worried his words would go fatherless into the world, reaching sundry readers with nobody present to explain what was meant or to clear up misunderstandings.'[5]

A principle of *schole* was the use of time to exchange ideas collectively as the basis for ethical and political action. In a sense, the personal progress of Athenian citizens was measured in how much time they could devote to *schole*, particularly public action in the *agora*. Status depended on performance in the public arena. And this required putting time aside for deliberation and learning.

The citizen was not just expected to allocate a lot of time to public participation but was rewarded for doing so. In 451 BC, Pericles was the first to introduce payments for jury service. He argued that otherwise a poor citizen could not afford to spend the time on this work, which would run counter to deliberative democracy and leave the delivery of justice in the hands of the wealthy. He went further, in instituting a regular modest payment as a reward for participating in the deliberations of the *polis*.

Some years ago, I was invited to speak at an arts and

literary festival in Barcelona. Just before I was due to go on-stage, a TV producer ushered me into a studio to answer, without notice, a question asked of all the festival's keynote speakers: 'Besides Barcelona, which is your favourite European city?' I just had time to decide on one that epitomized a message I wished to convey in the ensuing talk. 'Paestum,' I said, to the bemusement of everyone in the studio. Asked for the reason, I said it was where the evidence of ancient deliberative democracy can still be seen.

Paestum was an ancient Greek city in present-day southern Italy dating from about 600 BC that was abandoned and left undisturbed and overgrown for hundreds of years until rediscovered in the eighteenth century, famously visited by Goethe. Besides the three majestic and well-preserved temples, the ruins include a tiered circle accommodating about 500 people that was the city's *ekklesiasterion* (citizens' assembly place) or, more probably, its *bouleuterion* (assembly place for a council of citizens that in ancient Greece ran a city's daily affairs). Before making judicial or political decisions, the 500 citizens on the council, selected using a randomization device called a *kleroterion*, were expected to listen to all points of view. Although Greek civilization was hardly egalitarian – women as well as *banausoi* could not be citizens – the *ekklesiasterion* or *bouleuterion* was a true symbol of deliberative democracy.

It was allied with the fifth use of time that the Greeks acknowledged and celebrated as part of the human condition. Thus Aristotle gave a special place to *aergia* – that is, laziness or idleness – seen as vital for the contemplation and deliberation needed for *schole*. As Arendt noted in her classic analysis of Greek thinking, abstention from certain activities was regarded as necessary to make time for a meaningful political life.[6] Indeed, Cato later coined the aphorism 'Never is [a man] more active than when he does nothing'.[7]

The sister concept is boredom. Most people do not like being bored. However, thinkers such as Archimedes, Isaac Newton, René Descartes and Albert Einstein have attributed some of their most profound ideas to periods of boredom.[8] Friedrich Nietzsche (1844–1900) thought likewise, noting that 'for thinkers and all sensitive spirits, boredom is that disagreeable "windless calm" of the soul that precedes a happy voyage and cheerful winds'.[9] Psychologists have also concluded that boredom is a more fertile mother of invention than necessity.[10] The philosopher Bertrand Russell (1872–1970) thought it was essential for children to be bored from time to time. But only the ancient Greeks made *aergia* a societal virtue.

Later, ideas of leisure soon blurred with recreation. For the mighty Romans, leisure was conveyed by the word *otium*, a use of time enjoyed by the nobility thanks to the labour of slaves. This was a regression from what the Athenians understood by *schole*. *Otium* signified the pure luxury of leisure, associated with hedonism, with pleasures of the flesh, with institutionalized idleness and relaxation. Undoubtedly, it contained elements of *schole*, of political engagement, but we should revive the ancient Greek distinction between recreation and public participation.

Disaffected with ostentatious displays of wealth and property, and political self-aggrandizement, the Stoics set a different, contemplative tone. Seneca, the best-known Stoic philosopher, captured the ethos of real leisure in his reflective writings, notably a moral essay in the form of a long letter to a friend, Paulinus, who held the high public office of superintendent of Rome's grain supply and may have been considering stepping down.

Written in about AD 49, when Seneca was forty-four, the essay has come down to us as *On the Shortness of Life*. It still resonates nearly two thousand years later. In it, he mocks those promising to take leisure time later, when it is too late, and those who are constantly preoccupied, lost in incessant activity. 'The preoccupied', he wrote, 'find life very short.'[11]

However, Seneca also recognized that leisure was a learning process. He advised that the way to gain time for leisure was to study all the great philosophers, thinkers of the past: 'Of all people only those are at leisure who make time for philosophy, only those are really alive. For they not only keep a good watch over their own lifetimes, but they annex every age to theirs. All the years that have passed before them are added to their own.'[12]

This sense of leisure as distinct from recreation and entertainment differs sharply from how leisure was to be shaped by capitalism and is consistent with the ancient Greeks' supreme respect for what the Stoics called the *vita contemplativa*. Again, in the quest for a Good Society, we should insist on making the distinction between leisure and recreation.

Philia: Civic Friendship and Care

Fellow citizens, why do you turn and scrape every stone
to gather wealth, and, yet, take so little care of your own
children, to whom one day you must relinquish it all?
— Socrates (attributed)[13]

A Good Society, as Aristotle emphasized, should include 're-productive' work: besides nurturing and caring, this should encompass regular, voluntary acts that help to maintain the community and reinforce empathy, strengthening *philia* or civic friendship. Citizens should put adequate time aside for acts of compassion, wanting well for the other person and able to put themselves 'in the shoes of the other'.

Ideas of civic friendship and citizenship overlapped with the idea of community, a word derived from the ancient Greek implying 'a sharing'. Community was *koinonia*, from the verb *koinoneo*, 'to share'. A community arises from groups doing a similar range of activities, from which they derive a sense of common interest.

A modern labour market and market society does not require civic friendship or community. In a sense, time-using activities involved in building, sustaining and reinvigorating a community stand in the way of labouring. They have no perceived value. But the ancient Greeks' division of time remains relevant to thinking on work, labour and leisure, even in the twenty-first century.

Foraging and Commoning

Another historical perspective on time dates from long before the ancient Athenians. Thousands of years ago, people in hunter-gatherer societies enjoyed what has been called primitive affluence. Of course, life in the long hunter-gatherer era was far from idyllic; it was often nasty, brutish and short, involving violent struggles for hard-won food.[14] Yet the amount of time devoted to work was minimal. Our distant ancestors did what was needed to achieve subsistence, and little more than that. They did not live with the fear of constant scarcity.

They had much more free time than workers in the materially far richer societies of the past two centuries. Anthropologists such as Marshall Sahlins, in his book *Stone Age Economics* (1972), and James Scott in *The Moral Economy of the Peasant* (1976), and before them Karl Polanyi in the neglected appendix of his classic book *The Great Transformation* (1944), have shown the absence of stimulated desire for material possessions. Absent, too, was external pressure to labour in order to meet perceived wants.

Foraging societies also practised demand sharing.[15] In early societies (a better label than the condescending 'primitive'), those able to gather the most normally shared their bounty with the less able. This limited any tendency for inequalities to emerge. It took thousands of years, and a class-based society, for 'possessive individualism' to displace 'natural egalitarianism'.

We cannot be sure whether demand sharing arose mainly from requests from needy recipients or offers from fortunate donors. At some stage, a more moralistic tone must have emerged, with notions of charity and a vocabulary and imagery appropriated by prospective donors. Demand sharing as a mechanism among rough equals requires balanced reciprocity understood as an integral part of the way of life, formalized or implicit. Perhaps it was a distributional principle that was also a form of community insurance, a survival strategy based on reciprocity between generations, which is best suited to compact, relatively small, closed communities. People work more to gain more in order to share more, in case at some future moment they need to receive from others.

This motivation to work is weakened when structured reciprocity is not feasible or is risky. Flashing forward to the twenty-first century, we can easily see that informal demand sharing and personalized forms of reciprocity are most unlikely to coexist with open market economies, flexible labour markets, fragile household relationships, and structural income and wealth inequalities. They must be either societally generated or replaced by a state-based set of mechanisms.

One feature of a demand-sharing system is asset sharing. Gifts are more likely to be given for a purpose other than wealth or property accumulation. If the purpose is for practical use rather than for property accumulation, it is easier for the recipient to pass the gift on later to somebody else. This will tend to reduce the price or market value, increase use of the gift and reduce the pressure to do more labour to gain more income to spend on gifts. Such recycling, in my mind, is linked to the generous African idea of *ubuntu*, the propensity to share time and gifts, which stems from a belief that a person's humanity is developed through their relationship with others.

The work done in demand sharing is best captured by the term 'commoning'. In traditional hunter-gatherer societies, possessors of a potentially scarce asset or a means of production would be asked to share it when or if they had no immediate need for it. This also applied to objects such as jewellery or clothing that would be gifted to others and then re-gifted within 'networks of mutual affection'.[16] Sharing and recycling define the archetypal commons.

A commons is an environment that, actually or potentially, provides amenities and resources for a defined community to access, use and – vitally – preserve and reproduce within agreed governance rules and through shared activities (commoning). It combines a sense of individualism – an individual right to use shared assets (known as a 'usufruct right') – with structured reciprocity and altruism. This tends to limit the degree and permanence of inequalities. All societies worthy of the name have some commoning activity but, as we shall see, it later came to be denigrated and made a residual use of time.

Until the Middle Ages, producing food and basic living needs depended largely on shared means of production and shared use of assets within communities. With the transition to agrarian economies, as farmers and landowners gained property rights, commoning retained its place, even though the amount of individualized or family work grew, and more people supplied labour, either as serfs or as free men.

The widening variety of work relations was matched by a diversity of property forms. However, the emerging system of common law rested (and still rests) on the fourfold distinction made in the late Roman *Codex Justinianus* (Code of Justinian, AD 529–34) between private things (*res privatae*), public things (*res publicae*), nobody's things (*res nullius*) and common things (*res communis*).

The Codex made it clear that private property rights were to be held in check. 'Nobody's things' were defined as those that had not yet been made the object of rights, perhaps because they had not been appropriated or had been abandoned. 'Common things' were, by natural law or heritage, held in common to humankind, including land, air, water, the sea and seashore. These were the commons, or 'common wealth'.

The mix of work, labour and commoning – the three forms of productive activity – has historically varied according to the predominant mode of production or the prevailing time regime. We can surmise that, in antiquity, for those who were not slaves or serfs, the amount of time allocated to work and commoning was much greater than the time spent in labour. But with the evolution of class-based society, for much of the population the ratio of labour to work increased.

Debt, Time and Jubilees

As far back as the Bronze Age, interpersonal debt – usually linked to harvests, illness and fluctuations in fortune – became normalized, providing the glue of society. It was to have a profound effect on how people allocated their time, then and throughout history.

Debt, as opposed to sharing, entailed new rules of reciprocity. If a debt could not be repaid, one or more of the debtor's family members was enslaved by the creditor until the debt was repaid. This often proved impossible, forcing family members to do unpaid labour and the debtor to do more work. From a societal point of view, it was a prescription for a small number of creditors first to accumulate economic power by having a large number of people in debt to them, and then to gain political power by turning their debtors into an army to overthrow the existing rulers.

The economist Michael Hudson has charted the rise of debt from ancient times, showing how rulers would periodically declare a debt jubilee, or mass debt cancellation or forgiveness, inspired by the fear that a small number of creditors could become an independent oligarchy.[17] Jubilee debt cancellations occurred regularly from about 2400 BC to AD 1100. The ancients knew the dangers of debt build-ups very well. As Aristotle noted: 'Many cities have constitutions that appear to be democracies, but they are really oligarchies.'[18] He predicted that every democracy would gradually become an oligarchy, as a wealthy elite turned itself into a hereditary aristocracy, lording it over the rest of society.

From those very early times, the state became an arena in which creditors, rulers and landowners vied for control. Rulers needed the peasantry to be free to give their time to serve in the army, to help build infrastructure or simply to work in order to pay taxes. But indebtedness gave control of their time to creditor oligarchs. Periodic debt jubilees redeemed the poor from debt bondage.

Jesus was at first seen as a messenger for debt forgiveness, exemplified by his ejection of the moneylenders from the temple, which incurred the hatred of the Pharisees and ultimately led to his crucifixion. But early Christianity gradually ceased to be about defending the interests of the poor as debtors. This was symbolized by one change above all others. The original English translation of a line in the Lord's Prayer that is common to all Christians was 'And forgive us our debts, as we also have forgiven our debtors'. This now reads, 'And forgive us our trespasses' (or 'sins', in some branches of Christianity). The first written form of the Lord's Prayer was in Aramaic, where the same word meant both debt, including non-financial forms of obligation, and sin. However, the encompassing reference to forgiveness of financial debts has now been lost.

What is the lesson of the history of debt for our narrative? When debt cancellations were common, individual debtors could expect to recover control over their time sooner or later. Once a creditor oligarchy gained control of the state, the poor's control over their own time could be lost for ever. But there is a wider political reality of current relevance. No government or monarchy has survived for long once a financial oligarchy of creditors has gained ascendancy.

Looking Back

If we are to make sense of how we use time today, we must recover the distinctions made by the Athenians, between labour and work and between recreation and leisure (*schole*). As a general point, we may say that labour is done for exchange value, for a wage, paid in cash or kind. This reflects the fact that labour is fundamentally instrumental, to gain income.

Work as self-directed activity involves not just the expenditure of time in a specific activity but also the pauses, reflections and inbuilt inefficiencies, the personal usefulness of working, in which pressure and motivation come from within ourselves. There is no space for that in labour, in jobs, in employment, where the economic imperatives of productivity and efficiency prevail. Dignity is an incidental by-product, not intrinsic to the activity itself, however decent the boss might be. It thus makes no sense to praise 'the dignity of labour',[19] as social democrats and communists have done in identifying with workers in their struggle for emancipation and against exploitation and oppression. And, of course, defenders of capitalism have been only too keen to praise labour.

Magna Carta and the companion Charter of the Forest, sealed together in London on 6 November 1217, clearly recognized the distinction between work and labour in restoring and protecting rights of access to the commons and its resources for 'free men' (commoners) to work and gain subsistence, which contrasted with the labour required of serfs and tenants on manorial lands. The Charter of the Forest was the first and perhaps only constitutional document ever to give proper meaning to the right to work. In many respects, it was far more radical and subversive than the Communist Manifesto of 1848 or the UN's Universal Declaration of Human Rights of 1948. Crucial for a real right to work, there must be a prior right to access resources (raw materials) and means of production (tools, machinery, and so on). This primary right was the core of the charter.[20] And implicit in that was a right – and a power – to refuse labour, because in extremis a free man could survive in the commons without subjecting himself to labour.

For a long time after that, at least in England, it made sense to differentiate work, as serving personal, family and communal needs, from labour, as a set of duties serving the perceived needs of those in positions of power. For the commoners of the time, the optimal situation was sufficient independence to avoid doing labour. Numerous local struggles marked attempts to avoid or minimize it.

What counted as work and labour evolved with the changing nature of production. The social division of labour and work also evolved, with men and women doing different activities and young men and women doing activities that differed from those typically done by their older counterparts. While these structural shifts were taking place, social thinkers were wrestling with weighty matters, trying to decide what activities could be classed as productive or worthwhile.

For the eighteenth-century Physiocrats, a group of mainly French thinkers writing in the 1760s, only agricultural labour counted as productive work, since in their view the wealth of a country depended solely on what was produced on the land. Similarly, the great contemporary Prussian philosopher Immanuel Kant (1724–1804) thought anybody providing what we now call services was unfit to be a citizen, a status that should be reserved for those who produced goods.

For Adam Smith (1723–90), generally regarded as the father of modern economics, services in general were unproductive. Writing in 1776, he dismissed as unproductive labour all occupations concerned with ethical and reproductive activity, including 'menial servants' and 'churchmen, lawyers, physicians, men of letters of all kinds; players, buffoons, musicians, opera-singers, opera-dancers, etc.'. Many modern admirers of Adam Smith would have been regarded by him as non-productive. For Smith, service providers did labour that 'perishes in the very instant of its production'.[21]

The tortured relationship between labour and citizenship crossed the Atlantic. In the early years of the United States, labourers were denied the vote and full citizenship precisely because they had no property, and government was seen as the defender of private property. It was only with the development of industrial capitalism that labouring became the desirable norm; Democrats and Republicans alike praise labour and ritually promise to create more of it, in the form of jobs. Still, prominent neoliberal economists, notably Nobel Prize winner James Buchanan (1920–2013), have supported government by property owners, portraying those reliant on labour as only fit to be governed.

By the early twentieth century, what counted as work reached new heights of stupidity. Only labour done for income was considered to be 'work', and only labour boosted economic growth, which became the yardstick of progress. Thus the work most women do more than any other, that of caring for their children or other relatives, ceased to be regarded as work. For the ancient Greeks, that would have seemed very odd. So, as the economist Arthur Pigou famously noted in his book *The Economics of Welfare* (1920), if a man hires a woman as a housekeeper, economic growth and employment go up. If he then marries her, and she continues to do the same work, economic growth and the number of jobs shrink. Our national income statistics perpetuate such nonsense to this day.

The romanticizing of labour is linked to the modern fetish in favour of jobs. Social democrats, communists and most Marxists have supported the idea that every able-bodied adult should do labour, have a job, and that society should aim for so-called full employment. Yet Karl Marx (1818–83) himself saw this as folly. He characterized labour as 'active alienation, the alienation of activity, the activity of alienation', because people did labour for the means of living but had no intrinsic interest in what they were producing.[22]

The idea of alienation in the context of labour has gone out of fashion. But for most people who are doing jobs, it is surely real. Doing labour in a job is to be in a position of subordination. This is why, in the twentieth century, the development of labour law was based on a presumption of the master–servant relationship, and why labour law is the only branch of law that presumes an unequal relationship.

The Jobs Fetish

Two concepts representing time and work took shape as capitalism evolved – the idea of occupation and the language of jobs. From early in human history, most people have defined themselves by what they do with their time, which has usually meant referring to their occupation. Even in ancient Rome, work and labour were organized in clearly defined occupations.[23]

In England, an array of standard surnames today stem from a person's identification by their occupation – smith, carpenter, tailor, farmer, and so on – and into the nineteenth century population censuses classified people by their usual occupation, not their labour-force status. The essence of occupation is a process, a narrative of personal development: learning, acquiring reputable abilities, rising status within a community and, crucially, increasing control over use of time. This is quite unlike defining oneself by a labour relationship. Yet in the twentieth century the language of jobs took over. Significantly, population censuses, those societal records of who and what we are at a particular moment, ceased to show the occupational profile of the population and now give only job and labour status.

In modern economics and modern political discourse, the number of jobs in existence at any moment, and the number added or subtracted in the recent past, are held up as signs of a country's economic success. People are told that being in a job brings happiness and social integration. Modern social democrats and liberals even propose that government should operate a job-guarantee scheme – discussed in Chapter 7.

Yet for thousands of years, and certainly for much the greater part of British history, being in a job was something to avoid if possible. Historically, the term 'job' had a negative connotation. The terms 'jobbing' and 'job work' were used to describe incidental bits-and-pieces labour. In a job, a person is expected to carry out a predetermined set of tasks and activities. A job is a teleological concept: its end is defined in its beginning.

By contrast, an occupation is ontological: a person is constantly evolving. An occupation suggests a career, a niche, occupying a space perceived as expanding and enriching. The word 'occupation' stems from the Latin *occupare* – to seize – and the sense of occupy as 'filling the mind' dates from the mid sixteenth century. Someone in a job will mostly do labour; someone with an occupation will over time do a lot of work that is not paid labour, even if part of that work is intended to improve their performance of labour, in a waged job or as a finite project or task.

In a 'jobholder' society, there are only weak relational links between jobholders; relationships are predominantly instrumental. In a society based on 'occupational citizenship', in which social, cultural, civil and economic rights are grounded in occupational communities, there are much stronger linkages, providing a federated sense of social solidarity. These are profoundly different ways of looking at life and the time patterns that comprise it.

The Alienation of Leisure

What has happened to the idea of leisure during human history is no less odd than what has happened to the idea of work. The old distinction between recreation and leisure has been lost. Both are needed for a Good Life, but the distinction is vital. Equating work with labour easily falls into linguistic and conceptual traps that block radical thinking. An example is the stylized fact cited in an article, 'Time for post-capitalism', by journalist Paul Mason in 2019:

> In the UK, the average annual number of hours worked per worker has fallen from 2,200 to 1,700 since 1950. There are 8,760 hours in a year. If we deduct 2,920 hours for sleep that means the average worker enjoys 4,140 hours of leisure time per year (presuming five weeks holiday, the weekend, bank holidays and other leaves-of-absence).[24]

The political right could cite that with pleasure – capitalism results in less work and lots more leisure. But had Mason used the ancient Greek concepts, he would not have made the same deduction. It is true that many more people are paid for less time in labour than used to be the case. But that does not mean they are doing much less work. As discussed later, many people must do much more unpaid work-for-labour (at and away from the workplace), work-for-reproduction (such as retraining), and work-for-the-state (form-filling), none of which is counted in official statistics.

Somewhere along the line of history, the idea of leisure lost its emancipatory meaning. At the turn of the nineteenth century, Thorstein Veblen (1857–1929) captured the spirit of his age in his classic book of 1899, *The Theory of the Leisure Class*. For him, the leisure class consisted essentially of the bourgeoisie. And the leisure was embodied in the time of the bourgeois wife, who was not expected to do any work or labour, but instead to indulge in conspicuous consumption. This conceptual slippage would have perplexed and alarmed the ancient Greeks and the Roman Stoics. As we shall see, it has come to define the existential malaise of the twenty-first century.

There is one other reflection on leisure as *schole* to take from this very brief review of the ancients' approach to time. The ancient Greeks' idea of citizenship, which has shaped the ideas of republicanism, is that freedom begins with having the time, energy, knowledge and opportunity to participate in political life outside the household. Freedom is not static, existing or not. It evolves through public action. For the Greeks, a citizen had to be able to escape from 'slavish occupations', and only through working in the company of others could freedom be developed. They made a distinction between hedonic and eudaemonic happiness, the former linked to consumption and pleasure-seeking, the latter to escape from labour, which granted the ability to be a public person.

Hannah Arendt was to take this perspective forward in *The Human Condition*. For her, freedom is disclosed in the togetherness of people deliberating and acting in concert. She deplored the jobholder society and what Jürgen Habermas was later to call civic privatism.[25] Unless collective action is promoted and supported by the state, citizens become merely consumers and labourers. The Greeks and Romans failed, with their sexism and slavery. But the goal of gaining leisure as *schole* has remained critical to the politics of time ever since.

The Agrarian Time Era

Ideas about time and how it is used have changed with the structure of the economy.[1] Broadly speaking, we may distinguish between three different time regimes: agrarian (in economies predominantly based on agriculture); industrial (based on manufacturing in factories); and 'tertiary' (based on services).

Our agrarian ancestors lived within numerous local time zones. The allocation of time was determined mainly by the weather and seasons, and activities in the commons played an integral role in daily and annual life. In agrarian society, it made no sense to think of standardized working weeks. When, where and how much work and labour were done depended on the vagaries of the climate for growing crops and rearing livestock. That is still roughly the case today in many rural societies, but it was the overwhelming norm for ordinary folk for many centuries.

In the hunter-gatherer period there was minimal 'work', but work increased in agrarian societies because of a new preoccupation with scarcity, the belief that there would not be enough to eat unless people cultivated and stored more food.[2] While scarcity was a reality for early agricultural communities, whose crops and livestock were vulnerable to weather, pests and soil degradation, this preoccupation grew with the expansion of cities and the need to feed a growing urban population. However, one should recognize the role of class as well, and the ability of class-based elites to contrive scarcity even amid abundance by denying a majority access to resources. In Europe, beginning in the Middle Ages, the main way elites did this was by enclosing common land and exploiting its resources for their private gain. A growing proportion of people were then forced to labour or to work more to produce commodities for sale, to pay landlords for what they had previously obtained from the commons for free. For hundreds of years, the owners of land and its natural resources wielded huge power, which they used to extract ever more labour. Those on the political right tend to argue that growing labour participation was driven by an appetite for new consumer goods, meaning that common people needed more money. In fact, people were being denied access to land and its resources; it was a period of contrived impoverishment.

That was why so much turned on the struggle over land ownership in the English Civil War in the seventeenth century. After the extensive enclosures of the Tudor period, the Stuart monarchy, mainly under Charles I, launched a fresh round of land enclosure, forcing the citizenry to provide more labour to indulge the lavish lifestyle of the king and his court, and to help the monarchy pay down its debts. Centuries of rising tensions finally erupted in the parliamentary rebellion, whose victory under Oliver Cromwell briefly slowed the labour extraction process.

Before the class-based enclosures, much of the land was commons, where local people (commoners) had rights of access and use, and much of the work was commoning.

Crafts, trade and what were mostly menial services took place in small towns and cities. However, commons traditions continued to prevail in urban areas until the late fifteenth century, when loss of access to commons sparked social unrest across England.[3]

The rhythm of agrarian societies was based on seasonal festivals, whose rituals and celebrations served to cement community ties. Doing regular work or labour during these often lengthy festivals was frowned upon. Otherwise, the demands on time varied, but they were modest demands. Just as fields were left fallow every few years to restore soil fertility, a certain amount of fallow time was needed to cope with sudden contingencies. A difference between farmer and hunter-gatherer communities was an orientation towards the future: planning, planting, harvesting, breeding, feeding, killing. But time horizons were mostly short and cyclical, in the expectation of unchanging patterns of life.

Daily time, meanwhile, was very localized. In medieval England, a person could travel from one village to another and find that the church bells tolled the hours earlier or later than the place they had just left. In a relatively small, island-based country, consisting largely of very loosely interlinked villages and towns, it took generations before the state could impose a national time system, finally achieved in 1880.

The notion of time in the daily or weekly sense was hazy. The sundial was ubiquitous, even guiding churches on when to ring their bells. However, it was hardly functional on rainy days or in winter! Hourglasses were essential. The ancient ideas of time – as a destructive force in the ravages of old age and as eternity – predominated. Only late in the era of agrarian time did time come to be perceived as linear and progressive, as measured by the clock and calendar, rather than cyclical and repetitive, as measured by the positioning of the stars and the revolving seasons.

A consciousness of the passage of time is said to distinguish humans from all other living creatures. Gerald Whitrow, the pioneering philosopher of time, said that 'we have good reason to believe that all animals except man live in a continual present'.[4] But as Whitrow and others have demonstrated, throughout the medieval period, cyclic and linear concepts of time were in tension. By the thirteenth century, while scholars influenced by astronomy and astrology focused on the cyclic concept, on recurrent cycles, the rising mercantile class, steeped in the money economy, focused on the linear one, of planning, postponed leisure, accumulation.

As long as the main source of power derived from the ownership of land, time was perceived as plentiful and was associated mainly with belief in an unchanging cycle of the soil and seasons. Once money became an independent source of power, emphasis shifted to the linear way of thinking, of time passing and time lost. In the fourteenth-century Italian city-states that were the crucible of mercantilism, all public clocks struck on the hour every hour of the day and night, which told people they should be doing something and counting the time in doing it. The notion that 'time is money' was on the march. Those public clocks signalled the end of the era of agrarian time.

Meanwhile, gradually, a third perspective had joined those of linear and circular time: the notion of time as 'progress', as 'improvement'. This perspective, which crystallized in the eighteenth century, was linked to the evolution of science and the foundation of industrial capitalism based on the application of scientific advances to productive systems. According to this perspective, we accumulate more knowledge over time; it is additive. A way of expressing this sense of time is that humanity has a 'social memory'. We build on the knowledge gained and distilled by our ancestors. But there is also what could be called 'social forgetting', loss of vernacular knowledge through disuse or rejection, or a crowding out of the old thinking by what is new and topical.

The Age of Commoning

In medieval England, considerable time was spent on commoning, in doing largely self-governed, shared activities within local communities. Commoning was not usually the main activity, let alone the only form of working in the commons. But the shared activities helped preserve the commons as a way of living and as a social organization.

Commoning took on a political character as well, such as the time-consuming activity of 'beating the bounds'. This was an annual collective exercise in which whole communities would walk round the boundaries of their designated common land, to ensure there had been no encroachment by landlords or others in the preceding year. The rounds usually ended with the proverbial 'cakes and ale'.

Commoning was relatively easy to sustain when the resources for producing subsistence – such as land, water, wood and clay – were abundant. But as elites and rulers started to arrogate land and resources for themselves, they forced more commoners to provide labour, often in the form of rent for the privilege of residing on land that had been part of the commons. Among the consequences were increasing pressure on commoning and increasing difficulty in managing the commons.

Commoning had to be defended. The most successful instance followed the civil unrest around the time of the French invasion of England in 1216 and the defeat of the invading army at the Battle of Lincoln in May 1217. This victory united the barons behind the English monarch, but the barons also recognized that the grievances of the common people needed to be addressed to ensure their support.

The outcome was the Charter of the Forest, sealed in November the same year in St Paul's Cathedral by the regent for the ten-year-old King Henry III (r. 1216–72) and a cardinal from Rome. It was the most emancipatory piece of legislation in British history, and the most long-lasting, repealed by a Conservative government only in 1971. The charter not only restored to the commoners the rights to common land illegitimately taken since the Norman conquest of 1066 by kings, barons, courtiers and the Church. It also enshrined for the first time the right to subsistence, through activity in the commons including commoning.[5] The commons thus acted as a social protection system, aptly described as 'the poor's overcoat'.[6]

The charter legitimized commoning as a systemic use of time, quite distinct from labour and from work. Work was done mostly in and around the home, which was as much a 'workplace' as a 'homeplace'. Commoning had a different rhythm, with time set aside for rituals an integral part. These embodied many socializing and solidaristic functions, including, when operating well, activities limiting inequalities and socio-economic differentiation.

Commoning has always been oriented to reproduction, to the cycles and preservation of life. Take the venerable art of coppicing, a classic activity in the commons. Trees are periodically cut to ground level, stimulating growth from the base for use later as firewood or material for fencing, flooring or tools. Coppicing is a reproductive activity, reflecting an understanding that tomorrow's subsistence depends on careful commoning today.

Because there is no intention to turn the tree into a commodity, coppicing typically encourages social constraint on personal behaviour. Excessive taking of branches would be criticized. But when a tree is turned into private property, rules and regulations are required because the probability that coppicing will be replaced by tree felling is much greater. It is then just a commodity, one tree among many for converting into timber for sale. Commoning helped preserve trees, especially old trees, which are particularly valuable for biodiversity.

Alongside foraging, another classic form of commoning historically has been gleaning, which was a way of maximizing use of the crop and minimizing waste. This was mainly done by women, as celebrated in the well-known painting *The Gleaners* of 1857 by Jean-François Millet, depicting three peasant women in a field bending to pick scattered stalks of wheat after the harvest. When the painting was first displayed, just nine years after the French revolutions of 1848, bourgeois critics complained it glorified lower-class work; they were not impressed by the implied tribute to the women's solidarity. However, to avoid over-idealization, it should be noted that gleaning is also an example of the gendered division of labour within commoning, with women doing some activities, men others. This remains a feature of commoning in artisanal subsistence fisheries, especially around coral reef flats and estuaries.[7]

Gleaning and other shared activities are expressions of the physical and emotional closeness of commoners to commons resources, reproducing sustainable relationships between nature and human activity. Normally, a commons is bound together by a body of knowledge, of what, how and why things should be done. To an outsider, some of the practices and norms may appear strange or counterintuitive. But, to the extent that they have stood the test of time, they fit into a complex, sensitive set of relationships that preserve the overall social system.

A commons has usually prioritized certain types of knowledge and ways of building or adapting knowledge on which actions are based. This 'situated knowledge' is inseparable from the knowledge holders and the local environment.[8] The commons embodies the social memory. At its best, it embodies a morality of time, shaping how time should be used, for the benefit of family, neighbours and the wider community.

Commoning includes activities that are about adapting and reinforcing indigenous knowledge, sometimes known as folk knowledge, which is important for monitoring strains on the environment.[9] Commons knowledge depends on relationships and connections between living beings and non-living entities, based on understanding cycles of interdependency. This was embedded in local communities in the Middle Ages, shaping the architecture of agrarian time. Such knowledge systems might have held back 'progress' but they

were the means of preserving social reciprocity and reproduction of both nature and the community.

Particularly from the fourteenth century onwards, major
events weakened traditional commoning. Most influentially,
the Black Death or bubonic plague of 1346–53, which may have
killed a third or more of England's population, hastened the
demise of feudalism and triggered an accompanying transformation in how commoners used their time. Peasants demanded
better conditions in any labour they were required to perform
and payment in cash rather than in kind, such as a share of the
harvest, or an allocation of firewood, with rent also paid in cash
rather than labour service. All this eroded commoning.

Because of its leisurely character, in which social, economic and cultural activities interacted and blended, commoning was readily criticized as a form of idleness by keen
apostles of the emerging capitalism, while the rural commons
were portrayed as zones of wickedness and debauchery. One
seventeenth-century observer sneered that forests were

> so ugly a monster as of necessity will breed . . . more and
> more idleness, beggary and atheism, and consequently
> disobedience to God and the King . . . wherein infinite
> poor yet most idle inhabitants have thrust themselves,
> living covertly without law or religion, 'rudes et refractori'
> by nature, among whom are nourished and bred infinite
> idle fry, that coming ripe grow vagabonds, and infect the
> Commonwealth with most dangerous leprosies.[10]

It was around this time that the terms 'commons' and 'commoners' lost their previous dignifying, universalistic character and became associated with being lower class and

inferior, which contributed to a delegitimation of popular political participation.[11] By the Tudor era, commoners were expected to know their place and do jobs for employers, as the way to uphold the 'Commonwealth'.

But commoners did not give up meekly or silently. All the great social revolts and protest movements throughout British history can be ascribed to defences against loss of commons and commoning. They include the Peasants' Revolt of 1381, whose demands included an end to serfdom and oppressive labour laws, and the 'camping time', or Kett's Rebellion, of 1549, almost spontaneous occupations of land perceived to be commons, akin in some ways to the Occupy movement of 2011, but with rather more tragic outcomes.

Then there was the Western Rising of the early seventeenth century, the Levellers of 1648, the Diggers of 1649, and the 'blacking' protests of the early 1720s against enclosure and encroachment of the commons, which so traumatized the elite that they made the blacking of faces a capital crime. Perhaps most celebrated of all were the Chartists in the nineteenth century, whose democratic demands – universal male suffrage, secret ballots, abolition of the property requirement to become a member of parliament – seem so mild today. These and other protests were the only form of political action available to commoners, who lived in a society that was not remotely democratic and was controlled by and for a landholding elite.

The relentless marginalization and demonization of commoning went with the almost total disappearance of the very word 'commoning' in the English lexicon. While we should not over-romanticize commoning, or the flexible mix of time uses that was often involved, the most relevant point for discussion of today's politics of time is that the emerging capitalist system sought to suppress both commoning and work that was not labour.

Even in the sixteenth century, the upper classes waged a societal campaign against the enjoyment of times of idleness by low-income people. They started to chip away at the previously large number of holy days and saints' days linked to the liturgical calendar of the Catholic Church, many of which also marked seasonal changes such as planting and harvesting times and were celebrated with singing, dancing, playing games and feasting. Failure or refusal by the lower classes to do labour was also castigated as vagabondage or idle wandering, leading to the passing of the first Vagabonds Act in 1531. This described 'idleness' as 'the mother of all vices' and dictated that those found guilty of vagabondage should be whipped and 'put to labour'.

Subsequent Vagabonds Acts were even more vindictive. The most severe, passed in 1547, mandated that for a first 'offence' a person was to be branded with a V and subject to two years of forced labour, and for a second offence punished by death. Over 100,000 people were hanged in the space of just a few years. Most of the population was forced to 'want' labour. Wanting to labour was clearly not a natural human impulse.

While this was a brutal feature of the early evolution of industrial capitalism, later apologists did their best to find an intellectual justification for it. The founder of modern thinking on the alleged supremacy of private property rights, John Locke (1632–1704), claimed a moral justification for what he openly acknowledged as the theft of the commons by a minority, because it enabled increased agricultural output. Others welcomed land enclosure as restricting independent thought by the commoners, who would reject the social power structure.

Symbolically, Robert Walpole (1676–1745), Britain's first and longest-serving prime minister, set mantraps in Richmond Park near London, enclosed as a hunting park in 1637 by Charles I, to capture and mutilate any desperate commoners breaching the enclosing walls. This both set an example and epitomized the eighteenth-century war against commoning, a long-drawn-out campaign to change how people used their time. It was a deliberate strategy by ruling elites to make and keep the lower classes poor so that they had to labour to survive.

Arthur Young (1741–1820), an influential agriculturalist who became the first secretary of the Board of Agriculture, asserted in 1771 that 'everyone but an idiot knows that the lower classes must be kept poor, or they will never be industrious'.[12] He advocated further enclosure of common land and the mass settlement of the indigent poor on waste land nearby. This ideological posture gave rise to the widely repeated dictum that workers should be kept poor so that society could become rich.

Among the prominent thinkers who shaped such pro-capitalist attitudes to labour was French philosopher and mathematician René Descartes (1596–1650). Since humans were the only species with minds, he argued, only when they were separated from the land and from attachment to nature would they develop their human quality. Otherwise, they would indulge in bodily pleasures, living like mindless animals!

Here, we have a narrative of a strategic reshaping of time: more people forced to focus almost exclusively on labour, with less time for commoning, informal leisure, reproductive work – care for family, home, self and community – which became increasingly domesticated, and less time for passive recreation in which to regain the required energy for intensified labour.

At all stages, the upper classes used the legal system to penalize the poor who were not doing labour and justified these penalties in moral terms, with the enthusiastic backing of establishment religion, always the servant of the state. It took much longer to convince those not doing labour that being in a job was the source of happiness and joy, and that to be without a job was a source of unhappiness and 'scarring'. That sophistry did not appear until well into the twentieth century.

Working Time in Occupational Guilds

Of course, not everybody lived and worked in the countryside in the agrarian era. For hundreds of years, going back at least to ancient China, urban working life was shaped by several types of guild – merchant guilds, occupational guilds and religious or communal guilds. The English word stems from the Anglo-Saxon verb *geld*, meaning 'to pay or to contribute'; the noun meant an association of persons contributing to a common set of purposes.

Some anthropologists have traced the origin of the guilds back to the last ice age, which ended around 11,500 years ago, and the very early traditions of long elaborate episodes of feasting, which reinforced religious and kinship structures. The sharing of a common meal has been a universal feature of guilds across the world and persists in the City of London guilds into the twenty-first century. Another universal feature was paying communal dues, enabling a form of risk pooling. In ancient Greece, the near equivalent of a guild was the *eranos* – originally meaning a meal or banquet to which all the diners contributed – founded on principles of mutual aid, with monthly meetings.

In the Middle Ages there were numerous synonyms for the term 'guild', including 'fraternity'. It conveyed a sense of Aristotle's *philia* – civic friendship – and the *convivium* (literally 'a feast', from which the word 'convivial' is derived) described by the Roman historian Tacitus in reference to the voluntary bodies known as *collegia* that operated in the late Roman Empire. These *collegia opificum* (trade associations) generated the idea of colleges, initially guilds of students, which in turn led to the first universities at Bologna (1088), Oxford (1096) and Paris (1150).

All these terms suggest that economic activity in guilds – work and labour, as well as commoning – was accompanied by social and even political functions. Members of these essentially self-regulating and self-policing bodies were expected to allocate part of their time to work that was not directly productive and which blended into leisure and recreation. Indeed, if someone did not fulfil those functions, they risked suspension or even excommunication from the guild. Much of the quasi-political activity occupied a lot of time and often took the form of organized leisure, in the Greek sense.

The social activities and the uses of time within guilds aimed to foster collective respect for standards of excellence in the work being done, while legitimizing and reinforcing certain ways of behaving, including what was acceptable 'competition' between members. The guilds acted like a commons and often promoted commoning in the form of shared activities.

Merchant guilds – whose modern near-equivalents are chambers of commerce – facilitated international trade over a period of several hundred years. They offered insurance for their members and for those with whom they traded. They helped enforce contracts, even to the extent of making themselves corporately liable for debts incurred by members. There were commercial reasons for all this, but as self-regulating institutions they imposed considerable demands on the time of their members – a form of commoning.

However, it was the occupational guilds that shaped occupational practices and communities to this day. They usually operated as a hierarchy of master craftsmen, journeymen and apprentices, with young apprentices aspiring to become journeymen and then master craftsmen. Masters employed journeymen, typically on short-term contracts or on contracts that were expected to be short term. Hence journeymen generally mixed labour and work while waiting for an opportunity to become masters, which depended not only on their own skills and experience but on openings in the restricted community of master craftsmen.

The guilds were self-governing quasi-monopolies, with state-granted entitlement to collective property and with designated legal privileges. While not democratic in granting every member equal voting rights, decisions on standards, practices and discipline were usually made by majority vote from the ranks of the master craftsmen.

Young men entering the craft community were obliged to spend a long period of apprenticeship, while 'grandfathering' protected the privileges of older master craftsmen beyond their 'sell-by' date. This way of distributing income helped to preserve the community. The older members performed rituals of governance and oversaw the guild's 'reproductive' social and political activities, a form of commoning that had a use value, within the occupational community and in society.

Guilds reached their peak of political and social influence in fourteenth-century Florence, when the twenty-one registered guilds provided members of the city's governing council on a rotating basis. Guild members were expected to devote considerable time to governance activity, both inside the guild and in the wider political community. Just as work and labour blurred into each other over the course of a person's life and career, so work, commoning and the Greek idea of leisure overlapped.

Between about 1150 and 1400, guilds represented the main way of organizing work in European cities and towns, loosely based on associations of rough equals, a *universitas*. They were part of the elaborate architecture of the state. Among their functions was maintenance of work quality, setting minimum standards for their products and services. They thereby fostered transparent exchange, while determining prices and wages according to the guild's reputation for quality. They also provided social protection, extending credit to members, providing mutual insurance, aiding members in legal cases, helping the children of members to afford apprenticeships and dowries, and helping to pay for marriage and funeral costs, among many other functions.

Guilds operated a system of incentives and sanctions. If members contravened the rules or failed to meet expectations, perhaps by delivering poor service or not repaying debts, the guild imposed penalties that ranged from public reprobation to expulsion. It is relevant to modern debates about labour regulation that a guild's rules could not supersede common law; the collective interest of the occupation could not override the rights of individuals set by the legal system. The guilds were not a state within a state.

It would be wrong to characterize guilds simply as market manipulators and social-protection bodies. They also played powerful religious and cultural roles. At their peak, they were a channel for the pursuit of religious salvation and eternal life. They were part of societal management, acting to help maintain social discipline, piety and socially responsible behaviour, with rituals to encourage sober dedication. They also helped to limit labour time by requiring their members to observe religious holidays and to participate in bonding social ceremonies.

Guilds may have limited economic growth by constraining competition, but they helped preserve society. Following the Black Death, at a time when families were shattered and the Church was impoverished, they fulfilled a fictive kinship role, helping to sustain families and individuals through a pandemic crisis. Such periods induce a sense of social reciprocity, giving help today in the expectation of needing it tomorrow. And the threat of pandemics at that time may explain the emphasis placed on righteous living and moderation. Social responsibility was vital: survival of the community depended on social solidarity. The guilds gave associational protection in an era of state retreat.

The guilds also helped define the class structure of pre-industrial societies and did so in ways that were to remain relevant to this day. In Florence, seven 'major' guilds represented what we would call professionals, such as lawyers and doctors, while fourteen 'minor' guilds represented artisans, or craftsmen, such as stone masons, blacksmiths and shoemakers. Although between them guilds dominated political life, about three-quarters of the city's population were not in guilds. These were the labourers, doing what we would call jobs.

An intriguing feature of the Florentine structure was the large amount of time that guild members were expected to devote to politics. The city government was run by nine nominated guild members, six from the major guilds, two from the minor, and one chosen to be the city's 'standard bearer', its senior magistrate and custodian of the city's banner. All were elected for periods of two months, during which they had to live away from home and devote most of their time to administrative matters.

Work and *schole* – political participation – were integrated, institutionalizing a sense of social solidarity. The closest modern analogy is jury service, a practice that goes back to the Athens of Pericles. Regarded then and now as a citizen's duty, it could be called a form of commoning, a shared activity representing commitment to the communal interest.

One way of looking at the norms of that time was that an initial period of labour, often for minimal wages, was the price an apprentice or artisan paid in order to qualify for a life of work. For lower-class women, periods of labour were often a precursor to a life of work in the home, although many had to continue doing labour all their lives.

Artisanal practices were another part of the pre-industrial structure of time use. Artisans devoted much of their time to develop, apply and refine skill in producing something useful, usually utensils or items from the decorative 'minor' arts such as ceramics or glassware. The time used in work by artisans was partly determined by the individual and partly by the status that individual had in the modest hierarchies that existed in most occupations, whether the artisan was working for a master or independently as a journeyman.

The word 'artisan', borrowed from the French, comes from the Latin *artire*, 'to instruct in the arts'. It also has a Japanese equivalent that captures the essence very well. The ancient Japanese word for artisan or craftsman was *shokunin*, which also implied having a pride in one's work, not only in technical skill but in attitude and social consciousness, an appreciation that the work had real value for potential customers and for society.

As in other cultures, for the *shokunin*, work blended into forms of time-using social activity that reflected bonds between nature, means of production and the community of activity. On New Year's Day, sharpened and cleaned tools were put in a container or box (*tokonoma*) and two rice cakes and a tangerine were placed on a sheet of rice paper on top of each toolbox.[13] The ritual honoured the tools and expressed gratitude for having been able to perform the work.

The guilds were weakened by the Reformation and by Protestantism. The emerging industrial capitalism was incompatible with their values and their uses of time. They were largely suppressed in England in the 1530s and 1540s, although some were allowed to continue with payment of large sums to the monarch, and some professional guilds were to make it through into the twenty-first century. In France, they were banned during the Revolution in 1791, and Napoleon disbanded them in countries occupied by the French army. The Napoleonic Code abolished guild controls, setting up bourgeois rights to establish businesses and free trade across continental Europe. The old order of integrated work, labour, commoning and leisure was relegated to the margins.

The guilds persisted, to some extent. Their privileges were formally abolished in 1835 in Britain as the drive for a laissez-faire market society accelerated. They were also abolished in Austria, Germany and Italy in the nineteenth century, and in Russia and China after revolutions in the twentieth century. But it should not be forgotten that for hundreds of years they shaped the way time was used, when the values of work and commoning held sway over the dictates of labour.

How Work and Labour Evolved

In the Middle Ages, social thinking about work was shaped partly by religion, but also by philosophers and political and economic thinkers. In the heyday of feudalism and towns built around guilds, it made little sense to separate work, labour and commoning. They formed an integrated whole. But with the coming of agrarian capitalism and early industrial capitalism, scholars started to differentiate between 'productive' and 'unproductive' activity.

In feudal society, most labour was done by the serfs, just as in ancient Greece labour was done by the slaves and metics (resident aliens). Free men did as much as they could to avoid doing labour, although young men typically went into ill-paid apprenticeships that lasted for years, and for much longer than necessary, to learn their trade.

The mainstream attitude to work and labour changed dramatically during the eighteenth and early nineteenth centuries, linked to the spread of what the German sociologist Max Weber (1864–1920) called the Protestant ethic in his influential book *The Protestant Ethic and the Spirit of Capitalism* (1905). This was based on the belief that diligent hard work and labour were God's calling, to be done for their own sake and for displays of virtue within one's family and community, not for profit per se. But 'the spirit of capitalism' of Weber's book title came to predominate. Gradually, the promotion of 'disinterested work', done without concern for the output, was overtaken by the interests of those exploiting the people doing hard labour.

The man who most represented the transition between work as part of life, to gain the basic necessities, and labour as the centre of life was the American polymath and statesman, and one of the Founding Fathers of the United States, Benjamin Franklin (1706–90).[14] Described by Weber as embodying the spirit of capitalism, Franklin dismissed idleness as 'the Dead Sea that swallows all virtues'.[15] And despite calling himself 'the laziest person in the world', he was one of the most inventive. Among his abiding contributions to humanity, he invented bifocals, the Franklin stove and the urinary catheter, and was one of the most important diplomats in history.

In 1784, he wrote to a friend: 'If Every Man and Woman would work four Hours each Day on something useful, that Labour would produce sufficient to procure all the Necessaries and Comforts of Life.'[16] However, those fortunate enough not to have to use all their waking hours trying to procure life's necessaries had a duty to be productive with their time. He carried around a list of thirteen virtues by which he would judge his daily conduct, one of which was 'industry', meaning 'lose no time; be always employ'd in something useful'.[17] He made daily resolutions, allocating blocks of time each day for work, meals, chores and, towards the end of the day, 'enjoyable distraction'. This was a mechanical lifestyle for a mechanical age.

In his widely read *Poor Richard's Almanack*, published yearly from 1732 to 1758, he extolled the need for hard work, asceticism and saving, and scorned sleep, opining: 'How much more than is necessary do we spend in Sleep, forgetting that the sleeping fox catches no poultry, and that there will be sleeping enough in the grave.' For good measure, he added: 'Sloth, like Rust, consumes faster than Labour wears.' Yet he chose to retire at the age of forty-two, when he took on a partner to manage his printing business, priding himself that 'by the sufficient tho' moderate fortune I had acquired, I had secured leisure during the rest of my life, for philosophical studies and amusements'.[18]

Franklin represented the evolving rationalization for labour in the transition from agrarian to industrial time. Shortly after his death, a crucial development took place in the United States: the mass production of clocks. The price of watches had already fallen to the point where British and American artisans could afford them as status symbols. However, in 1816, the American inventor Eli Terry received a patent for a low-priced wooden clock that revolutionized the clock-making business and made the possession of clocks and watches almost universal.[19] This ushered in the age of industrial time and a profound restructuring of work, labour, leisure and recreation.

As commoning was squeezed and as independent work was made harder to sustain and less remunerative for many, reliance on wage labour grew. This had tragic consequences. A growing number of families were unable to support those who could not labour. Many elderly and disabled people came to feel they were a burden on their children and grandchildren.

As a result, the eighteenth and nineteenth centuries saw the indigent pushed out to depend as well as they could on parish relief, which was stretched and mean-spirited and usually resulted in the early death of those who sought it. This was also the period that saw the institutionalization of the infamous workhouse, foreshadowing the modern state, where mainly elderly rejects spent their last years labouring in abject conditions, a visible disciplinary warning to others that they must do labour or face the same fate.

Analogous to today's 'deaths of despair', many older people turned to suicide. During the eighteenth century, the over-fifties may have accounted for 40 per cent of recorded suicides, twice their proportion in the general population.[20] Suicide was interpreted as an act driven by medically rooted 'insanity'. But for many it was more about time. Their time was worthless, socially and demographically. In opting to shorten their lives, they took their residual time with them. Had commoning been preserved, had enclosure and privatization been reversed, had independent work been fostered, dependency on labour would not have become the sole means of survival. But industrial capitalism was being built on jobs and labour, and those unprepared, unable or unwilling to devote their time to labour were consigned to history.

The shift from work to labour, and the erosion of people's capacity to combine work with commoning, thus started in the countryside. And it was given huge impetus by the introduction of the Speenhamland system of poor relief that began in the eponymous Berkshire village in 1795 and spread rapidly to other rural areas of England. This scheme gave modest income support from the parish to the landless poor but only if they remained in the parish and laboured for paupers' wages for local landlords. This type of conditional wage subsidy was to stay as part of the armoury of capitalism right into the twenty-first century, in the form of tax credits. But at the time, it served a particular purpose, inducing more labour when there was a reluctance to do so, at a price that was extremely advantageous to employers.

In 1832, a royal commission recognized that this had led to 'universal pauperization'. Landlords and employers had been able to obtain full-time labour, knowing that the low wages would be topped up by means-tested benefits and that the poor could not leave the area. But the Speenhamland system was ended for a more structural reason. As the nineteenth century advanced, owners of the mills, factories and mines in and around urban areas favoured an influx of rural workers to provide them with cheap labour. Marking the end phase of the agrarian time regime, the Speenhamland system was a preparation for creating a surplus rural population that, following the 1834 Poor Law Amendment Act, would be released into the growing mill towns and industrial centres.

CHAPTER 3

Industrial Time:
The Triumph of Labourism

Although putting dates on social and economic change can be arbitrary, the turn of the nineteenth century can be said to mark the transition to the industrial time regime. Its defining feature was the division of life into distinct blocks of time. Time spent in independent work and commoning was squeezed and diminished, while time in labour sharply increased.

The status and role of commoning had already been shrinking, but it had remained an important use of time, giving a semblance of security to lower-class families and communities, particularly to women and children. Independent work was still preferred to labour and was still for most people the mainstay of their income, status and community integration. This was to change, however, in the first decades of the nineteenth century.

The beginnings of the industrial time regime can be traced to the achievements of a self-made textile industrialist, Richard Arkwright (1732–92), who is often described as the 'father' of the modern industrial factory system. While he is best known for introducing the water-powered spinning frame, a more lasting legacy was his development of the factory system and the rigid labour-time arrangements underpinning it, initially in his cotton spinning mill at Cromford in the Derbyshire Dales, which was chosen for its good supply of fast-flowing water.

He instigated two overlapping thirteen-hour day and night shifts six days a week. Bells were rung each morning at 5 a.m. and again at 5 p.m. to announce the beginning of each shift, and the factory gates were shut an hour later at 6 a.m. and 6 p.m. respectively. Any worker not inside by the allotted time was excluded from the factory and lost two days' wages.[1] Arkwright encouraged weavers with large families to move to Cromford so they could supply more labour as a family, with the men weaving at home and the women and children doing labour in the factory. By the time he died, nearly two-thirds of all those working in his factory were children. Employees were given a week's unpaid holiday each year, on condition that they stayed in the town. In effect, he set up the precursor of the company town that became widespread in the nineteenth and early twentieth centuries.

Arkwright was an important influence on (though not a member of) the Lunar Society, a club of like-minded scientifically inclined men who helped shape the industrial time regime of the ensuing century.[2] Set up in Birmingham in 1765, its core members included Matthew Boulton (1728–1809), whose metal-working Soho Manufactory was at that time the largest factory in the world; his business partner James Watt (1736–1819), inventor of the steam engine; Josiah Wedgwood (1730–95), the pottery manufacturer; and Erasmus Darwin (1731–1802), who anticipated the theory of evolution, though it was his grandson Charles who developed the fully fledged version. Among those who corresponded with or visited the club were Thomas Jefferson (1743–1826) and Benjamin Franklin.

This distinguished group held regular meetings to discuss how to harness new ideas in science and technology to speed up and automate production, which they then put into practice in their own and other people's businesses. Thus Boulton, working with Watt, installed hundreds of Boulton & Watt steam engines in factories around Britain, enabling widespread mechanization. This made possible the Industrial Revolution, based on industrial time. The machine age was to be the age of the factory system, and a shift to mass production dominated by capitalist entrepreneurs, often linked to entrepreneurial inventors. It was subsequently bolstered by financiers who, by the late nineteenth century, had become masters of the universe, on both sides of the Atlantic.

As with other transformations in the way people allocated their time, the spread of machines and the new mode of production met with resistance, notably from the Luddites. However, a historical apology is owed to the mythical Ned Ludd (also known as Captain, General or even King Ludd), whose name is associated with the riots and the smashing of weaving machines by hitherto self-employed weavers that began in 1809.[3] Ever since, the word 'Luddite' has been bandied about as a pejorative term to imply opposition to progress or technology in general.

In fact, as their pamphlets and actions made clear enough, the Luddites were mainly against the disruption and destruction of a way of living and working, not against machines per se. There had been machine-smashing riots before – in 1779, for instance, Arkwright's cotton mill was burned to the ground – so the Luddites were not the first. And they were selective, even to the point of breaking machines in factories owned by capitalists known to be particularly exploitative while leaving those of others intact. Many of the machines they destroyed had been in existence for generations, such as the power loom and the gig mill (which raises a nap on cloth).[4]

Weavers previously had an integrated life based on independent work in or near home coupled with commoning, perhaps with seasonal or occasional labour. That time pattern was brusquely destroyed by the shift to a system of jobs, in alien workplaces. Trekking to and from workplaces took up an increasing amount of people's time. As in Arkwright's factory, employers often sent round 'knockers up' to wake workers unused to the time regime that was being imposed.

The Luddites were opposed to the herding of workers into factories as wage labourers, while their artisanal work and livelihoods were threatened by cheaper factory-made textiles. They were also against the loss of guild-like traditions, such as apprenticeships and the life-cycle reciprocities that ingrained a code of community ethics. They were objecting to the displacement of work by labour.

Thomas Carlyle (1795–1881), a Romantic and one of the more perceptive social observers in the nineteenth century, recognized this deleterious change in his 1829 essay 'Signs of the Times', when he said that the weavers were against becoming 'mechanical in head and in heart, as well as in hand'. The Luddites were the primitive rebels of their day – that is, knowing more about what they were against than having a clear vision of an alternative future. Their reference point was a perceived lost past; they even circulated public letters that began by citing Magna Carta and ended with '[sent from] Ned Ludd's office, Sherwood Forest', hideout of the equally fictitious Robin Hood, a thirteenth-century defender of the commons.

The symbolism of the Luddites' actions was, or should have been, obvious. But it suited the ruling classes to present them as an obstacle to progress, along with their ethos of work and commoning. Parliament hastily passed a law to make frame breaking a capital crime punishable by hanging, and the army was deployed to hunt the perpetrators down.

This was the moment in history when the third notion of time, as improvement, became predominant. Science and technology promised that things become better with time – more advanced, more scientific, more productive – so obstructing change was retrograde, to be prevented and deplored. This coincided with the rising power of financial capital, for which investment was solely for the purpose of yielding more income and wealth in the future.

Financialization thrives on the notion of 'improvement', a presumption that change is positive. Cultural theorist Raymond Williams (1921–88) long ago wrote a perceptive essay on the etymology of the word 'improve'; how it originally meant 'to make a profit' from something, but later came to mean 'to make something better', even when that involved taking something away, depriving communities of a viable way of allocating time according to their perceived needs.[5] The notion of change as improvement meant there was a bias in favour of constant change.

In his book *The Great Transformation* (1944), under the heading 'Habitation versus Improvement', Karl Polanyi

(1886–1964) attacked the 'mystical readiness to accept the social consequences of economic improvement, whatever they might be', including 'catastrophic dislocation of the lives of common people' and 'literally robbing the poor of their share in the common'.[6] Referring to the Industrial Revolution in England, he described it as 'improvement on the grandest scale which wrought unprecedented havoc with the habitation of the common people', who were finally rescued, in the late nineteenth century, by 'legislative acts designed to protect their habitation against the juggernaut, improvement'.[7] Polanyi understood that finance speculated solely on expected improvement, with no regard for dislocation or inequality.

The first technological revolution to have shaped production, society and time use around the world was the widespread introduction of the water mill. The Domesday Book, compiled in 1086, records more than 5,600 water mills in England, and by 1300 this had risen to as many as 15,000. While these concentrated production, markets and work and labour in areas near rivers, they fitted with the agrarian time regime. Water supply depended on the season and weather, making for flexible working conditions, with short spells of inactivity followed by long days of labour.

Arkwright's water-powered factory system, with its mills and canals, was the second technological revolution. However, it was soon followed by a third in 1829, when Robert Stephenson's steam locomotive, *Rocket*, heralded the age of steam, rail and coal. Because coal-based power and the steam engine did not depend on seasonal factors, they made continuous production feasible. This enabled capitalistic employers to manufacture enough goods to satisfy a growing demand for exports, as international trade boomed in the era of *Pax Britannica* after the Napoleonic Wars. Although coal-based steam power did not provide cheaper energy than water power, and water was still widely available, 'water followed its own clock – not that of the factory', as Andreas Malm has put it.[8]

A fourth technological revolution came later in the century in the USA, with the opening in 1875 of Andrew Carnegie's steelworks using the Bessemer process that enabled the mass production of steel. This led to a revolution in transport and building, halving the price of steel and facilitating the 'engineering age'. And in 1908, Henry Ford's assembly lines can be said to have started the fifth technological revolution.

Moreover, the coming of the railway made the old system of varying local times untenable, forcing the standardization of time based on the synchronization of clocks. Britain finally adopted Greenwich Mean Time (GMT) for the whole country in 1880, while other countries used GMT plus or minus a correction based on the brilliant invention by John Harrison (1693–1776), a self-educated English carpenter, of the marine chronometer for measuring longitude at sea.[9] The ability to measure distance travelled east and west, which revolutionized navigation and increased the safety of long-distance seafaring in the eighteenth century, established the basis of common time zones in the nineteenth century.

All these technological developments cemented the industrial time regime. They transformed the way time was organized, bringing dramatic changes in the social and technical divisions of labour and making capitalism a societal system, not only a productive one defined by what took place on factory floors or in mines. Capitalism came to redefine society and the way time was used in all spheres of life.

To help legitimize the shift to industrial time, the Factory Act of 1833 prohibited employment in textile mills of children under the age of nine and capped the hours of older children, while the Ten Hours Act of 1847 was the outcome of a public campaign for a maximum ten-hour labouring day. By then, the use of steam power was already more profitable in keeping production running than requiring children and adults to spend every waking hour at the factory. Rather, it imposed a more uniform time regime, accelerating the regimentation of labour time.

This was the first period in history to be dominated by the clock, which was used to standardize and discipline labour, clocking in and clocking out and timed tea and lunch breaks. As the great historian E. P. Thompson has argued, the clock orchestrated the intensification of labour in this period of proletarianization of workers.[10]

It also became a symbol of labour achievement; workers who had been employed for many years were given a watch for 'years of service'. This was part of a more general acquisition of status. As Thompson pointed out, 'When any group of workers passed into a phase of improving living standards, the acquisition of timepieces was one of the first things noted by observers'.[11]

Daily and weekly life became defined in terms of blocks of time – getting up early, labouring for ten or more hours, returning home, dropping exhausted into bed, mostly for six days of the week, with Sunday set aside for rest and recuperation. Women's time regime varied somewhat, though less so in the initial phase of the industrial time era. In England, women outnumbered men as industrial wage workers at the outset of the Industrial Revolution, participating as part of family labour groups or individually.[12]

However, women also had the double burden of domestic work as well as labour, and in addition often spent years of their short lives preparing for and recovering from childbirth. Many women fortunate enough to survive childbirth became worn out by repeated pregnancies and the demands of child rearing. These domestic pressures contributed to the gradual conversion of women into a secondary labour force as the industrial labour market evolved.

Special paternalistic legislation governed the time-use patterns of women in wage labour – prohibiting night-time labour, limiting hours of labour, limiting child labour, and so on. In themselves, these may have been well intentioned. But they sharpened gender differences in time use, with male 'breadwinners' and female 'housewives'. This coincided, not coincidentally, with time spent in unpaid care work disappearing from statistical representations of the world of work.

In the USA, the old homestead-based production system, based largely on self-sufficiency, broke down in the 1820s as men took much of the wage labour away from the home. Most work had previously taken place on domestic premises, where women were the primary producers of many basic goods. As wage labour spread, women became what the historian Ann Douglas refers to as disestablished.[13] They lost civil and social rights and vanished from certain occupations as these became professionalized.

The industrial time regime sharpened the divide between

the home and the workplace, which became 'the factory floor', 'the plant' or 'the office'. Much later, Max Weber characterized the workplace as based on scientific and rational criteria, while the home was based on affective and emotional norms. Such was the bias in favour of the industrial workplace that, even as late as the 1930s in the USA, it was illegal to employ home workers to produce certain knitwear, clothing and jewellery, ostensibly to prevent exploitation by unscrupulous employers.

Distinct blocks of time also defined the life cycle of the mass of workers. A short period of schooling was followed by decades of labour, succeeded by a short period of 'retirement' for the minority who had survived the rigours of labour. Schooling for the masses was essentially preparation for labour; it was short, sharp and very basic. Retirement, a word that dates from the 1600s, was derived from armed service and was linked to the idea of a pension.

In addition to the standardization of time and use of the clock to discipline workers, the transformation of time use was driven by proletarianization. This meant much more than simply becoming a wage worker. It meant being disciplined to be a steady supplier of time to wage labour, and to see that as a normal way of working and living. But creating what might be described as false consciousness, that labour was a proper and desirable way of working and earning a living, did not come naturally or quickly. Most people qua workers did not want or like labour; it was servitude.

It is an irony of history that, in the mid nineteenth century, it was employers who promoted labour security, to persuade workers to stay in jobs from which many wished to escape as soon as they could, to set up on their own in some way. Led by mine owners, employers offered inducements to provide regular labour and pressed for legislation to give employment security. Sometimes longer-serving employees were given perks, or non-wage compensation; other employers set up company stores that provided goods on credit, essentially obliging workers to stay in the job to pay back the debt.

A third aspect of the transformation of time use was the commodification of labour and labour power: workers' labour time was bought in a market just like apples and pears. This was because of what are called the two freedoms: workers were made 'free' of ownership of the means of production and the raw materials needed for production and were accordingly made 'free' to sell their time, as they had no other means of survival.

Technically, a worker does not sell his or her labour power, which Marx defined as 'the aggregate of those mental and physical capabilities existing in a human being, which he exercises whenever he produces a use-value of any description'.[14] In the mid nineteenth century, for the average worker in the process of being proletarianized, the difference between the labour being used and their capabilities would have been relatively small, given the lack of formal education. But nearly two centuries later, the divergence between what a person is required to do in a typical job and the capabilities they possess has become a gulf. For example, between 2011 and 2019 nearly half of recent university graduates in Britain were in non-graduate jobs, defined by the Office for National Statistics as not normally requiring 'knowledge and skills developed through higher education'. The picture is similar in many other industrialized countries.

The Marginalization of Commoning

As the commodification of labour proceeded, commoning and work that was not labour suffered. In aggregate, work may have shrunk as labour expanded. But women did a rising proportion of unpaid or non-earning work. And because they were obliged to labour as well, there may have been a diminution in the *quality* of the work. A wry comment about poor English cooking and cuisine claims that most women did not have enough time to cook elaborate meals, unlike women in France, where industrialism was far less developed.

As for commoning, in 1804 James Maitland, 8th Earl of Lauderdale (1759–1839), an amateur political economist, wrote a brilliant, incisive essay that has remained relevant in the twenty-first century. Entitled *An Inquiry into the Nature and Origins of Public Wealth and into the Means and Causes of its Increase*, it put forward what is known as the Lauderdale Paradox, the essence of which is that as private riches grow, public wealth shrinks.

As elites acquired more of the commons, they concentrated the ownership and use of what became private resources, creating 'contrived scarcity' and shrinking what was available for commoners. This had implications for patterns of time use. The affluent were acquiring more land, more means of production and more control of private property of all kinds, obliging commoners to labour more to obtain less. In the process, the commons shrank and withered the scope for commoning as a way of life and as a means of social protection. This became the reality in Britain (and later elsewhere as well).

Commoning in Britain lived on through the nineteenth century, but as a residual activity, in pockets of forest set aside as commons and in allotments that had emerged in the seventeenth century. It was a victim of the industrial time regime.

Intellectual Resistance to Industrial Time

The development of industrial capitalism and proletarianization prompted unease in some intellectual circles. Jean Sismondi (1773–1842), the Swiss writer who influenced Karl Marx, warned that factory labour of this sort would turn people into drones. And John Stuart Mill (1806–73) railed against the paternalistic prevailing philanthropy that treated labouring men and women as 'perpetually a child . . . the approved condition of the labouring classes'.[15]

The Victorian era of dark satanic mills, the poorhouse and workhouse, disease, and the short brutalized lives of the industrial proletariat is etched in English literature, notably in the works of Charles Dickens (1812–70) and later in the rural–urban class tensions poignantly captured in the novels of Thomas Hardy (1840–1928).

Earlier, William Wordsworth (1770–1850) had lamented the alienated labour of those in industrial jobs, a theme of his *Lyrical Ballads* (with Samuel Taylor Coleridge) of 1798. In the tragic poem 'The Last of the Flock', Wordsworth shows how work linked to nature, to reproduction, was being lost by commercialization as work gave way to labour. Caught in a vicious poverty trap, the shepherd in the poem utters the memorable lines, 'And now I care not if we die, / And perish all of poverty.' This theme of lost control over time and work is extended in the poem 'Simon Lee: The Old Huntsman', which bewails the increasing inability of even hard labour to provide sustenance.

After Carlyle's more direct lament in 'Signs of the Times', quoted earlier, perhaps the most celebrated critique of the industrial time regime came from John Ruskin (1818–1900), the essayist and art critic. In 1853 he observed:

> Men were not intended to work with the accuracy of tools, to be precise and perfect in all their activities. If you will have that precision out of them, and make their fingers measure degrees like cog-wheels, and their arms strike curves like compasses, you must unhumanise them. All the energy of their spirits must be given to make cogs and compasses of themselves . . . On the other hand, if you will make a man of the working creature, you cannot make a tool. Let him but begin to imagine, to think, to try to do anything worth doing; and the engine-turned precision is lost at once. Out comes all his roughness, all his dullness, all his incapability; shame upon shame, failure upon failure, pause after pause, but out comes the whole majesty of him also.[16]

Ruskin's call for an end to the artificial division of labour in which some were allowed 'to think' and some were made to labour was nevertheless overtaken by reality.

The latter part of the nineteenth century saw an ideological struggle between several visions of work and leisure by those calling themselves socialists, communists or anarchists. It was a pivotal moment in the opposition to capitalism.

The struggle was shaped by the emerging class structure. In the background, capitalist producers were manipulated by financiers, as both made huge profits by the standards of the past. The bourgeoisie were gaining income and assets in increasing comfort. The proletariat was growing, increasingly habituated to long hours and long weeks of stable labour.

But there was a new dangerous class – often called just that – consisting of craftsmen, artisans, artists and intellectuals of a sort that Hungarian sociologist Karl Mannheim (1893–1947) was later to call 'free-floating intelligentsia'.[17] They were politically dangerous because they stood against both bourgeois respectability and capitalistic progress, and against the labourist mindset being inculcated into the labouring proletariat class. The most energetic and imaginative agitators and pamphleteers came from this part of 'the working class', and the debate was enriched by emigrés in London and Manchester from Russia, Prussia, other German states and elsewhere. At stake was an intellectual conflict over political strategy as well as the vision of the future.

One side was led by people around William Morris (1834–96), textile designer, artist, poet and activist, whose doctor put as cause of death 'simply being William Morris and having done more work than most ten men'.[18] Morris wished to build a society freed from labour where craft work and guilds thrived, and leisure and work blended, in communities of workers in search of beauty. He did not use the language of commoning, but this was the core of his ethical position. At the other extreme were those who wanted the proletariat to overthrow capitalism and be equalized in generalized labour. This was to reach its apogee in the Leninist dictate that 'he who does not labour shall not eat', later enshrined in the Soviet constitution, which regarded those not doing full-time labour as parasites.

The defence of crafts and craftsmanship was a reaction to what some called the American system of mass production based on standardized parts, which enabled the worldwide success of the Singer sewing machine. The Arts and Crafts movement, associated with William Morris, briefly flourished. But mass production and labourism marched on, driving such activity into the economic margins.

Labourism triumphed in political terms too. Morris's Socialist League floundered in the 1890s, while communist and labour parties emerged strongly, and trade unions shifted from craft unions to industrial (labour) unions, in different ways in various countries. In the end, labourism came to suit capitalism. Of course, there was a struggle for the division of income generated by capitalistic production. But both sides wanted as many people as possible in stable wage labour. Labourism became the hallmark of time in the twentieth century.

There were a few concessions. Following the steady loss of the many holy days that characterized the agrarian time regime, the proletariat won the establishment of May Day, the First of May, as International Workers' Day or Labour Day. This was first celebrated internationally in 1890, after a meeting the previous year of twenty socialist and labour parties in what was known as the Second International, which called for demonstrations in favour of an eight-hour labouring day. A century later, in 1990, it was an official holiday in 107 countries. Ironically, Hitler's Germany was the first after the USSR to make May Day a public holiday, with Franco's Spain and

Vichy France following suit. Remarkable in retrospect is how cautious trade unions and social democratic political parties were towards this symbolic holiday, this break from labour.[19] For the most part, initially they were not very keen on the idea.

By this time, both social democrats and communists were committed to the ethos of labourism. Communists believed in generalized labour and a long-term strategy of what we should call fictitious labour decommodification. This amounted to a withering of money wages, as the state took over the provision of what in modern parlance would be called universal basic services, or cradle-to-grave welfare. It was fictitious decommodification because the worker was not freed, as the term decommodification might imply, but was obliged or coerced to labour, without being able to determine the price for that labour, or its timing or location.

Social democrats too took a labourist perspective; witness the reaction to a contribution to the seething debates by Karl Marx's son-in-law, Paul Lafargue (1842–1911), co-founder of what would become the French Socialist Party. His pamphlet *The Right to be Lazy* (1883) was instantly popular in European socialist movements. But it aroused an equally instant hostile reaction from 'workerists', who dominated the main social democratic party of the time, the German SPD, which set out to suppress it. When Friedrich Engels (1820–95) gave the task of translating the pamphlet to Eduard Bernstein (1850–1932), the leading intellectual of the German SPD, he removed several passages and reframed the pamphlet as a caricature of bourgeois morality, rather than the intended critique of capitalism and a demand for freedom from the labour underpinning it.

Opposition to labourism came from the anarchists,

whose political philosophy embraced self-government and cooperation. In *Mutual Aid* (1902), his most articulate and still influential publication, the leading anarchist intellectual, the Russian prince Peter Kropotkin (1842–1921), argued that species that practise solidarity and rely on mutual, reciprocal assistance become more numerous and more prosperous, a version of Darwinism opposed to the individualistic 'survival of the fittest'. 'The unsociable species, on the contrary, are doomed to decay', he wrote in the concluding chapter. In his other famous book, *The Conquest of Bread* (1892), he expressed what we might now regard as an extreme view, but which conveyed a valuation of the commons:

> the means of production being the collective work of humanity, the product should be the collective property of the race. Individual appropriation is neither just nor serviceable. All belongs to all. All things are for all men, since all men have need of them, since all men have worked in the measure of their strength to produce them, and since it is not possible to evaluate every one's part in the production of the world's wealth.[20]

Kropotkin advocated a society oriented to the wellbeing of all, through the abolition of private property and a return of land, machinery, factories, means of transportation, and so on, into the hands of the community. In his view, this would end the capitalist exploitation of labour, since both the means of production and the goods produced would become common property.

The ideas of mutual aid, community production and systems of social solidarity have come through to the twenty-first century. However, these messages were submerged in the violent and bitter ideological conflicts of the early twentieth century. Labourism emerged as the dominant theme. And it wasn't just communists who took it to extremes. Leading members of the Fabians, the dominant social democratic movement in the United Kingdom, Australia and New Zealand, most notably Beatrice Webb (1858–1943), openly advocated labour camps for unemployed youths. The so-called left embraced labourism. It was one of the great historical errors of modernity.

Stress and Suicide

By late in the nineteenth century, many men and women had lost control over their way of using time. Occupational control had been lost, coupled with the disappearance of institutions, including the guilds and means of commoning, that had buttressed old ways of living. Proletarianization, the commodification of time in labour, in jobs, and the intensification of time in labour gave rise to widespread mental and physical disorders, including what were called occupational neuroses and hysteria – derived from *hustera*, the Greek word for 'uterus', and typically dubbed 'female hysteria'. Their ultimate expression was an epidemic of suicides, highlighted in the classic study by the French sociologist Émile Durkheim in 1897, simply titled *Le Suicide*.

Working-class men (but not women) found some relief in their various social clubs, fraternal societies and support organizations. Membership required a certain standard of decency that their women were expected to bolster, aimed at weeding out the bulging *Lumpenproletariat*, or underclass, of the time – the destitute and other wounded souls. Those who could not adapt often drowned their sorrows in cheap alcohol and opioids such as laudanum. Or, particularly in the case of women, victims simply lost the will to live. An agonized public discourse concerned women in distress. The wrench from long-established patterns of time use led to what was given the generic name of 'nerves'.

The predictable response of the state was to try to control social behaviour, by criminalizing public drunkenness and categorizing illness and disability as social ills to be curbed. Meanwhile, the old presumption that people with mental or physical disabilities would be cared for by their families and communities ceased to apply, partly because time used in labour and the intensity of labour increased, leaving little or no time for care. The number of lunatic asylums increased dramatically in the UK, USA, France and elsewhere, as did their size and number of inmates. In England, in 1806, the average asylum housed 115 patients; by 1900, the average was over 1,000. The numbers rose steadily, but particularly following the Lunacy Act of 1845. In 1866, a prominent physician hailed the asylum as 'the most blessed manifestation of true civilisation the world can present'.[21] Modern historians have been rather less impressed.

The ascendancy of the asylum came about as part of the development of psychiatric treatment for all sorts of stresses arising from the new way of labouring and living. The most celebrated analysis of its role in inducing conformity and acceptance of the new order was Michel Foucault's *Folie et déraison: histoire de la folie à l'âge classique* (1961), published in English in 1965 as *Madness and Civilization: A History of Insanity in the Age of Reason*. According to Foucault, the asylum was a means of 'moral imprisonment' in which anyone not adhering to the norms of desired behaviour was supposed to internalize the values of the socio-economic order or become a warning to others to conform. The high number of wrongful confinements, the use of physical restraints and the overuse of sedatives marked a crisis in the transition to the labourist society.

The state took the lead, but less emphasized was the privatization of asylums, another trend with echoes in the twenty-first century and the privatization of care homes, mental homes and prisons. The private asylums tended to adhere to what was essentially a new, Darwinian psychiatry, which suggested that insanity – a loosely used word to cover a multitude of behaviours – was evidence of an evolutionary struggle, the inevitable consequence of remorseless 'progress'. This required the insane to be separated from the sane.

The twin development of psychiatry and asylums was extremely harsh for women. The new profession was entirely dominated by men – only in 1894 was the first woman allowed to become a psychiatrist – and was infused with preposterous male prejudices. Women's time was not to be their own, and if they did not conform they were subject to enforced 'rest cures' or committed to asylums. In the late nineteenth century, women could still be committed to mental institutions merely at the whim of their husbands, fathers or brothers, and numerous women were locked up permanently for having opinions that male society did not like. The mix of oppression and repression was systemic, not marginal.[22]

While the new quasi-medical professions offered a cure for present ills, another reaction was a search for reward in the hereafter and the revival of institutionalized religion. A lot of time was devoted by a lot of people to the promise of future compensation for a bewildering current existence. Marx's jibe about religion being the opium of the masses was aided by the state, keen to placate and subdue the disoriented.

The clubs and societies offering men in the labouring class some respite and mutual support were a sort of commoning, blending time in leisure (political in character) and in reproduction (recovering from labour). And they anticipated the later development of workers' education that drew the participation and enthusiasm of luminaries such as Karl Polanyi, Raymond Williams and the economic historian R. H. Tawney (1880–1962).

Set up in 1903, the Association to Promote the Higher Education of Working Men was renamed the Workers' Educational Association two years later. It was never very radical politically and was openly supported by subsequent Conservative governments. Critics have claimed it was set up to steer workers away from Marxism.[23] Still, it has proved one of the great institutional survivors, today being the UK's largest voluntary body providing adult education.

However, workers' education, while labourist in perspective, nevertheless contrasted with 'vocational training', which was always employer and state driven, aiming to make workers more efficient, more docile and more disciplined. Workers' education was about liberating people from a false consciousness, about extending citizenship, about empowering people to seek to improve their social position and to understand that the workplace was a site of contestation, a place of struggle for forms of labour and work that would better suit their needs and aspirations.

Taylorism and Scientific Management

Proletarianization reached its peak in the early twentieth century, with a revolution in the way labour time was used based on the precepts of 'scientific management' set out by American engineer Frederick Winslow Taylor (1856–1915). The word 'Taylorism' is still used today to describe the extreme division of labour and concept of jobs that he advocated. A hyperactive individual, he apparently strapped himself into a straitjacket to be able to sleep at night.[24]

His own boundless energy led him to frown on what he saw as 'the natural instinct and tendency of man to take it easy'.[25] Even when he had no material need to do so, he insisted on labouring on factory floors himself, where he would use his time working out how to achieve maximum efficiency. He reckoned every second of labour done in a factory was potential profit and so impressed Henry Ford (1863–1947) that Taylor was hired in 1905 to design a new production process for the rapidly expanding Ford Motor Company.

The essence of Taylor's management technique was to break every set of tasks into repetitive components, based on the idea that 'conception' should be separated from 'execution'. In his view and that of his primary convert, Henry Ford, a worker should not think or have the capacity to do his job in any way other than the way in which he was instructed to do it. As Taylor argued in Chapter 2 of his globally influential magnum opus, *The Principles of Scientific Management* (1911): 'It is only through *enforced* standardization of methods, *enforced* adoption of the best implements and working conditions, and *enforced* cooperation that this faster work can be assured.'

Under Taylor's influence, the Ford Motor Company cut production time dramatically and, by breaking down the technical division of labour into relatively simple, repetitive jobs, reduced the need for skilled mechanics. De-skilling was inherent to the system. And workers on the job were not expected to use time in 'thinking', just 'doing'.

Taylorism was lauded not only by industrial capital, but also by Vladimir Lenin when moulding the Soviet Union after 1917. Clearly, there have been embellishments since those early years, largely to take account of the obvious criticism that such a management process deadens creativity among workers. 'Human resource management' has used various techniques to improve worker 'happiness'. Nevertheless, in 2001 the Institute of Management in the UK voted Taylor's book the most influential management text of the twentieth century. He and his disciples shaped the nature of jobs across the world. Perhaps the greatest testament to the hegemonic success of the industrial time regime is that social democrats have led the way in defending 'the dignity of labour'.

Meanwhile, Taylorism was extended through Fordism, a term popularized by the Italian Communist Antonio Gramsci in his *Prison Notebook* 22 of 1934. This was a management method ideally suited to mass production of a standardized commodity, where the technical division of labour meant jobs could be narrowly defined, involving just a few tasks routinely performed, and 'static', involving little scope for broadening and increasing in complexity. Calling it 'scientific management' suggested that it was all about following natural laws of time and motion. It was actually about imposing direct control by supervisors and foremen over those performing subordinated labour, in which workers were expected to execute what management and engineers instructed them to do.

The other tenet of Taylorism and Fordism was that money wages should incentivize labour productivity and rise with it, so that employees could afford to buy the commodities being produced in the factories, including the black Model T Ford. Henry Ford believed in the 'family wage', to be paid to the male 'breadwinner', and he insisted on hiring men who were or who intended to be married, with wives at home. He even set up a social department with investigators and support staff to check on workers' behaviour, promising a form of profit sharing for those adhering to this family model.

He also introduced the five-day, forty-hour workweek in 1926, well before that became the norm, which was intended to boost productivity and enable workers to increase their consumption. He famously, but no doubt opportunistically, declared, 'It is high time to rid ourselves of the notion that leisure for workmen is either "lost time" or a class privilege.'[26] Admittedly, he also made it clear that workers had to expend maximum effort in their labouring hours if they were to enjoy any such leisure.

While Fordism evolved, Taylorism shaped the jobs that were idealized across a wide political spectrum during the twentieth century. The separation of concept and execution, intended to de-skill labour and increase management control, was to be memorably analysed by the American Marxist Harry Braverman in 1974, by which time the approach had long been extended to service sectors as well as manufacturing.[27] The proverbial clerks, like factory workers, were expected to do repetitive jobs without learning the mysteries of the professions they were serving.

Taylorism was subject to some refinements during the twentieth century, most notably in the 'Hawthorne experiments' in the Western Electric Company in the 1920s, associated with the Australian psychologist Elton Mayo (1880–1949). Whereas Taylor assumed that workers in jobs did not enjoy their work and thus had to be closely monitored and controlled, motivated only by money, Mayo and his colleagues argued that they could also be motivated by judicious emotional nudges, including team solidarity and supportive managers. The Hawthorne experiments essentially represented an attempt to humanize an engineering model of jobs.

It was left to the Japanese to take labour control to the next stage after the Second World War, in what came to be known as Toyotism after the Toyota Motor Corporation. Drawing on a corporate paternalism of *oyabun-kobun* (roughly translated as 'simulated kinship'), Toyotism took time control to a more sophisticated level through such devices as the 'just-in-time' inventory system.[28] This reached its peak in the 1980s. It was suited to a working class and a salariat attuned to Confucian dictates of conformity and respect for elders and superiors, and to a society resigned to subordination following its traumatizing defeat in the Second World War.

Toyotism also suited what had become by then, given incipient globalization, a more volatile economy than when Taylorism took hold, and could be adapted more easily to changing consumer demands. Most significant at the time was that its adoption by Japan and later by the newly industrializing countries (NICs) of South-East Asia greatly helped in making their manufacturing goods competitive with those produced in the industrialized countries of the West.

At the same time, when conducting large-scale surveys of factories in Malaysia and the Philippines in the 1980s, I witnessed the increase in what was dubbed 'running amok', a form of collective hysteria induced by the extreme intensity of routinized labour in electronics factories, analogous to the hysteria manifested in the early days of proletarianization.

Toyotism was the penultimate variant of the industrial time regime. The ultimate was what could be called Shenzhenism. In the late twentieth century, the city of Shenzhen became China's first special economic zone, which grew rapidly to over 12 million inhabitants and emerged as the world's largest supplier of manufactured goods. So great was the labour intensity at factories operated by Foxconn, the giant contractor that makes many of the world's electronic devices, including Apple's iPhones, that some workers threw themselves out of windows, preferring death. To curb the practice, the firm put huge nets around the factory walls, a classic case of treating the symptoms rather than the cause.

Shenzhen was also the first city to come close to being a 'social factory'. By early in the twenty-first century, there were over 200,000 surveillance cameras installed across the city; by 2022, there were nearly 5 million.[29]

The CCTVs are part of a mass surveillance system called Skynet, designed to create a huge zone of behavioural control. With as many as 540 million cameras in mainland China, Skynet is the largest video surveillance system in the world, now using facial recognition technology and big data analysis. However, it would be a mistake to see this just as a creation of the Chinese Communist Party. Much of the technology and equipment used in tracking people on and off jobs and workplaces was initially supplied by American multinationals, such as General Electric, Honeywell and IBM. And many other countries are using similar systems, including the USA, Britain, India and Brazil, while China is exporting its own surveillance technology to autocratic regimes around the world.

The tightening of industrial labour time had two implications. First, the disciplinary control system put increasing restrictions on the agency of workers – that is, the time and scope to think for themselves and to act as they would wish. If agency is a defining attribute of decommodification, then the production process was profoundly commodifying. This spread from factories to bureaucratic offices. The Fordist/Taylorist/Toyotist model acquired 'labour power' for blocks of time, buying people's time and effort for a fixed working day, for a fixed number of years of service.

The so-called company man – or, in Japan, salaryman – was trapped in a gilded cage. Even civil servants and lower-level salaried service employees were cowed, fearful of causing offence to superiors in case they were dismissed. The model of labourism was further entrenched because not only family income but social benefits (pensions, sick pay, paid holidays, and so on) were tied to continued employment as well. Employees embraced labour security in return for accepting subordination. The quest for dependable conformity was a feature of the era.

Second, the evolution into Toyotism of time control in jobs also undermined the model of labourism pursued by the

International Labour Organization. The ILO was established in 1919, in the aftermath of the First World War and the Russian Revolution of 1917, to advance an international agenda of social but not economic rights. It ignored work that was not labour and was geared to labourism from the outset, predicated on industrial unions – rather than craft unions, occupational guilds or cooperatives – alongside collective bargaining between labour unions and centralized employer bodies. Among its first acts in 1919 was a bid to cap labour time with the Hours of Work (Industry) Convention, No. 1.

The ILO was devised as an international instrument to advance decent labour, not emancipation from labour, let alone the values of work in a broader sense of occupational freedom. There was no place for the guilds or for unpaid care work and there was certainly no place for commoning. Its primary role was to set international standards with the goal of taking labour costs out of international trade. In other words, if countries had similar labour standards, their goods would compete on other costs and comparative advantage.

However, the wording of ILO conventions and recommendations always allowed for national variations in interpretation. And governments could select standards they wished to ratify and ignore those that were inconvenient. Perversely, the USA stood back from being a founder member (only joining in 1934) and has been reluctant to ratify its conventions and recommendations ever since.

A premise of the ILO labourist model was that labour standards could be higher in rich countries because they were competing with each other in selling manufactured goods, while developing countries were producing and exporting primary goods such as food and raw materials. But suddenly, here were upstart NICs openly competing on the basis of low labour costs. Toyotism symbolized a new stage in the globalization of labour, which made clear that the conditions and remuneration of labour were indeed part of international trade and competitiveness. The era of 'labour market flexibility' was about to begin.

The Right to Work

In one sense, the claim that there is a right to work was enshrined in Magna Carta and the Charter of the Forest of 1217, as the right to subsistence through work in the commons. This was a very radical emancipatory assertion for that era. In another sense, the right to work goes back even further, to the Code of Hammurabi of ancient Babylon, composed in around 1755–1750 BC, which established who had the right to practise certain kinds of work; this was extended through regulations in ancient Rome and the guilds of the Middle Ages.

The term 'right to work' is ascribed to Charles Fourier (1772–1837) and is derived from the French Declaration of the Rights of Man and of the Citizen of 1789. A utopian socialist, Fourier is also credited with the invention of the term 'feminism', of which he was a proponent, and the idea of 'attractive work'. He was to have an important influence on anarchist thinkers later in the nineteenth century and subsequently on thinkers in the 1960s, particularly Herbert Marcuse (1898–1979) in his book *Eros and Civilization: A Philosophical Inquiry into Freud* (1955) and in the book that was to be so influential in the protests of 1968, *One-Dimensional Man* (1964).

Fourier sparked a debate that has continued to this day about the right to work. His idea of 'attractive work', or *travail attrayant*, despite using the word *travail* rather than *activité*, was close to what the ancient Greeks had in mind. Attractive work was envisaged in an environment of 'liberated passion', within communities housed in 'grand hotels' he called *phalan-stères*. In each community, consisting of hundreds of people, individuals would undertake a variety of activities based on their desires and interests, while necessary but unpleasant menial jobs would have higher associated incomes. He fore-saw a unity of manual and intellectual activity, a liberation of work in play. This was in sharp contrast to the emerging la-bourism of industrial capitalism, of a separation of thinking and doing, that was to come into hegemonic prominence at the beginning of the twentieth century.

Fourier fumed that politics 'vaunts the rights of man but fails to guarantee the first right and the only useful one, which is the right to work'.[30] But how could this exist in a capitalist economy? The French aristocrat and social thinker Alexis de Tocqueville (1805–59), best known for his two-volume *Dem-ocracy in America* (1835 and 1840), perspicaciously saw the perverse implications of pursuing such a right in a capitalis-tic economy in 1848:

> To grant every man in particular the general, absolute and incontrovertible right to work necessarily leads to one of the following consequences. Either the State will undertake to give to all workers applying to it the employment they lack, and will then gradually be drawn into industry, to become the industrial entrepreneur that is omnipresent,

the only one that cannot refuse work and the one that will normally have to dictate the least task; it will inevitably be led to become the principal, and soon, as it were, the sole industrial entrepreneur . . . Now, that is communism.

If, on the contrary, the State wishes . . . to provide employment to all the workers who seek it, not from its own hands and by its own resources, but to see to it that they always find work with private employers, it will inevitably be led to try to regulate industry . . . It will have to ensure that there is no unemployment, which means that it will have to see that workers are so distributed that they do not compete with each other, that it will have to regulate wages, slow down production at one time and speed it up at another, in a word, that it will have to become the great and only organiser of labour . . . What do we see? Socialism.[31]

One could quibble with the names Tocqueville gave to those two tendencies in a market economy. But he captured them well. At about the same time, a scarcely noticed Karl Marx was writing dismissively that under capitalism the right to work was 'an absurdity, a miserable, pious wish'.[32] How could there be a right to work if workers were effectively denied the means of production and the raw materials or even the space in which to produce?

The notion of a right to work has been strongly linked to paternalism, in which those in a position to do so have a moral obligation to provide employment. Pope Leo XIII, a progressive paternalist, pushed it in his papal encyclical *Rerum novarum* (subtitled 'On conditions of labour') of 1891, although this depicted labour ideally as embedded in medieval guilds. The Speenhamland system at the end of the eighteenth century was often presented as fulfilling the state's obligation to create labour for the poor. At almost the same time, the Prussian Civil Code of 1794 was making the same commitment. Putting the poor into labour, for as little pay as possible, was for a long time a primary way of dealing with them.

Around the turn of the twentieth century another strand took hold in the United States, taking the right to work in a different direction altogether. In the country's founding period in the eighteenth century, the idealized citizen was a male landholding head of household. It was hardly the land of the free, as eulogized by self-satisfied modern Americans. Not only was there institutionalized slavery until the Civil War but all other household members, including women and servants, were disqualified from full citizenship and the vote by their perceived dependency on 'the master'.[33] It is also largely forgotten that wage earners were also non-citizens. Republican Americans likened wage labour to slavery and gave status to the self-ownership of time and assets, and the right to make contracts to sell or buy labour. In this, they drew in part on ancient Greek thinking about work and labour, and more explicitly on Magna Carta.

Early radical workers accepted that, without ownership of productive property, the act of supplying labour could not be free. But after the abolition of slavery in the 1860s, with the adoption of the Fourteenth Amendment of the US Constitution, the notion of 'free labour' lost its attachment to property ownership, becoming defined by 'liberty of contract', interpreted to mean the 'right' to sell one's labour and to buy

the labour of others in a labour market free from state interference. And under the 'due process' clauses of the Fifth and
Fourteenth Amendments, the US Supreme Court could rule
that interference with liberty of contract deprived employers
and employees of liberty without due process, unless it was
done to protect public health and safety.[34]

This was a major step towards the full commodification
of labour. It led to the most influential legal case in history
relating to labour, *Lochner* v. *New York* of 1905, which struck
down a state law establishing maximum hours that wage-
earning bakers could be required to labour, on the grounds
that doing so would violate liberty of contract. The ruling
ushered in what has been called the Lochner era, which lasted
from 1905 to 1937; subsequently, after the Supreme Court re-
pudiated its earlier ruling, a raft of New Deal legislation regulated the labour market. Thus, the National Labor Relations
Act (the Wagner Act) of 1935 protected union representation
and the Fair Labor Standards Act of 1938 established minimum wages and maximum hours, protecting employees.

These symbolized the partial decommodification of
labour and influenced the international negotiations within
the ILO that took place in Philadelphia towards the end of
the Second World War. The delegates from countries linked
to the winning side of the war agreed on a document, the
Philadelphia Declaration, that was to define the world of
work and labour in the post-war era. The key was a one-line
paragraph: 'Labour is not a commodity.'

The declaration prefigured the post-war commitment to
full employment, the labourists' interpretation of the right to
work. It was always a sham, because in practice it excluded

many women. But perhaps the starkest interpretation came in Japan's 1947 (and current) constitution that was drafted by officials of the US occupying forces. Article 22 asserted a right to choose an occupation, which meant no more than a right to choose an employer. Article 27, paragraph 1, states: 'All people shall have the right to work and the obligation to work.' This led to a slew of labour legislation in the following decades, much of it modelled on the US Wagner Act of 1935.

Again, it was partial labour decommodification. But to obtain protection and benefits a person had to perform labour and devote time to it. Those protections or benefits could not be obtained from doing other forms of work. In effect, the partial decommodification of labour was achieved by the increased commodification of people as 'workers'. Take-home income was less dependent on the time given to labour, but being in stable labour was necessary to obtain take-home income in the first place.

The right to work was often cited by politicians and commentators in the early decades of the twentieth century as industrial citizenship took shape. The prevailing view was epitomized by a leading English sociologist, T. H. Marshall (1893–1981), who conspicuously excluded economic and cultural rights in his portrayal of citizenship based on civil, political and social rights, matched by corresponding 'duties'. Thus there was an 'essential duty' to work and a duty 'to put one's heart into one's job'.[35]

It was a classic prescription for subordination, which became an implicit part of the social compact of the post-1945 era. Employers and managers were granted the right to manage and direct in return for accepting progressive income tax and labour regulations providing labour-based security for conventional employees. That is key to understanding the historical compromise of social democracy. At no stage in their evolution in the middle decades of the twentieth century did state socialism or social democratic welfare states honour the right to work as 'the right to follow the occupation of one's choice' or to do the type of work of one's choice. The labourist view of work and labour-based social-security systems made sure of that.

Subsequently, the right to work was interpreted by the mainstream as a right to employment. This reached its apogee in the ILO's Employment Policy Convention of 1964, which calls for governments, in the ILO's words, 'to declare and pursue an active policy designed to promote full, productive and freely chosen employment'. By then, labourism had moved a long way from a cry for 'the rights of labour' to a bourgeois comfort zone of claiming there was a right to labour, to a job. Of course, a job was better than being unemployed and impoverished, as was the case for millions during the 1930s Great Depression. But it was a peculiar sort of right, to be put in a subordinated position and to have one's work or labour dictated by another.

The era of labourism and fictitious labour decommodification coincided with an international discourse on human rights, which reached its zenith in the 1960s. The Universal Declaration of Human Rights in 1948 was followed by regional human rights declarations and then the UN's International Covenant on Economic, Social and Cultural Rights of 1966, in which Article 6 states: 'The States parties to the Covenant recognize the right to work, which includes the right of everyone to the opportunity to gain his living by work, which he freely chooses or accepts, and will take appropriate steps to safeguard his rights.'

This was issued just after the ILO's Employment Policy Convention, but the ILO never came to terms with the ambiguities and contradictions implicit in the convention. In its reports on compliance by countries that had ratified the convention, it focused almost entirely on what was happening to official unemployment rates. Work was interpreted as synonymous with employment, and workers as synonymous with employees – that is, wage workers. This omitted all those working on their own account and all those devoting most or all of their time to unpaid care work.

As for the much-used term 'freely chosen', this was interpreted to mean nothing more than condemnation of precapitalistic forms of labour, such as slavery and bonded, indentured, forced or child labour. By neglecting situations in which people were forced by penury or insecurity to accept jobs they would not otherwise wish to take, the convention allowed countries to push people on benefits into subordinated employment, in what was to become known as 'workfare'. The right to work as a freedom right was simply not considered.

Between 1945 and 1969, when it received the Nobel Peace Prize, the ILO was the main means of legitimizing and globalizing the industrial time regime. But soon afterwards this model began to unravel, with the neoliberal revolution in economics and deindustrialization in the rich member countries of the Organisation for Economic Co-operation and Development (OECD).[36] Full-time manufacturing jobs began a rapid decline, and the number of workers in what was later to be called 'the standard employment relationship' started to decline as well.

Class and Time Under Industrial Citizenship

In the pre-industrial era, work as occupation was elevated in status, while jobs were for those with no other choice. In the emerging industrial era, jobs became the main form of labour, with professional jobs split from manual jobs and a sharpening difference between their time patterns.

New layers of services spread around the contrived distinction between professions, crafts and manual labour. But the professions were to become subject to the same disciplinary devices, with increasing proletarianization, discipline by the clock and routinization, in which a sense of autonomy and agency were whittled away, along with traditional guild practices with their mix of leisure, commoning and work.

The industrial time regime reached its absurdist limit in the professions, and the sprawling legal profession in particular. As the range of legal services expanded, feeding off the contract culture linked to capitalism, a class structure took shape within it. An elite emerged, with fancy titles, elite credentials, and so on – barristers, QCs or KCs (Queen's or King's Counsel, for top barristers of the English bar) and judges – alongside a salariat in stable employment, and a mass of people in more lowly positions initially subject to proletarianization. Self-regulation by the profession, backed by the state, enabled the elite to control access to its ranks via qualifications, and establish fee structures and codes of behaviour for different forms of employment, with bodies set up as monitors and enforcers of the rules.

Particularly in the USA, proletarianization was encapsulated in the practice of 'the billable hour', which still holds today. Both legal 'partners' (the elite) and 'associates' (juniors) are required to bill clients for the hours they put into their service and are under explicit or implicit instruction to maximize the hours they bill, backed by incentives and sanctions. Not only is this highly stressful, it also leads to less time spent on the more reflective aspects of legal work, including the study of jurisprudence (the philosophical basis of law, its systems, institutions and principles), which is constantly evolving.

By the 1970s the time regime was complete, epitomized by a campaign by the American Bar Association to 'preach the gospel that the lawyer who keeps time records makes more money'. Corporatization of law, a feature of recent decades, made billable hours an easy way of imposing labour discipline. But the system also prefigured an aspect of the tertiary time regime. It was soon estimated that, for each billable hour, the salaried lawyer had to do at least half an hour in unremunerated or less well remunerated work, attending meetings, dealing with internal correspondence and doing administration. Often lawyers had to work twelve-hour days to achieve the target number of billable hours.

The loss of control over time was debilitating. Billable hours were often broken into six-minute elements. And the regime led to the marginalization of informal services that the profession had traditionally provided, such as general advice to longstanding clients. As the president of the American Bar Association later lamented, 'The billable hour is fundamentally about quantity over quality, repetition over creativity.'[37] But that is not the worst of it. Fraudulent practices have dogged the profession throughout its history. The time-control system invites and rewards sharp practice, giving substance to George Bernard Shaw's quip that the professions 'are all conspiracies against the laity'.[38] The client is rarely able to determine how much time is put into the service, and the output cannot easily be related to the time. Even if the lawyer is scrupulously honest, suspicion is bound to arise, turning a service into a potentially tense transaction.

The system of time control also has ramifications in crowding out time for desirable work, as reflected in the squeeze on collegiality, on free or pro bono work for low-income clients and social causes, on training and other courses, and on participation in the governance of the profession.

Similar though not identical trends have characterized other professions, notably medicine and teaching. The combination of commodification (of knowledge), proletarianization, standardization and routinization has fragmented professions into distinct classes, including an emerging precariat at the bottom with unstable jobs and little hope of advancement. During the twentieth century, the proletarianization of occupations, and in particular the so-called professions, typically involved the commodification of the knowledge associated with the occupation. This tended to shift the allocation of time from prolonged practical experience and collegial exchange of knowledge within the professional community to periods of learning new 'skills' outside the community, by way of diplomas, modular training and 'refresher' courses. Standardizing job requirements also made it easier to substitute employees, generating an insecure precariat within wider occupational communities.

The early twentieth century, in all but name, marked the triumph of the 'labouring class' over the 'working class' (artisans, craftsmen, professionals, care workers). The craft unions that had led the opposition to industrial time in the nineteenth century, and the earlier occupational guilds, were largely displaced by the big battalions of industrial or labour unions, mostly representing unskilled and semi-skilled manual workers. Their priorities were raising money wages and non-wage benefits, while controlling labour time on the job.

Labour market regulations, collective bargaining between unions and employers, tripartite bodies (which included the state as the third partner) and the tripartite ILO itself prioritized labour relations over the right to work as a right to pursue occupational development. When the ILO celebrated its centenary in 2019, it could not identify a single one of its two hundred or so conventions that gave priority to occupational security, or one that gave dignity to forms of work that were not labour.

Labour as False Consciousness

One feature of the industrial time regime was that the goal of ever higher 'productivity' in the workplace became internalized by workers and their union and political representatives. In the process, managers effectively pursued what Marx called 'a closer filling up of the pores of the working day'.[39]

The labourist obsession permeated all labour and socialist political parties and movements, including the Soviet-bloc communist parties. Its most alienated extreme came in the real figure of Alexei Stakhanov, a Russian coal miner, who shot to international fame in 1935 after he reportedly used basic tools to extract 227 tonnes of coal in a single shift, more than fourteen times his quota. He was feted in the Soviet Union as a model worker, with Stalin himself putting his name to a gushing pamphlet. He was equally celebrated in the USA as epitomizing a new labour movement dedicated to increasing productivity, even appearing on the cover of *Time* magazine.[40]

Since he came from a nominally socialistic state and was seen as a self-motivated 'worker', it was hard for social-democratic political parties to oppose Stakhanov's status, even though it should have been obvious that he exemplified self-exploitation, setting superhuman expectations in the interest of the state or of capital, depending on where he was being celebrated. It jelled perfectly with Taylorism, which was equally lauded in Soviet as in American factories.

The labourism associated with Taylorism and Fordism was clearly paternalistic from the outset. Workers were steered to allocate their time in specific ways and to adapt their lifestyle to the factory system. The early industrial-relations scholars recognized this trend; some mildly deplored it. Writing in 1929, just before the Great Crash, the man regarded as the founding father of industrial relations, Sumner Slichter (1892–1959) opined:

> But is there no need among wage earners for more initiative and enterprise, for more mental independence, and for more disposition to rely on co-operative self-help than modern personnel practice is disposed to encourage? Is it not, in general, desirable that men be encouraged to manage their own affairs rather than that they be

deliberately and skillfully discouraged from making that
attempt? And if much paternalism is inevitable, would
it not be more satisfactory from the standpoint of the
community that it be paternalism of the government rather
than the paternalism of the employers?[41]

He was to have his wish in the 1940s, on both sides of the Atlantic, with the formation of welfare state capitalism. In 1948,
when he was president of the US Industrial Relations Research
Association, he aptly described the USA as 'a laborist state'. He
could have been describing Western Europe as well, and even
more so the Soviet bloc. Labour unions, and social democrat
and labour parties, went along with all that this implied.

The concept of 'high performers' of labour evolved steadily during the twentieth century, bringing with it the verbi-
age and imagery of 'human resource management', and belief
in fostering a 'meritocracy'. One outcome was the 'performance appraisal'; an arbitrary 20 per cent of the workforce
became a norm for the share of employees given incentive
rewards within corporations or bureaucratic organizations.
This allowed a system of discretionary favouritism to permeate their 'culture'.

That has spread into a more invasive form of 'ratings' in
platform capitalism. It has also contributed to the spread of
karoshi (death from overwork) in Japan and elsewhere. In
London in 2013, twenty-one-year-old Moritz Erhardt, a financial intern with Bank of America, was found dead in the
shower of his flat, having spent three days and three nights
in continuous labour.

The false consciousness that the fetishization of 'jobs'

engenders has also made people feel that, unless they are in a job, they are useless and have no purpose in life. In a graphic example, Professor Vere Childe, a world-famous Australian archaeologist, retired from his job aged sixty-four in 1957 and shortly afterwards jumped off a cliff to his death. He left a letter for a friend declaring that the elderly were parasitic rentiers, with no useful work to do. He also criticized the elderly for doing any work, as if to prove they were still useful, whereas in his view they were an obstacle to progress, robbing 'younger and more efficient successors' of the opportunity for promotion.[42] A more alienated consciousness one can scarcely imagine.

Industrial Citizenship: The Mantra of 'Full Employment'

In the 1930s and 1940s, 'full employment' became the social democratic mantra, and it has continued to be so. It was always bogus. All work that was not labour was ignored, and women were mostly excluded from the unemployment statistics. Full employment became a political trap for pushing more people into full-time jobs. The ILO model moved from being a potential means of 'freedom from labour' to being largely a means of subordination in decent labour, further marginalizing and delegitimizing the use of time for work that was not labour.[43]

By the 1950s, and through into the 1970s, the institutions and policies of social democracy provided not only labour-based security for families with male 'breadwinners' but also a greater sense of control over the near future for those families. Those in stable full-time jobs had their material needs safeguarded, as long as they stayed in those jobs and obeyed their managers. A Keynesian framework of macro-economic policies oriented to full employment limited the range and depth of economic uncertainty. That is why the late era of industrial time deserves to be described as one of industrial citizenship.

The social democratic ethos that shaped politics in the post-1945 era, even in political parties of the right, involved a decommodification of labour. The money wage shrank as a share of the social income of workers, so that the performance of labour was increasingly rewarded by access to non-wage benefits relative to wages, in the form of occupational pensions, medical insurance, subsidized canteens and other perks. And there was an extension of social 'rights' to those who were in industrial labour, or in services linked to economic growth, if they were in stable full-time jobs or married to someone who was. It was not an era of equal citizenship rights for all people classified as citizens. If you did unpaid work, or combined it with part-time or casual labour, you did not have the full range of available 'rights'.

One area where progress was made was the shortening of the standard labouring week of those doing full-time labour. The long struggle was inspired by the historic call in 1817 by Welsh textile manufacturer Robert Owen (1771–1858), founder of the cooperative movement and a progressive educational reformer, for workers to have 'eight hours' labour, eight hours' recreation, eight hours' rest'. Known as 'Mr 8-8-8', as well as the 'father of British socialism', Owen inspired a century of struggle for shorter labouring days and weeks. By the early twentieth century, the eight-hour labouring day was widely adopted, mainly achieved through sectoral collective bargaining between industrial unions and employer organizations, rather than legislation.[44] But many workers were not protected from long workweeks until the European Union's Working Time Directive came into effect in 2003.

Leisure: From *Schole* to Time Off

A crucial transformation of time in the industrial time era was the conversion of leisure into 'time off'. Instead of being a zone of potentially subversive and radical activity, leisure became just the opposite of work or, more accurately, the opposite of labour.

Before industrialization, leisure time was something possessed and shared by most classes, albeit in different ways. It was always implicitly linked to political or social involvement. This changed with the coming of industrial time. For the upper middle class, the bourgeoisie, it became increasingly the conspicuous consumption described in Veblen's *The Theory of the Leisure Class* (1899), mainly performed by the women who ran the home, the domestic side of family life. For a man, having a wife who did not work, let alone labour, symbolized economic and social success. But for those pushed into the labouring class, there was a steady reduction in days of leisure, and a replacement of dozens of 'holy days' by far fewer 'holidays'.

It is a mistake to think that in the nineteenth century a new way of taking time as 'holiday' reflected growth in 'leisure time'. It was primarily a reflection of a changing time regime. The annual holiday as an escape from labour was made real by the spread of the railway and cheap train tickets to coastal towns such as Bournemouth, Blackpool, Brighton, Hastings, Great Yarmouth and Scarborough. But it is too sanguine to say that people in general had 'more leisure time to dedicate to travelling'.[45] It was an upper-class and middle-class phenomenon.

One block of time took decades to crystallize. There is a pertinent scene in the TV series *Downton Abbey* when the ageing aristocrat played by Maggie Smith asks, 'What is a weekend?' It was still a valid question in the mid 1920s, since the notion of the weekend was very much a twentieth-century invention. Traditionally, Sunday had been 'the day of rest'. Then, gradually, employers introduced a half-day on Saturdays. Only in the 1930s did the full weekend become the norm.

While industrial capitalism phased out the leisurely lifestyle of numerous holy days, in the later stages it began to replace them with official 'days off' from jobs. In Britain, a significant step was the passage of the Bank Holidays Act of 1871, the long-term result of which is that most people in the UK and Commonwealth countries now have about eight 'bank holidays' a year. This was the brainchild of a close friend of Charles Darwin, Sir John Lubbock (1834–1913), an eccentric but brilliant man, who besides being a Liberal MP was a prominent banker, philanthropist and scientist. He had the wisdom and humility to recognize that he was able to achieve so much only because he was wealthy enough to be able to do what he wanted. He understood, and said so repeatedly, that having adequate leisure and rest were essential for creativity.

Even that was a give-and-take measure. Before 1830, banks closed on the forty days of the year declared as saints' days, after which the number fell to just four days. The 1871

Act allowed any day to be a bank holiday, not just saints' days. Leisure as recreation and family togetherness became formalized blocks of time, a reward for prolonged and intensified labour. The term 'bank holiday' symbolized the connection to finance, a permitted break from money making, even though banks welcomed the extra spending that such holidays promised.

Leisure as time off labour was a dismal replacement for the leisure eulogized by the ancient Greeks and Romans. It was permitted recreation. And when it began to expand during the twentieth century, it was intended to enable labouring families to spend more money to keep the economy growing. But if you could neither labour nor consume, you were increasingly likely to be dubbed 'lazy' and 'scrounging off the state'.

If leisure is interpreted as private recreation, entertainment and consumption, it not only loses its subversive, solidaristic, public place in the allocation of time. It means that leisure as *schole* is marginalized to the point where politics can be converted into a voluntary, superficial form of consumption itself. Quality time is necessary to participate as an active political citizen. One of the scarcely noticed outcomes of the transformation of leisure into recreation-and-consumption time was that political messaging gradually became 'dumbed down', converted into a zone of commodification commanded by advertising minds. The average number of words on a political message shrank, and political soundbites became shorter and more platitudinous. It was to become much worse under tertiary time.

Tertiary Time: Labourism's Last Legs

Since the 1970s, the industrial time regime has been overtaken by what one might call a tertiary time regime, accentuated by the information technology revolution. The concept of 'tertiary' derives partly from the conventional depiction of the economy as consisting of primary (farming, fishing and mining), secondary (manufacturing) and tertiary (services) sectors and partly from being the third era following on from the preceding agrarian and industrial time regimes.

In rich countries, such as the UK and USA, about nine in ten people in the labour force are in service jobs, jobs that Adam Smith dismissed as 'unproductive labour'. Most produce intangible outputs and are 'stretchable' in terms of the time they take. Tasks can be done rapidly or slowly, depending on the worker and the degree of pressure. Increases in productivity or efficiency can be the enemy of the service or its quality, and often are.

Tertiary time is characterized by a blurring of time uses, a breakdown of boundaries between types of activity, and a tendency for multiple activities to take place within any given period. Neither the vocabulary and rhetoric around work, nor mainstream politics and social policies, have adjusted to tertiary time. They are still tied to industrial time.

The structural change began in the 1970s with the displacement of Keynesian economics by a neoliberal revolution. This was marked by the ascendancy of the Chicago School of law and economics, or what was dubbed 'the Washington Consensus', backed by the Washington-based International Monetary Fund (IMF) and World Bank, which centred on the primacy of private property rights. The key developments were liberalization of financial markets and of trade and international investment, and a re-regulation of the economy in favour of capital and employers. The labour securities of the industrial citizenship era were suddenly portrayed as impediments to economic growth, maintenance of which was regarded as the supreme political and economic objective.

Financial institutions became all powerful. They aided major corporations to dominate their sectors and to become multi-industrial as well as more multinational in character. The strength of large financial and corporate capital enabled its representatives, mainly through compliant politicians, to establish institutions, regulations and policies to produce a profoundly new type of market economy, best described as 'rentier capitalism'. More and more of the income has flowed to the rentiers, the owners of property – financial, physical and 'intellectual' – while less and less has gone to those who rely on labour and work for their livelihoods.[1] In this way, the machinery of the state has been used to increase all forms of inequality. It is misleading to characterize the era as one of a withered state or of 'deregulation'.

A feature of tertiary time is that many people are spending more time in labouring and working than used to be the case but earning less than they or those like them used to earn.

And the average worker, who is doing more work and labour, has fallen further behind those higher up the income scale.

Rentier Capitalism and the Global Class Structure

The development most relevant to this narrative is the evolution of a new global class structure, which may be defined in three dimensions.[2] A class has distinct relations of production, signalling a pattern of work and labour, or time uses; it also has distinct relations of distribution – that is, a mix of sources of income; and it has distinct relations to the state – that is, a range of citizenship rights and entitlements.

At the top of today's class structure is a plutocracy, loosely defined as the world's billionaires. Most 'work' but do no labour, earning almost all their income from assets or property, rather than from how they use their time. It is scarcely an exaggeration to say they gain more money while they sleep and play than when they are awake and work. And they are global citizens, having rights anywhere they wish. They can buy the time of many others and can do so more lavishly than most ancient feudal barons could.

Many plutocrats are far from 'the idle rich'. Some devote themselves to work to what is surely an unhealthy degree. Elon Musk has boasted that for years he worked 120 hours a week, and he reportedly has a practice of holding a series of meetings, each of which must last no longer than five minutes. It is doubtful whether he or anyone else could work nearly seventeen hours a day for seven days a week without impairing their mental judgement and sanity. But we should not presume the plutocracy spend most of their time in recreation and sloth.

Below them in the income spectrum is an elite (top managers, senior partners in legal and financial firms, and so on), who do some labour, gain income from salaries as well as from forms of rent, and have a full range of citizenship rights. Then there is a growing category of 'proficians' (consultants, self-employed professionals such as architects or veterinary surgeons), who choose to be independent of employment, work frenetically for high money incomes, and possess a full range of citizenship rights. They are prone to burnout, spending too much time on work and taking too many risks.

Below proficians in terms of average earnings is the salariat (state and company employees doing non-routine service jobs with regular pay packets and indefinite or long-term contracts). They have employment security and relatively predictable earnings, along with an array of non-wage perks and access to state benefits. They also gain increasingly from ownership of property and financial assets. This means they do not identify with old labourist politics, on collective bargaining, labour law and social assistance.

At the height of the industrial time regime, the salariat tended to have an aspirational public service mindset and supported moderate Christian democrat or social democratic politics. That has largely gone, with the withering of public services and more emphasis on individualism, which has led to disengagement from politics in favour of a focus on career and personal interests. But the salariat is shrinking all over the world; young people, including the offspring of the current salariat, have less chance of joining it.

Despite above-average incomes, the time the salariat allocates to labour, and work associated with it, has increased.

According to official statistics, they labour longer on average than those on lower wages, a reversal of the situation during the industrial time era. In effect, the salariat has made a Faustian bargain – high earnings in return for an obligation to work and labour at almost all times and places, with a risk of burnout, stress, and drug and alcohol addiction.

Below the salariat in the income spectrum is the proletariat, as forged in the industrial time era, doing manual or routine service jobs. For them, the three dimensions are clear: extensive blocks of time in labour, with well-defined workplaces and labouring hours; a mix of wages and non-wage benefits, with access to state benefits if needed; and an array of rights in the state. But the proletariat has been shrinking steadily, with many of those remaining in it fearing a fall into the group below them.

This is the precariat, the growing mass class of 'workers' who rely almost entirely on labour and work for their income, with the following combination of the three dimensions. In terms of relations of production, they usually experience unstable and insecure labour in jobs, and find themselves living a bits-and-pieces existence, without a clear occupational narrative or identity, or a corporate or sectoral one, to give themselves. They rarely have fixed workplaces or fixed labour time. They must do a lot of work that is not paid labour, and they are the first class in history whose average level of schooling is greater than needed for the type of job they are likely to obtain, creating status frustration. They have no sense of control over their time.

Although the precariat typically has labour that is both unstable and insecure, these terms are not synonymous with 'precarious'. In today's production systems, capital wants lots of unstable labour, meaning that the amount can be varied easily with minimal cost to employers. Such labour may be 'secure', in so far as the worker has a quasi-permanent contract, but in most cases it is not. Indeed, the precariat lacks all seven forms of labour-based security that the core of the proletariat had obtained by the later stages of the industrial time regime.

These seven forms of security are: labour market security (ample good employment opportunities); employment security (secure contracts, with compensation for employment loss); job security (a niche or secure type of work); skill security (possession of viable skills and access to the means of improving them); work security (safeguarded health and safety in the workplace); income security (predictable, adequate income, with comparable compensation if losing employment); and representation security (access to collective and individual voice to defend and enhance rights, or agency).

The absence of these forms of security, which the salariat and proletariat had, has implications for what the precariat must do with their time. Whereas the average worker in the proletariat was being proletarianized – that is, habituated to a norm of stable, secure labour if they conformed to management rules – the precariat is being 'precariatized', pressured to internalize a lifestyle of insecure labour and work.

In terms of the precariat's distinctive relations of distribution, they rely almost entirely on monetary remuneration, in money wages or commissions on projects, without non-wage benefits or entitlements. They also have diminishing entitlements to state benefits, while losing community and

family benefits and support, which insecure workers historically had through access to the commons. Most find themselves 'bowling alone', unable to rely on a close network of
relatives or friends, meaning they lack what might be called
relational income security.

Living alone is more common than it used to be.[3] Feelings
of solitude and loneliness are growing.[4] This has been accompanied by increasing loneliness in jobs. In a 2018 global
survey, two in five office workers reported being lonely.
Studies have found that lonely workers are less motivated,
less productive and more likely to quit.[5] This makes the insecurities experienced by the precariat more threatening
psychologically and financially.

The precariat is also systematically, not incidentally, exploited through rental mechanisms, mainly by debt. Most are
living on the edge of unsustainable debt, in which one accident, illness or mishap can plunge them into absolute poverty.
In the United States, for example, the bottom 50 per cent of
income earners had a negative annual savings rate of about
7 per cent in the period 1995–2019, implying they were simply
running up debts as they earned.[6] In the UK, the gap between
earnings and spending has risen steadily, as the precariat try
desperately to maintain living standards or just survive.[7]

As for its relations to the state, the precariat is the first
mass class that has been losing citizenship rights – civil,
social, economic, cultural and political. They are essentially
supplicants, denizens not citizens, reliant on discretionary
favours and decisions by people in positions of authority, including decisions taken to deny them benefits without any
respect for due process.

Being a supplicant adds to their lack of control over time. The Latin origin of the term 'precarious' (*precarius*) was 'to obtain by prayer [*prex*]'. Praying for relief, for attention, for relevance, for opportunity takes up a great deal of time, much of which in a good society would be redundant. Yet social and economic policies have increased the amount of time used in supplicant activity.

The class structure outlined above exists in all sectors of the economy and in all occupational groups, including the professions. For example, in the legal profession there is an elite, a large salariat, a small proletariat and a spreading precariat. In the medical professions, it is much the same. Often the precariat is crowded into categories such as paralegals, paramedics and teaching assistants, with limited qualifications and limited chances of upward mobility within the occupation. However long you labour as a paralegal or paramedic, you do not become a lawyer or doctor. No sector is immune from this class-based fragmentation.

Some commentators argue that neoliberal policies have reduced most people to self-exploiting, isolated individuals, unable to mobilize for collective action because they lack a collective consciousness. In this view, the precariat blame themselves for their insecurities and frustrations, directing their anger inwards. In the words of the influential Korean-born German philosopher Byung-Chul Han, they become 'depressive, not revolutionary'.[8] While such feelings may be widespread, this seems too pessimistic an analysis.

A crucial point in the evolving class structure is that the control of time and the allocation of time to various types of activity – not just the amount of time spent in labour, in jobs – are differentiated by class. This is a form of inequality, one rarely considered in conventional assessments of the growth of inequality and insecurity, which is often described in gender or generational terms, focusing on alleged differences between 'Millennials' and 'Baby Boomers', 'Generation X' or whatever.

Defining groups in age terms diverts attention from class-based differences within generations. Although more of today's younger generations are in the precariat, many in older age groups are also in it, while some of all ages are in other classes. The task is to identify the different time patterns of the classes that characterize the tertiary time regime.

In particular, the precariat has lost (or never gained) control of time in ways quite different from the loss of control by the proletariat in the industrial time regime. A growing number of people have neither control over their current time – today, this week, this month – nor control of their future time, knowing (or at least imagining) where and how they are going forward, or what they are likely to be doing in a year or more's time. Many also feel they have no control of their past time, with no worthy narrative of what they have done or been, no narrative of identity and status that they can tell themselves or their offspring and peers.

Time in Schooling

For the majority set to join the proletariat in the industrial time era, schooling consisted of a few years to habituate them to labour, through rote learning and respect for time discipline. Meanwhile, the offspring of the bourgeoisie and aristocracy received a liberal education over many more years, designed to fit them for the professions and for government. That dualistic model has evolved to fit the era of tertiary time, with a steady extension of social control through schooling institutions.

The average number of years of schooling has risen, but more interesting is the political portrayal of education as 'the education industry'. The purpose at all levels, primary, secondary and tertiary, is to increase 'human capital' – that is, to increase the income-earning capacity of students. There has been a reduction in learning time dedicated to subjects regarded as unrelated to jobs. Why devote time to history, philosophy, literature or music, if that does not lead to a job? The values extolled as the essence of education for the past two thousand years are being trashed. In a commercialized society, learning for its own sake, the pursuit of knowledge, culture and morality that the ancient Greeks called *paideia*, has been relegated to the margins.

Today, schooling at all levels promotes neoliberal values of competitiveness, self-entrepreneurship and individualism. And the resultant credentials are increasingly so-called 'positional goods', where status and success depend on having more or better credentials than others, leading to credential inflation. Economist Fred Hirsch encapsulated this when he said, 'If everyone stands on tiptoe, no one sees better.'[9]

Nevertheless, students are being pushed into spending most of their waking hours, for many years, in a bid to outcompete their peers. With a limited supply of good job opportunities, the education system has become a treadmill, which commercial interests have eagerly exploited in offering private after-school tutoring and 'shadow schooling' – private, fee-paying extra schooling outside regular school hours. In the UK, the share of 11–16-year-olds doing such informal schooling has risen sharply, presumably giving performance advantages to children whose families can afford it, but also using up a lot of time that could be spent in social and socializing activities instead.

In China and South Korea, high-stakes tests determine where children go to school and then whether they enter a prestigious university, which raises their chance of being offered a rewarding job that can also provide old-age security for the parents. Parents pressure their children to study hard for exam success. In Chinese cities, pupils spend 10.6 hours on average every week in after-school tutoring.[10] The stress on students and parents has become so great that both countries have tried to limit time spent in studying outside school hours. South Korea imposed a 10 p.m. curfew on cramming schools in 2009. In 2021, worried that families were reluctant to have more children because of the cost, the Chinese authorities banned for-profit tutoring of core school subjects and barred tutoring companies, which had built up a $100 billion business, from listing on the stock market. President Xi Jinping described the sector as 'a stubborn disease that is difficult to manage'.[11]

Ironically, credential inflation has accompanied the de-skilling of large parts of many occupations, as they have become fragmented along class lines. Thus, the growing precariat is not able to use the education they nevertheless need to acquire to obtain a 'port of entry' job. For instance, you do not need a graduate degree to *perform* paralegal labour, but you may need it to *obtain* the job. In the past, many legal professions did not require a university degree. Now it is standard. Described as 'a race to professionalization', this forces students to increase the amount of time spent on acquiring credentials for jobs, even though they know credentialism is a sham. Nor are they fooled by extensive job 'uptitling' – giving jobs fancy names to pretend they are more complex and skilled than they really are.

As part of the more regulatory state, there has also been a standardization of schooling curricula alongside creeping commodification of teaching, teachers and students, increasingly paid by (and paying for) blocks of teaching time. And there is a credo of lifelong learning, including more time for so-called training, discussed later, and more for courses organized by outside bodies. Schooling never stops, with both negative and positive implications. (The latter includes the University of the Third Age (U3A), a nationwide network in the UK that encourages older people to share with others their knowledge, skills and interests. U3A is a form of commoning: people give their time for free, while participation strengthens social and community ties.)

Already entrenched are MOOCs (Massive Open Online Courses), standardized packages often produced by celebrity 'academics' that are sold to schools and universities all over the world. The latest development is the metaverse: avatar-driven virtual reality courses have the potential to displace human teachers. Meta (formerly Facebook) is taking the lead globally, along with Microsoft.[12] The prospect of further standardization and harmonization of what purports to be knowledge is a worrying trend towards control over time and mind.

Fees for higher education, and the student debt that

results, have also led to the commodification of other time, in some cases to an extraordinary extent. In the United States, young women students can reduce their debts by donating their eggs, for up to $20,000 a cycle, if they have the right genetic characteristics. For this they must spend time at commercial clinics and can do so several times. As one student explained, 'The first and second time I was unemployed or barely employed, so in a way I needed the money but I wasn't desperate for it.' On those occasions, she used the money to pay her rent; on the third, she used it to pay tuition fees.[13]

More mundanely, the commodifying process obliges more young adults to devote time to jobs to help pay for schooling costs. In doing so, they swell the precariat ranks and diminish the time they can devote to learning around their core examination subjects. Meanwhile, commercial pressures have reshaped how time in schooling is allocated. Not only have cultural studies been crowded out, but donations by powerful commercial or political interests, for buildings, research or university chairs, have directly or indirectly discouraged political thinking, the basis of *schole* since ancient times.

Thus the Koch Scholars Program in the USA, sponsored by far-right billionaire Charles Koch, aims to steer students in an ultra-libertarian direction,[14] while establishment of the Oxford Centre for the Analysis of Resource-Rich Economies with a generous grant from BP has arguably muted criticism of the company's damaging activities in West Africa.[15] More generally, the search for commercial and job-related relevance has displaced a search for truth. 'Jobs first!' is the mantra.

Homo neoliberalis

When neoliberalism swept into ideological hegemony in the 1970s and 1980s, many interpreted it as a revival of nineteenth-century free-market capitalism. The neoliberal ideal type is a 'self-entrepreneur', producing and selling oneself. This concept, associated with French philosopher Michel Foucault (1926–84), reflects the neoliberal fixation with 'individualization', a belief that each individual is his or her 'own capital' and 'own producer'.[16]

It sets the scene for a modern Hobbesian world of all-against-all, of hyper-competition, in which a few winners confront legions of losers, victims of bruised encounters, shredded nerves and existential stress. They are encouraged to blame themselves for any inadequacies, by the state, by advertisers and, most of all, by the smug rentiers secure in their wealth and the power and status that go with it.

If people see themselves as self-entrepreneurs, they will be more inclined to internalize 'capitalistic' values and not the values of work, caring, commoning and leisure as *schole*. Time spent on these activities is then seen as lost time, branded as 'unproductive' or even 'scrounging'. The sharing of ideas too becomes a betrayal of oneself as entrepreneur because it means giving up a source of advantage. Hence the notion of 'intellectual property', allowing individuals and firms to patent inventions or to copyright writings, music, designs and much else to prevent others making use of them. Turning ideas into intellectual property is now pervasive.

Consistent with this neoliberal ideal type, building an occupational career involves investing time in accumulating a portfolio of competences, activities, experiences and networks. Yet much of this investment may be seen retrospectively as 'a waste of time'. For artists in particular, a career 'consists not in filling "vacancies", but in engaging in a multitude of often very heterogeneous projects'.[17] Many projects may overlap, and may involve applying for several while still undertaking one or more, inducing a sort of pathological mindset of 'I project, therefore I am'. If I am not projecting right now, I am lost.

The Tertiary Workplace

The industrial model produced a historically unique division of place and time, which severed the prior embeddedness of home and work. Work around the home and work in the community (the essence of commoning) shrank, while labour in workplaces became the norm. Tertiary society has seen a blurring of the boundaries defining workplace, commons and homeplace, and of related uses of time. The division between labour and work has become fuzzy, while the pressure to 'play' and to 'recreate' (as in recreation) squeezes out leisure as *schole*, including what might be called 'social stewardship', in the form of public participation in political activity.

Architects and town planners are designing buildings and the land around them to facilitate modern forms of labour, work and recreation, allowing people seamlessly to combine activities. This pre-dated the seismic impact of the Covid-19 pandemic in 2020–22. More than a decade earlier, *The Economist* noted the growth of what was termed a modern urban nomadism.[18] 'Virtual' firms, in which most employees and partners do not have an office or fixed workplace, had also increased in number for the previous two decades.

Another feature of the tertiary time regime is the advancing panopticon surveillance system. This began in the late industrial time era, epitomized by Shenzhenism which, as noted in Chapter 3, established a 'social factory' model with sophisticated surveillance mechanisms to monitor how workers were using their time both inside and outside factories. Later, in the guise of an initiative entitled 'Safe Cities', the Chinese government required all internet cafés, restaurants and 'entertainment venues' to install video cameras with feeds to local police stations. This was part of a gigantic project known as Golden Shield, or the National Public Security Work Informational Project, which started in 1998 with technology provided by Western companies from the USA, UK, Israel and elsewhere, led by Cisco Systems. Today, all online and mobile communications are monitored, and Golden Shield has created a database covering almost every person in China. It is the panopticon state operating at full throttle.

The fact that more labour and work-for-labour is being done away from fixed workplaces has implications for the body of labour law and labour regulations built up during the twentieth century, which is based firmly on 'the workplace'. Tertiary workplaces, and the tertiary production system in general, also imply a blurring of the 'ownership of the means of production'. The Marxian notion characterizes the proletariat as 'freed' from ownership. But today's precariat, proficians and part of the salariat carry around the 'means of production' in their electronic devices, along with the 'raw materials' of their trade.

This conjures up a picture of work and labour in almost constant change, of place, personnel and time. There is an immortal line from T. S. Eliot's poem 'The Love Song of J. Alfred Prufrock' (1915) – 'I have measured out my life with coffee spoons'. Some see it as reflecting an orderly life. But it also portrays an image of a life of anomic emptiness. This is well understood by the burgeoning 'artistic community', chasing for projects, moving workplaces opportunistically, rootless and too often directionless, just waiting.

Tertiary Labour

Tertiary labour is a system of time uses without strong boundaries. One change from industrial time is the shift from a standard nine-to-five, five-day week to a far more varied pattern. No hour or day is sacrosanct. For instance, by 2010 one in every five employees in the USA laboured more than half their hours outside the hours of 6 a.m. to 6 p.m.[19] In 2015, across the European Union, half of all employees were doing some labour on at least one Saturday each month, while a third were doing so on at least one Sunday, and about a fifth were doing labour at night.[20]

Numerous types of flexible labour have proliferated, including prolonged internships, zero-hours and variable-hours contracts, part-time casual jobs, agency labour, phoney self-employment, and so on. This diversity partly reflects the modern 24/7 production system and ubiquitous electronic connectivity, sometimes called 'the continuous working week'. A growing share of employees are doing shifts, rotating blocks of time without any regular pattern. Such systems have deleterious effects on mental health, and contribute to heart and gastrointestinal problems, as well as harm to family life. Yet in rich economies, these patterns are spreading.

The terms 'non-standard' and 'atypical' employment have been used for too long. Large numbers of people are in jobs covered by these terms. And the growth has occurred in even the most prosperous economies. In Germany by 2020 – that is, before the impact of the Covid pandemic was felt – 11.5 million people, or a third of the officially counted labour force, were in so-called mini jobs, part-time or fixed-term temporary jobs.[21]

There has also been a double 'feminization' of the labour market globally – women have been displacing men, and jobs are increasingly characteristic of those traditionally taken by women (light manufacturing, most service jobs).[22] Globally, women comprise over half of all college students, giving them a competitive advantage, and more men drop out of college. And higher female labour-force participation is inducing more flexible forms of labour.

Information technology and algorithmic control systems have enabled sophisticated labour management techniques to match 'just-in-time' production with 'just-in-time' labour arrangements. Firms can calculate how much labour is needed at any one time and automatically inform workers when and for how long they will be needed. This leads to scheduling insecurity for the worker, which is not the same as employment insecurity.

In the UK, the Living Wage Foundation estimated in 2021 that 38 per cent of all workers – about 10 million people – were in jobs where they were given less than one week's notice of their labour schedule; 7 per cent were given less than twenty-four hours' notice.[23] Among low-paid employees 55 per cent were given less than a week's notice of their schedule, and 15 per cent were given less than twenty-four hours'. Another study covering forty large firms that used zero-hours contracts found that thirty-five sometimes cancelled shifts at short notice and only four compensated workers for doing so.[24] This is a modern source of economic uncertainty, causing stress and anxiety, especially when people must arrange childcare or other commitments. Time put aside for jobs is simply wasted.

Another contrast with the industrial workplace is the relationship between labour time and productivity. In manufacturing, an increase in the technical division of labour raises productivity, as Adam Smith pointed out for pin production. He noted that production of pins could be increased if, instead of each worker making a whole pin, the task was split into components with some workers making pinheads, others making the points.[25] Taylor's scientific management was based on the same idea. But Taylorism's separation of 'conception' and 'execution', or 'thinking' and 'doing', surely generates more resentment and frustration when workers have secondary or tertiary education. In these circumstances, limiting job responsibilities may well reduce productivity rather than increase it.

A service-oriented economy also challenges the claim of mainstream economics that economic performance should be measured by productivity growth. In manufacturing, and even in agriculture, growth in the amount of output per unit of input increases economic growth (as measured by Gross Domestic Product, GDP), provided it can be sustained without accelerating the rate of depreciation of machinery or the quality of land or resources. But in services, increases in 'output' per unit of input can easily cause a deterioration in quality and effectiveness of service delivery, for example in education, healthcare and care work, where personal relationships are important. Using less labour time to deliver a service may motivate financiers, managers and auditors, but higher productivity does not mean a better service for the recipient and may well mean a worse one.

The link between productivity and labour time is further weakened by platform capitalism, in which labour time is commissioned online and through apps. Three main forms of labour relationship look set to dominate labour markets of the future.

One is a new set of servant or 'concierge' activities, including delivery services for meals and other goods, taxi services, and household services such as cleaning or performing odd jobs such as putting up shelves.[26] These commodified services, with the online platform acting as labour broker, have grown to permeate almost every aspect of life in the rich world. For the consumer or client, they should free up time for other things (though fiddling with the app may offset some of this). But for the service providers, time is controlled by the app. Once logged in, they may have to wait around for orders, only to respond immediately once an order comes in. Failure to respond quickly leads to loss of earnings or, at some point, loss of the job.

Other personal services are being offered online to subscribers, with no physical contact. For instance, one company is giving online dance classes to people who pay through Patreon, a crowdfunding website.[27] Some so-called 'creators' (aka 'influencers') gain thousands of pounds every month by charging users to view their online videos or recordings. The claim is that everyone can profit by monetizing their abilities and interests. Not surprisingly, such creativity is extensive among sex service workers.

Another form of increasingly app-mediated labour could be called 'beck-and-call' labour, where no hours of labour are stated. According to one survey in the UK, there were 770,000 people in zero-hours or variable-hours contracts in 2019, and 2.4 million workers who were 'contractually exposed' – that is, in employment contracts that did not stipulate regular, predictable hours of labour.[28] In addition, there were 4.9 million self-employed, many of whom were freelancers with no employment security. Probably many more had variable-hours contracts or contracts with variable, unstable earnings. Others may have predictable hours of labour but no employment security, including many of those employed by temporary-employment agencies, another rapidly growing form of labour.

Even more disruptive of time and income distribution is 'cloud labour', doing discrete tasks remotely for a company or organization that are allocated through online platforms. Now the biggest growth area for labour time, this remote labour ranges from mini tasks such as tagging photos for training algorithms, commissioned through Amazon Mechanical Turk, to outsourcing of legal and medical support services and project work by professionals, including engineers and architects.

Cloud labourers, mostly deep in the precariat, are sometimes called 'telemigrants' because the labour, but not the worker, migrates between countries and communities. Online freelancing platforms broker millions of contracts for short-term projects. Upwork, one of the largest, had over 12 million freelancers on its books in 2022, the biggest number being in website and app development.

The growth of cloud labour, and remote labour more generally, is globalizing the labour process and weakening the bargaining position of those who rely on labour for their living, since jobs can be farmed out to any capable person, anywhere in the world, prepared to offer their services for the lowest price. If you phone London's Heathrow Airport to ask about lost baggage, you may speak to a service worker located in Bangalore.

After the USA, the countries generating the most revenue on Upwork are India and the Philippines. And one factor accelerating this form of labour has been the improvement in machine translation. Since 2016, apps such as Google Translate have routinely scored as well as human translators. Before then, Google Translate was graded at 3.6 out of a perfect score of 6, much worse than the average human translator; in 2016, it scored 5, and has since been refined further.[29]

In short, the very notion of jobs is being chipped away. And the size of the labour force in a country like Britain is an unknowable number.

Work-for-Labour

In industrial capitalism the worker was exploited and oppressed in labour, and mostly left to play and recuperate in 'free time'. Now workers are paid for fewer hours but are expected to do much more 'work-for-labour' outside labour hours. This is unremunerated work that we must do or feel we must do to enhance 'employability' and to function successfully as 'flexible' workers. Measured time in labour may be declining, but time in work-for-labour is mounting, crowding out time for other activities. We are in near-constant panic; as there is no standard of excellence, no amount of work-for-labour makes us feel secure.

One aspect of service-oriented labour is that time worked can vary in intensity much more than in the industrial time regime, and typically involves regular or occasional unpaid overtime. This also means reported hourly wage rates are over-stated in official statistics. An official National Health Service Staff Survey in 2019, before the Covid pandemic struck, found that British doctors, nurses and support staff were doing on average two to three hours of unpaid overtime every week.[30]

Unpaid overtime is also a burden for casual and sessional staff employed by universities and colleges – course teachers often referred to as the academic precariat – hired on short-term contracts and often paid by the contracted hour. This group has grown rapidly in the anglophone world as universities have become increasingly dependent on tuition fees and research grants for their income rather than more stable government funding. In Britain, a third of academic staff are on fixed-term contracts (and two-thirds of research staff).[31] In Australia, most teaching staff are on casual (hourly paid) or fixed-term contracts.[32] In Canada, half of university professors and assistant professors are on temporary contracts.[33] And in the USA, three-quarters of the faculty in universities and higher-education institutions are now on short-term contracts, often paying poverty-line wages.[34]

Everywhere, the academic precariat faces severe demands on their time, preparing lessons and courses, grading students, and so on, involving a lot of unpaid work-for-labour, since the amount they are paid is rarely sufficient to cover the hours of work they must put in. And they are not paid for scholarship, keeping their subject knowledge up to date and relevant, let alone for the research and the writing of scholarly articles on which their diminishing chances of gaining a permanent or continuing contract depend.

A commonly held view among economists and other commentators is that the ongoing technological revolution, often dubbed the fourth industrial revolution, will displace labour and create mass redundancies. Putting a positive spin on it, Andy Haldane, then chief economist of the Bank of England, asserted in a public lecture in 2019 that 'the fourth industrial revolution will deliver billions of hours more free time to people who live longer'.[35]

This is far too sanguine. On the contrary, so far this is the first technological revolution that has directly generated more work, while probably reducing the amount of paid labour. The phenomenon has been termed 'heteromation' to contrast with automation. Automation involves machines displacing labour; heteromation involves machines generating more work for humans.

For instance, in the UK the average amount of time spent online more than doubled from ten hours per week in 2005 to twenty-five hours in 2019 and 2020. About 35 per cent of adults used the internet almost every day in 2005, while 90 per cent did so in 2019.[36] Many people are addicted, to the extent that they are online from the time they wake up until the time they go to bed, and often in bed as well. In the USA, nearly a third of adults say they are online 'almost constantly'.[37] Much of this is work-related, however; it does not deserve to be called leisure or even free time.

Most economists focus only on paid labour, not all the work around it, which leads to some dubious conclusions. For instance, Daron Acemoğlu, a professor at the prestigious Massachusetts Institute of Technology, told the US House of Representatives in November 2021 that automation and algorithms were producing 'a very sharp deceleration in the introduction of new tasks'.[38] He should have said they were generating many more tasks, but that they were unpaid. They are work-for-labour.

Project work by artists and academics, which is often organized in teams, also involves much work-for-labour. People in such project teams may have the illusion of self-control and like to think of themselves as free floating, without bosses or supervisors.[39] In reality, they often chronically overwork, because they are subject to social control, by 'power without a centre'.[40]

In sum, the spread of work-for-labour, particularly among lower-income groups around the precariat, further clouds the notion of jobs and makes a mockery of measured labour time.

Emotional Labour

A great deal of time in many service jobs goes under the name of 'emotional labour',[41] in which people are expected to put on a winsome display of emotions such as smiling, wishing people 'a good day', or enquiring after their health and the wellbeing of their children, parents or the like. This has been converted into a social skill, which some people can do almost naturally, others cannot and some simply refuse to do.

A related aspect is emotional intelligence, seen as boosting productivity. Consider this piece of promotional puff:

> *Learn to identify emotional intelligence when you see it.* Smart employers recognize the value of emotional intelligence in the workplace. In a survey of more than 2,600 hiring managers and HR professionals, HR company CareerBuilder found that: 71% said they value emotional intelligence more than IQ in an employee; 75% said they were more likely to promote a candidate with high emotional intelligence over one with a high IQ. Emotionally intelligent employees are invaluable because they help build chemistry. Great chemistry leads to great teams. And great teams do great work. But as an employer, how can you identify emotional intelligence when you see it?[42]

Good question. Answers on a postcard, please. Clearly, emotional intelligence can be learned as well as being innate. It places a new potentially valuable demand on time.

It is also well established that physically attractive people are more likely to be hired and may even be paid more. While this form of discrimination has always existed, it features more prominently in a tertiary time regime. It can induce a form of alienation, a factor in commodifying the body and encouraging beautifying operations such as nose jobs, breast enlargements, or bariatric surgery to lose weight. We tend to think of these as linked to sexuality, or pure narcissism. But they play a part in the modern labour process as well.

The need to supply emotional labour increases the time

used for work-for-reproduction, which now requires time to acquire emotional 'skills'. Improving self-presentation and acceptable ways of behaving towards clients and supervisors – becoming 'docile bodies' in Foucault's terminology[43] – all require time, and loom large in a tertiary time system. Many people cannot easily reproduce their labour power, their capabilities, because they do not have control over their time or the opportunity to do so. Others spend a lot of time doing so, only to find that obsolescence of what purport to be skills mocks the effort. Self-care is intrinsic to being in the precariat; neglect it at your peril.

Meanwhile, activities that used to be part of domestic work, or were rarely done at all due to time constraints, are now supplied by commercial firms to enhance emotional labour. Companies are supplying activities that previously the idealized family was expected to provide. Once commodified, there is a tendency towards standardization, with activities packaged as variants from which consumers can choose. This puts more pressure on consumers to do more work and labour to pay for them. Thus, the commodification of emotional labour is penetrating family life.

After all, the family is a zone of emotions, revealed by attitudes, behaviour and the way time is allocated. But the commodification of family life is corroding that zone. The market is identifying and commercializing emotional needs (or contrived needs), to the point of creating desired norms for what 'good' parents, wives and husbands should do. Instead of a carefree birthday gathering, which you may do 'badly', there should be a proper party organized by party professionals or fast-food chains, offering a menu of choice depending on your purse (cowboys-and-Indians, *Star Trek*, and so on). Dinner parties can be pre-packaged, even supplied with 'conversation animators'. Rent-a-mum services fill maternal care deficits. Dads never spend enough time with their kids; now the market offers solutions.

There has been a creeping use of commercial criteria for assessing domestic work. In the USA, some companies have provided their executives and senior employees with training and guidelines on how to manage family life efficiently so as to fit family activities within the demands of employment. Evaluation of the person's performance as parent and spouse is based on workplace programmes.[44] This is a commercialized service – family management, to free up time for more or better labour.

Its advocates might claim that emotional-labour services in the family domain enable family members to handle pressures and family life more efficiently. But in converting domestic work into emotional labour, the market is generating more labour, more 'jobs'. An idealized commercial norm is being created, whereas only an imagined one existed in the past. And in the process, time patterns are being shaped and manipulated. This commodification erodes the family's psychological capacity to be a barrier to commodification more generally. Personal reciprocities are weakened, contributing to the erosion of our understanding of compassion, altruism and social solidarity. What we do with our time is vital for the preservation of those values.

The blurring of the boundary between the workplace and home was highlighted by the sociologist Arlie Hochschild, in her claim that home was becoming subordinated to 'work', by which she meant labour in jobs. More than half the employees she interviewed said they felt more 'at home' on the job than at home, partly because they experienced more emotional support there.[45] This should not be seen as an endorsement of jobs, but as an indictment of the emotional paucity of commodified domestic life.

Work-as-Training

There is also a culture of incessant 'training-for-labour', a sort of anti-ageing pill for workers. One human-resource consultant told the *Financial Times* that everybody should expect to spend at least 15 per cent of their time every year in training.[46] You are never as good as you were, and you are never good enough for tomorrow. Do more training! And don't forget to pay for it!

In the industrialized world, most professions now require practitioners to undergo 'continuous professional development' (CPD). In the USA, these include lawyers, teachers, accountants, engineers, pilots, physicians, nurses, psychologists, pharmacists and architects. As the 'adviser on learning' at the UK's Chartered Institute of Personnel and Development put it: 'A certificate on the wall can no longer be accepted as a guarantee of competence.'

Workers must remodel and remarket themselves, often turning to commercial bodies to help. This is a big change, and a big user of time. Most professions in the UK have moved from a voluntary to a compulsory scheme, on the grounds that all professionals have a duty to maintain and update their skills. And firms and professionals these days must demonstrate to professional-indemnity insurers that they are regularly updating their skills if they wish to be insured against malpractice claims or accidents, even if there is no proven need or even evidence that any updating is taking place.

Training has been extended to personality traits beyond technical competence. The training knot is being tightened. There is training in 'leadership', 'team playing', 'learning to listen', 'responding to feedback', 'challenging ingrained expectations' and 'overcoming self-limiting beliefs'. Unlike the old proletariat, the salariat in the tertiary age is subject to proletarianization of the mind.

Not only must professionals undertake regular retraining, but often they are required to undertake it from specific training providers. Firms are increasingly outsourcing their training. According to the UK's Chartered Management Institute, 'The days of the paternalistic organisation that looks after the career development of its employees are over. Average managers today will have nine moves in their working lives.'

The expansion of training-for-labour is not confined to professionals and the salariat and has been a growing source of inequality. The precariat must do more of it, to reduce the probability of falling into a marginalized underclass. To please potential employers, they must be prepared to learn new bundles of skills, perhaps taking night classes, or the equivalent, in their own time and at their own cost. Yet this time is often wasted, and those doing the training know it.

Governments resort to training schemes for a variety of motives, and upgrading technical competences is not necessarily the main aim, whatever the rhetoric. Take the time-honoured idea of apprenticeships: apprenticeship schemes promoted by the British government have reduced the duration to such a short period that they mock the original concept. As one unemployed person wrote after introduction of a training measure in 2015: 'The Apprenticeships that the Tories harp on about are just 6 months of providing cheap labour. They are nothing like the 3 or 5 year apprenticeships that young people used to get in the 1970s when they learnt a trade properly.'[47]

Another job seeker was offered a training course by the Department for Work and Pensions (DWP) but turned it down because he thought he could not learn enough in the time provided. The training provider's admissions clerk candidly told him, 'I agree with you that six weeks is an inadequate amount of time to learn the curriculum, but the government has told us to halve the length of the training period so as to double the throughput from the dole queue.'[48]

Companies and organizations around the world spent a total of $370 billion on 'learning and development' in 2019,[49] but much in-house 'training' has little to do with improving skills or helping workers do their job. For example, another form of work-for-training is ethics training. This has long been an obligatory feature of some professions, notably medicine and the law, where taking courses in ethics is required for the 'right to practise'. But in recent years such courses have spread far beyond the professions.

In the USA, even when not required by law, they are mandatory for employees of just about every company and organization because, according to the Federal Sentencing Guidelines for Organizations, having 'an effective compliance and ethics program' can 'mitigate the ultimate punishment of an organization' accused of wrongdoing, such as corruption, sexual harassment or racial discrimination.[50] Yet despite the hundreds of hours spent on standardized and often simplistic online ethics courses provided by commercial companies, there is little evidence that they prevent ethical violations. On the contrary, if people believe the courses are there just to protect the boss's back, they are unlikely to take them seriously and likely to resent the time required to do them. And studies of unconscious-bias training, for instance, suggest that much of it has little effect or can even backfire by *reducing* diversity.[51]

That said, much tertiary labour is already in a zone of ethics. Many service providers, especially in the public sector, are regularly required to make ethical decisions, which take time and nervous energy. The financial crisis of 2008 and the subsequent austerity era have intensified the ethical strain on public service providers; cuts in social care, health services, education and cultural support have forced them to make more distressing decisions on what services to supply and for whom. The outcome has been depression and burnout on the part of providers as well as hardship or worse for recipients.

Work-in-Waiting

Then there is work-in-waiting, a neglected form of work encompassing several ideas, including 'waiting around', as in filling time anomically, waiting for sporadic labour, waiting 'on call' and 'waiting your turn' in queues, traffic jams, offices or clinics. These are mostly obligatory uses of time.[52]

Tertiary labour has increased the amount of time spent on work-in-waiting. In the past, standardized labour schedules compressed time use, to the detriment of the proletariat and lower rungs of the salariat, with regimented working days. But nowadays forcing workers in the precariat to wait for scarce labour hours has become a disciplinary mechanism, as well as an exercise of economic power. Waiting in a virtual queue for an opportunity to labour is part of the process of precariatization, reinforcing supplicant status with a reminder that some higher authority is calling the shots.

Every transformation has involved work-in-waiting as a way for the newly powerful to re-engineer labour to suit their needs. For instance, waiting was a feature of the *population flottante* of eighteenth- and nineteenth-century Europe, when hordes of itinerant workers waited around, hoping for odd jobs. In developing countries, waiting around consumes much of the time of the urban unemployed, stigmatized as surplus to requirements. But waiting around in rich countries is also linked to the increased complexity of the state, and the way social policy has become more directive and coercive.

Prolonged waiting for benefits or social services is one of the hidden tragedies of contemporary existence, severely constraining the time of millions of people. Ironically, the politicians most likely to bemoan the constricting effect of government regulations on businesses tend to be the most enthusiastic supporters of piling on time-using regulatory conditions to obtain welfare support, a point we will return to later.

'Presenteeism' v. 'Absenteeism'

Policy on labour absenteeism has largely concerned itself with defining 'legitimate reasons' for absence, such as sickness, and sanctions for absence for other reasons. But a peculiar feature of a jobholder society is 'presenteeism', the opposite of absenteeism. In 2019, before the pandemic, over three-quarters of British adults in jobs said they were reluctant to call in sick,[53] and this proportion had hardly budged in 2022.[54] Discussed here are the trends already firmly established pre-Covid, while Chapter 6 looks at how they have continued post-Covid despite changes in labour patterns.

In 2018, British employees took an average of just over four sick days a year, down from seven days in 1993.[55] This compared with a European average of ten days and was the fourth lowest in Europe (Switzerland was easily the lowest, with just 1.6 days). The avowedly industrious Germans took more than eighteen days.

A health-and-wellbeing survey found that the proportion of British workplaces with a reported 'culture of presenteeism' more than tripled between 2010 and 2018, from 26 per cent to 86 per cent. Employees on average took just 6.6 days of absence in 2018 and sickness rates were low – 2.6 per cent in the public sector and 1.7 per cent in the private sector. Sickness was highest among public health workers at 3.3 per cent. 'Leavism' – doing job-related work during annual leave – had also been growing. Nearly 70 per cent of those surveyed said it existed in their firms.[56]

In 2011, the UK prime minister David Cameron condemned what he termed the 'sicknote culture' as a drain on resources. There was no evidence that any such culture existed. But this attitude remains prevalent. Only 42 per cent of managers in British firms surveyed in 2015 said that influenza was an appropriate reason for taking sick leave, even though coming to work while sick could infect other workers.[57]

(One US study estimated that a 'one or two flu day' stay-at-home policy would cut workplace transmission by about 25 per cent for a one-day policy and nearly 40 per cent for a two-day policy.[58]) And less than 40 per cent thought back pain or elective surgery was an appropriate excuse. The same survey found that nearly 40 per cent of employees did not tell their manager the real reason for calling in sick, because they feared being judged or disbelieved. This proportion rose to over 60 per cent if the cause was related to mental health.

Increasing presenteeism has been associated with a rising incidence of mental-health conditions and subsequent stress-related absence. In the health-and-wellbeing survey, 55 per cent of respondents reported an increase in such conditions between 2016 and 2018. In 2017–18, Britain's Health and Safety Executive estimated that 15.4 million working days were lost to job-related stress, depression and anxiety, amounting to 57 per cent of all working days lost to ill-health.[59]

Empty Labour

Another widespread use of time in labour deserves more recognition than it has received. In an insightful book, Roland Paulsen defined the phenomenon of 'empty labour', encompassing the ways in which employees avoid doing labour in their jobs, or 'everything you do at work that is not your work'.[60] Slacking, 'ca'canny' (go-slow), working-to-rule, time wasting, pilfering and petty sabotage have always figured in labour relationships.[61] However, in the tertiary time regime the scope for what is known colloquially as 'soldiering' is greater than in the industrial time era, and is less visible or transparent.

Soldiering was defined by Frederick Taylor in his

'scientific management' book of 1919 as the practice of 'deliberately working slowly so as to avoid a full-day's work'. But in the tertiary time regime, as Paulsen noted, professionals demonstrate among the most invidious forms of time wasting, by exploiting clients' ignorance of what a job entails, such as lawyers saying a case will take much longer than is needed.

Some see empty labour as a form of passive resistance to labour they do not wish to do, or as a protest against low wages and poor working conditions.[62] Passivity flourishes when there is no progressive politics. As the Italian philosopher Federico Campagna has interpreted the dilemma: 'This is not a time for assaults, but for withdrawal.'[63] Empty labour is a classic form of withdrawal.

Estimates of time taken up by empty labour are hazy, for the obvious reason that much of it is clandestine. According to US research, two-thirds of employees admit to visiting non-work-related websites every day; nearly half say they spend time on social media and texting. A quarter waste time chatting to co-workers and a sixth say they do 'household activities' such as online shopping.[64] Contrary to popular prejudice, older workers are just as likely to waste time as younger ones, according to surveys in Finland and the USA.[65]

Even before the hybrid arrangements combining in-office and 'work-from-home' labour that became widespread after Covid, the scope for empty labour was increased by the trend towards more flexible labour hours and trust-based work time, intended to achieve better 'work–life balance' mainly for employees with care commitments.[66] Almost certainly, the main forms of empty labour are not political but consumerist in character. Most use of pornographic internet sites is during 'working hours', as is the case with online purchases of everyday goods and services. This reflects the fuzziness of tertiary labour time.

The most famous case of empty labour concerns a German civil servant who on his formal retirement in 2012 sent colleagues a farewell email, in which he stated, 'Since 1998, I have been present but not really there. So, I am well prepared for retirement – Adieu!' [67] The email was leaked to the press and became world news. He had been employed in the state surveyor's office since 1974, but a reorganization in 1998 had left him with nothing to do, because the authorities had constructed parallel structures. He had offered to do other tasks but had been ignored. In a subsequent statement, he announced that he had earned €745,000 for doing nothing.

Lest any reader feels inclined to attribute such behaviour to the civil service, another case was well described by somebody who had spent many years in the British insurance business, employed by several major companies. In his book *The Living Dead: Switched Off, Zoned Out*, David Bolchover commented:

> During the years 1997 to 2003, I was employed to do a full-time job. If I was to be given now all the work I had to do for my employers during those six years, and I worked hard using all my ability, I would be able to complete all of it very comfortably in about six months, working Monday to Friday, 9 to 5. One month of work for every year of employment. Sounds about right.[68]

Although these may seem extreme cases, they appear to be widespread. One US survey of 1,000 full-time employees found that nearly 80 per cent said they could complete their daily tasks in less than the eight hours they were obliged to be in the office.[69] Bolchover bemoaned 'endless spells of nothingness' in his job, wasting time in an enervating way, the only point being to gain income. Yet 'boreout', in contrast to 'burnout', has received minimal attention.[70]

Anybody who has been employed in a bureaucracy or large firm will know that empty labour is endemic in most workplaces. This makes the measure of labour time a very haphazard, if not arbitrary, practice. It may also help explain the much-commented productivity puzzle. Technological change is supposed to raise labour productivity, but the widespread adoption of information technology has seen only a weak correlation. 'Cyberloafing' – employees doing online activities unrelated to their job – could be part of the reason.

The difficulty of equating time in labour with productivity and output also led to the start in the 1990s of the now quasi-universal practice of 'auditing' labour. In 1997 the accounting professor Michael Power described the increasing amount of time devoted to checking and scrutinizing labour as part of the 'audit explosion' and the expanding 'regulatory state'.[71] Then, as now, pseudo-criteria proliferated, often encapsulated in long-winded, turgid manuals, which encouraged people to prioritize the appearance of diligent labour and adherence to arbitrary rules to prove they were performing as required, generating yet more dysfunctional ways of using time.

Occupational Licensing as Time Stealing

One of several reasons for saying that the neoliberal era was not one of labour market deregulation, as so many commentators have asserted, is the systemic transfer of control over labour, work and time within occupations from self-regulating, traditional guild-like institutions to the state. Occupational licensing by government-appointed or government-approved bodies has been a global trend, although most extensive in the USA, where over 1,000 occupations require licences in at least one state and one in four employees is subject to state regulation.[72] In the UK, licences are needed to practise as doctors, solicitors, veterinary surgeons, private security guards, gas installers, taxi drivers and drivers of heavy-goods vehicles, among others. Often, regulation is dominated by insurance and other financial interests.

The essence of occupational licensing is that an external body determines who can and cannot practise a particular occupation, what conduct is required and what constitutes behaviour justifying suspension or removal of a 'right to practise'. Among the consequences is that occupations have become more fragmented, with layers of job titles and restrictions on mobility from one layer to another.

The full implications of this modern form of state regulation are discussed elsewhere,[73] but for now we should be concerned with the implications for people's time. Imagine two extreme types of occupational labour market. In one, roughly corresponding to the industrial time regime, there is competition for base-level jobs, as trainees or apprentices, which are the single port of entry for the occupation.

If they abide by the rules and show competence and diligence, they accumulate experience and climb over the years in terms of skill, status, income and privileges. There may be many competitors at the outset, but fewer as the person rises through the ranks.

In the second model, people can enter at several levels but to move to a different or higher level they must spend time off the job acquiring new credentials and then applying for another port of entry. A person must go out of the occupation and then try to come back once qualifications have been gained. To the extent this model prevails, much more time is spent off the job gaining credentials and in preparing and applying for more ports of entry.

Neither extreme has existed in quite the way outlined, but the tertiary labour process is much closer to the second model than the first. More people have to use more time doing work that is not classified as labour, in work-related activities that are not directly productive. They have to devote a lot more time in proving they are abiding by state-imposed rules, norms and standards, and a lot more time gaining or regaining credentials in order to go up an occupational rung or even to return to one they had before. This has been taken to an extreme in the USA where, for example, the average interior designer must complete 2,190 days of education and experience to obtain a licence to practise.[74] To compound the demands on time, the greater division of labour makes it easier for employers or state regulators to convert job clusters into zones of the precariat, full of supplicants jostling for insecure and unstable jobs.

Work-as-Job-Seeking

The labour market is a place in which millions of people are preparing to search for jobs, are applying for jobs and then, possibly, are being considered for a job. These are three distinct phases, all requiring large amounts of time and all potentially traumatizing.

For the precariat, job searching is a major feature of life and a hugely time-consuming form of work-for-labour. One analysis has compared it to being on a religious pilgrimage, implying 'suffering, doubt and self-transformation, making job-seeking a trial of the soul'. Having interviewed dozens of unemployed, the author concluded that 'all too often people internalise stigmatising ideas derived from politics about "skivers" and "spongers" – stereotypes repeatedly refuted by research'. He backed this up by referring to several job-seeking guides.[75]

What Color Is Your Parachute?, an international best-seller that has sold over 10 million copies since it was first published in 1970, was written by an American Episcopalian clergyman, who suggested that becoming unemployed was a trial sent by God. Another best-selling book, *The Gift of Job Loss* (2011), portrays unemployment as an opportunity for personal transformation. A self-help guide, *Life Without Work* (1994), describes unemployment as a test, for which the person should consider themselves specially selected, adding that 'the difficulties we are given are there to help us grow, and . . . we are never given problems that are more than we can cope with'.[76] These authors seem to have lost touch with reality, which is perhaps why their works are best-sellers!

There is a wry joke, with more colourful variants, told among the precariat: 'Question: how many freelancers does it take to change a lightbulb? Answer: five hundred. All apply, but only one gets the job.' It captures a reality. But it only captures part of what is happening. We should differentiate between three things here: first, applying for short-term jobs (tasks), as in the joke; second, the more complex process of seeking financial support for 'projects', which is the reality for many artists, academics and freelancers; and third, the search for longer-term employment.

In all three cases, the time-using activity of job seeking is complicated by the need to game the recruitment algorithms increasingly used by employers of every description. Almost all big US companies, and many smaller ones, use applicant-tracking systems that on average weed out about 75 per cent of all job applications.[77] These systems, also widely used in other countries, including Britain, screen out many qualified as well as unqualified applicants before any human scrutiny on behalf of the potential employer.

Once through the tracking system, application processes may involve four or five further tests, also assessed by algorithms, before any prospect of an interview. These take up a great deal of time; the process is also stressful for applicants, impoverishing other areas of time use. But there is no cost to the firm. Instead of sifting through numerous application forms, it need only interview the final short-listed few whom the algorithms have deemed most successful in the multiple tests.

An extreme example of software screening, although probably not unique, concerned a company that received 25,000 applications for a standard engineering job. After six rounds of tests and interviews, all were rejected as supposedly not qualified. One candidate, a fully qualified experienced engineer, demanded to know why. He was told he had been rejected because his previous job, which he had taken to earn some money, was not in engineering.[78] In another firm, an applicant was told his previous job title did not match the vacancy, which carried a title unique to that company.[79]

More generally, if someone with a university degree or professional qualification takes a job below their level of competence, they risk being blocked by the recruiting algorithm from jobs they are qualified to do, perhaps because the algorithm gives undue weight to recent job experience, or perhaps because it is presumed that the person has lost skills or not kept up to date with technical developments. One reaction to such digital discrimination is not to take short-term jobs below one's qualification. But many in the precariat will not have a choice.

Recruitment has become big business. The commodification of job-seeking time is nurtured by recruitment agents and 'head-hunters', armed with batteries of tests, assessments, practice interviews, required demonstrations of behavioural traits and psychometric status, and the like. Firms are outsourcing recruitment procedures to human resource consultancies and companies specializing in talent assessment. The Chemistry Group, a US-based talent consultancy, has designed an online game to analyse the credentials and mental sharpness of candidates. In the UK, one of the most widely used recruitment tools are the psychometric tests published by the SHL business management consultancy that purport to test the diagrammatic, numerical and verbal reasoning of prospective employees.

Of course, many in the recruitment business are endeavouring to assist people in finding a job and may save them time in doing so. But job seeking is an increasingly complex time-using process. For the precariat, who must move between a series of short-term, insecure jobs and 'projects', there are likely to be many such job-seeking episodes.

On average, to get one interview, British applicants make twenty-seven job applications, each requiring extensive documentation, preparation and perhaps completion of those stressful and time-filling tests. To land a job, they may have to make even more applications, as typically they must attend five interviews for one job offer.[80] In the USA, it takes between twenty-one and eighty applications to obtain a job offer.[81] According to the Trendence Institut in Berlin, in 2013 new graduates in France, Germany and Italy sent out over thirty applications on average before obtaining a job, while in Greece and Spain they had to send out over sixty.[82]

Millions of people in the precariat are expected to go through a tortuous process, eating up a great deal of time and expense, mostly for no gain. Some will claim that taking time to hire appropriately qualified people is worthwhile, because hiring the wrong person could be more costly to the firm. But the cost of a complex process is borne almost entirely by the job applicants, in their time, morale and energy. And, ironically, despite the prolonged selection processes, major corporations still make the wrong choices, accounting for about a third of managerial hires in US manufacturing firms, for instance.[83]

In the UK, state-benefit recipients must prepare a continuously updated CV (curriculum vitae) and are required to keep diaries of their job-seeking activities. This illiberal scheme of time control is paternalistic and contrary to common justice, which states that any imposition on the vulnerable is unfair if it is not imposed on everybody equally. One unemployed person wrote to me about the amount of useless time spent in drawing up 'claimant commitments' to satisfy the DWP. He noted that its 'Work Coaches are institutionally clueless about the time-demand realities of tailoring CVs and Equal Opportunities job application forms to job description and person specification, etc.'.

Meanwhile, in the growing sphere of project applications, where people join together to apply for funds from a foundation or agency, individuals commonly find they are competing against themselves by being in more than one competing team. This has created chaotic rivalries and much wasted time.[84]

The job (and project) application process has become a way of disrupting thinking as much as disrupting work as an activity. Applicants must use up time in orienting themselves to what they perceive to be wanted and what they expect other applicants to be offering. It is not just a matter of competition based on competence to do the tasks of a job or project, but of attitudes.

For example – an extreme one, but perhaps becoming less so – in the application process for certain academic jobs at the University of California, 76 per cent of all applicants were ruled out of contention before their research, teaching skills or academic merits were even considered, because their diversity statements on gender and race issues were deemed inadequate.[85] In other words, the recruitment process had little to do with technical competence. Of course, it is reasonable to rule out people who hold racist or sexist views. But the screening of diversity statements seems to have been designed deliberately to favour recruitment of minorities and women, wasting the time of applicants who, unknown to them beforehand, had no chance of succeeding.

As for the unemployed, the state is constantly finding ways of using up their time. In a form of work-for-labour called a work trial, introduced by the DWP, employers can hire job seekers on DWP books for up to six weeks (thirty working days) without paying them a wage. During that time, they are paid only their jobseeker benefits – much less than an average wage. This is blatantly exploitative and adds further insecurity to the precariat. One nineteen-year-old woman, who took part in a work trial but was not taken on afterwards, ended up £20 out of pocket because she had to buy the shirt and trousers deemed the appropriate uniform for the job in question.

The DWP claimed in 2020 that it had no data on the number put on unpaid work trials. According to a DWP spokesperson:

> It is misleading and disingenuous to suggest that work trials are exploitative. If a customer volunteers for a work trial, the Jobcentre will first ensure the employer is offering a genuinely worthy opportunity that could

lead to employment. Work trials are usually five days and customers who volunteer are financially supported throughout by the Jobcentre.[86]

This is disingenuous. If the DWP does not have the data, how does it know how many people are working how many days without pay? And do the job seekers really 'volunteer' to enter a period of unpaid employment?

Work-for-the-State

> Do not impose on others what you do not wish for yourself.
> — Confucius, *The Analects*, *c.*497 BC

This leads to what may be called work-for-the-state, tasks undertaken to satisfy demands made on individuals by the state. Self-assessment for income tax is one example, but its greatest extent lies in work people must do to claim welfare benefits, including lengthy and complex application forms that, furthermore, must be done online, forcing those without internet access at home or computer skills to seek help.

Much of the work imposed on supplicants is deliberate, designed to dissuade those entitled to state benefits from applying for them, thereby 'saving' public funds – so-called 'taxpayers' money'. From the outset, successive reforms of the welfare system have enforced on the precariat a regime of extra work, an enforced use of time. An invidious example is Universal Credit in the UK, the main means-tested benefit for people without jobs or with low earnings from jobs. Its underlying objective has been to habituate members of the precariat to a precariatized existence. They must use a lot of time in the process of claiming benefits, keeping benefits if obtained, and coping with threats of sanctions and with lengthy stressful appeals against sanctions.

Even if they succeed (and many do not) in negotiating the complex application process, which can take days or even weeks, Universal Credit claimants must wait a statutory five weeks for the first payment, and in practice the wait is often longer. To receive benefit, those deemed 'able to work' must sign a 'claimant commitment contract' to perform various tasks each week for at least thirty-five hours, backed by financial penalties in the form of withdrawal of benefits for non-compliance. They must engage in intensive job searching or preparation and prove that they have done so, whether suitable jobs exist or not. If any of the designated tasks are not done, or not done to the apparent satisfaction of the 'work coach', the person can be sanctioned and have their benefit withdrawn, reducing or removing their only or main source of income.

The contract between claimant and work coach is asymmetrical in time as well as status. If the claimant is late for a prescribed interview, they may be sanctioned. (Missing or being late for an interview is by far the most common reason for sanctions.) If the work coach is late or cancels at the last moment, the claimant pays the price in lost time and travel costs. Similarly, if a claimant is required to travel to a 'job fair', and does not do so, they may be sanctioned. If they go and find it is only for jobs for 16–24-year-olds and they are older, they have wasted their time and money in travel, and are not compensated.

Ever since Magna Carta in 1217, common law has rested on basic principles, which include due process, proportionality of punishment and right of representation. None of these principles are applied in the Universal Credit scheme, which denies due process. The person is charged and found guilty by the same, often junior official, and then punished. Afterwards, they are allowed to appeal. That is not how a legal process is supposed to work.

Such has been the use of sanctions – which, after all, is a denial of the right to subsistence, and thus disproportionately harsh for whatever failings are being asserted – that, pre-Covid, over a million claimants had benefits withdrawn each year, more than the number convicted in magistrates' and sheriff courts. And the average income loss (fine) has been much greater for those sanctioned than for those convicted in the courts for genuine misdemeanours.

Appeals may take up to a year for a final decision, leaving people without income for months. The fact that a very high proportion of appeals are granted testifies to the arbitrary and inequitable process. One could say the welfare system has become the biggest legal-enforcement instrument in the country. No wonder it has been called 'Britain's secret penal system'.[87]

While working on this chapter, I received an email from a disabled claimant explaining his perspective on the process. His statement (with his permission) is worth quoting in full:

> Number-crunching of job applications per week is part-and-parcel of creating a hostile environment in a world in which claimants are processed as throughput by an abusive system in which normal contract law's references

to the legal terms 'bargaining power' and 'consideration' are disregarded. At a government-funded computer skills training centre in 1998, trainees were allowed only two hours' guaranteed access to a PC per day, while numerous classes were shunted through each training room per day, creaming off the profit at the expense of trainees' quality of experience.

The Head of Jobsearch told trainees, 'Unless you submit your Jobsearch Portfolio at the end of each week with a minimum of 16 job applications, you will be terminated from the course and have to go back to the jobcentre with your tail between your legs, having to justify yourself.' Instead of photocopying one CV for every job application, my customised CV for a post I was really interested in took days of waiting for PC access (no home PC) and a whole weekend on six drafts of the specified covering letter. The Head of Jobsearch responded, 'You have clearly not spent sufficient time on jobsearch activity . . .' Yet I got an interview. How many interviews would those recording 16+ applications per week have got?

The barely concealed rage was surely what most of us would feel. Another person wrote to me about the fact, reported in August 2021, that care workers had to labour for three months to earn what a director of care homes earned in just a day, adding:

The £8.80 an hour figure cited for care workers' pay amounted to £1,224 a month based on a 35-hour working week. Not stated was the fact that many care workers are or were on zero-hours contracts and now Universal Credit sanctions fodder-status. I was a zero-hours contract worker from May 2005 to April 2006, generally employed for three-hour shifts at £8.71 per hour as a domiciliary care worker to adults with learning difficulties in an inner London borough while declaring part-time earnings when signing on fortnightly as a Jobseeker's Allowance claimant at the local jobcentre.

To accomplish that work, I would walk at least six miles per day return journey to service users' homes in a neighbouring inner London borough as Jobseeker's Allowance (JSA) administration claimed wrongly that my six hours per week at £8.71/hr placed me above the JSA threshold and I was therefore 'not entitled' to JSA and was not paid for travelling to work. At that time, New Labour's Department for Work and Pensions' televised broadcasts and public billboards proclaimed they were 'targeting benefit thieves' even while Jobcentre Plus call centres were in meltdown, leading many claimants including myself to face the risk of destitution.

Then there is the wilfully punitive demand on claimants to prove eligibility repeatedly. As one disabled pensioner wrote to me:

> The UK has become more and more dominated by ID papers as gatekeepers for everything. As but one example, when summonsed to a 'Customer Compliance Section' interview at the jobcentre in 2014, I was instructed to bring six months of bank statements as proof of ID. Not only is such a task a psychological and stressful challenge, but it is time-consuming and almost wilfully designed to make it

hard for people in vulnerable circumstances to obtain their 'rights'.

Work-for-the-state is a major time stealer that has received little political attention. Ironically, its inherent unpleasantness is compounded by what might be called a 'work-for-state deficit', in that many people are never able to do enough to succeed or gain security. Think of the welfare claimant confronted with a fifty-page application form, with numerous explanatory notes and instructions. Stressed by other demands on their time, and fearful, they may spend an hour doing the work, when three hours might be needed to do so adequately, four to do it optimally. The trouble is that the time of the precariat is given no value at all.

Work-as-Care

The omission of unpaid care from depictions of work in the industrial time era was sexist and distortionary. But in the tertiary time regime, this has had even more distortionary implications. The extent of care expected, if not demanded, by society is much greater. In rich countries at least, more of the average person's life is spent in receiving care, partly because children spend longer in school, partly because more people live into dependent old age and partly because more people with disabilities are living longer. In addition, more time is used by more people in providing care of various kinds. The twin trends exist even though there has been commodification of care linked to its privatization via commercialized care homes.[88]

The treatment of unpaid care work as non-work makes no

sense. If I care for my elderly mother and you care for yours, apparently no work is done. If I pay you to care for my elderly mother and you pay me to care for yours, two jobs are created and national income goes up.

The neglect of care work by policymakers, economists and statisticians was a failure throughout the twentieth century. In capitalistic economies, exchange value takes precedence over use value, to the detriment of affective caring roles. A few social scientists focused on this, but their work was relegated to the margins. Feminists demanded it should be taken seriously, as did Marxists in debating productive, unproductive and reproductive labour. But on the political left as well as on the right, when it was not neglected, it was regarded as inferior.

Despite the recent vast literature on the subject, economists still tend to regard care work as a subject for sociologists or 'the welfare community'. Even lobbyists for inclusion of 'informal' work in economic activity have tended to regard caring as non-work, as I found in working over the years with SEWA, the Self-Employed Women's Association of India.

It is only recently that statisticians have tried seriously to measure the extent or incidence of care work, let alone its economic or social value. Implicitly, policymakers in the twentieth century were inclined to allow care work – unpaid care – to decline, because of the way economic growth was measured, and because GDP growth was regarded as the primary economic objective, linked to job creation. People doing mainly unpaid care work were, from this perspective, reducing growth and the number in jobs.

Positioning care work has not only been hard for

economists. The difficulty starts with the linguistic ambiguity in the idea of care and the activity of 'caring'. 'To care for someone' has several possible meanings that blur into one another. 'I care for Jane' may mean no more than I care *about* her, that I hope all goes well for her. Or it may mean I am, or want to be, her lover. Or it may mean I am taking responsibility for looking after her wellbeing. Or it may mean that I take care of her, through tending to her needs, perhaps because of a disability or frailty. This multitude of meanings has surely contributed to the neglect of care work in general social analysis and to its neglect in the measurement of work.

Another factor in such neglect is the universality of caring. Almost all of us have done something we would call care work and, barring those who are ill, frail or disabled, we all think we could do it if necessary or if we so wished. This perception of near-universal capacity has contributed to its undervaluation. It is nothing special, so the conventional view would claim. This is unfortunate, because the capacity to perform it well is acquired through the kind of experience and training required in many forms of so-called skilled work.

Another cause of neglect is the differing intensity of work involved. It may mean no more than being a presence, available in case of an accident or an untoward development requiring support for someone. Or, at the other extreme, it may mean almost constant attention to a bed-ridden invalid. This makes it hard for policymakers and statisticians to have a clear concept of care work. For instance, some social scientists have tried to separate maternal childcare time into primary and secondary activities, the former concerned with the direct care of the child.[89] Some have gone further in dividing primary activities into development time, such as reading aloud or playing with a child in order to teach them, and low-intensity time. Others have defined childcare more broadly still, including eating meals together, even in a restaurant.[90]

However, it is the growth of the perceived need for care for the elderly and those with disabilities that has made care work politically prominent. Their numbers have grown dramatically, and they and their carers have votes. Today, there are about 15 million people in the UK with a long-term chronic condition. And many younger people are facing the challenge of looking after frail elderly parents, often at considerable cost in time and money.

The growing commercialization of care relationships has generated a disturbing trend as care has moved progressively out of the family household. It is increasingly not just a two-way relationship, between care provider and recipient, but involves significant others. With the spreading commodification of care and a shift from public provision and state regulation to commercial and less-regulated provision, others (relatives, the state, local authorities, charities) may be providing financial or other assistance; social workers may facilitate care relationships; and public agencies may monitor care provided by private commercial firms.

In that complex set of possible relationships, there is considerable scope for exploitation, oppression and self-exploitation, in which guilt or anxiety can induce people to spend more time providing care than is good for their own health or mental wellbeing. There is also a suggestion that, in the twenty-first century, more time in care work will be about helping ourselves, our relatives or colleagues recover from, or deal with, the stress of the way we are living. Surely, reducing the need for that should be part of the new politics of time.

The Regulatory Stranglehold

Neoliberals in the 1980s called for labour market deregulation. Critics since then, most on the political left, have decried deregulation. Yet there has been no such development. The labour process in the tertiary time era has been more tightly and comprehensively regulated than in any previous era.

It starts with schooling, which has been redesigned to produce job seekers and the attributes required for the economic system. It continues with the increasingly tight state regulation of training and retraining schemes, with standardized commodified processes. It continues with the extension of state regulation through occupational licensing, giving governance control to insurance companies and financial institutions. The neoliberal revolution set out to destroy the remnants of guilds and the commoning that characterized them. Symbolically, a leading guru of the revolution, Milton Friedman, wrote his first book *Income from Independent Professional Practice* (with Simon Kuznets, inventor of the GDP concept), published in 1945, on the need to dismantle the self-regulation of the professions.

While state regulation of the schooling–training–occupational sphere was being strengthened under the smokescreen of deregulation, the state set out to regulate the lower echelons of the labour market through conversion of rights-based and insurance-based welfare into means-tested, behaviour-tested 'workfare'. The surveillance state was on its way, not only shaping how the precariat used their time but raising the costs of non-conformism. There has been a tightening of state regulation of how people allocate their time, not deregulation at all.

The next chapter looks at the implications of these developments. However, this assessment of tertiary time should make clear that the dichotomy of work and leisure clouds reality. Even before the impact of Covid, people were doing work and labour in many places and at all times.

The notion of a fixed workplace was fading, while hours of work as conveyed by labour statistics had become more misleading and distortionary. Homes were becoming an extension of workplace, and vice versa. Increasingly, people were taking their labour home, while many were taking play to their nominal workplace. More were performing labour in several workplaces, while the work done outside home and nominal workplace was a growing part of their total work and labour.

Meanwhile, industrial notions of skill, and seniority systems based on a presumption that skill is refined through years of practice, have crumbled. Now that the historic guild system has been destroyed by the neoliberal onslaught, occupational splintering and restructuring are accelerating; fewer people can practise the occupation for which they trained.

All forms of work that are not labour are unremunerated in financial terms, but most impose costs on those doing them, as well as the risk of lost income if they are not done. The costs are intensified by uncertainty about outcomes.

Which time use offers a higher return? How much time should I devote to this work-for-labour compared with other possible activities? Such questions are hard, if not impossible, to answer.

The economic value of work that is not labour has surely risen. But measuring that is hard and largely arbitrary. One estimate in the UK suggested that taking account of digital work might add between one-third and two-thirds of a per cent to measured economic growth annually. As the report stated, 'the increased opportunities enabled by online connectivity and access to information provided through the internet have muddied the boundary between work and home production'.[91]

Unpaid for much of what we do as work, we are faced with time in disarray, bombarded with things to do. In the background, a double question lingers: how much time do people really have for recreation and how much for leisure in the classic sense of participating in the public and political domain? Hobbies, sport (or at least watching it) and screen watching surely win out, much of that being passive or needed to recuperate from alienating labour and the work around it. Besides the further marginalization of commoning, the great loser in the tertiary time era has been what the ancient Greeks regarded as the main claim on the time of a citizen, namely *schole*, public participation in political life.

CHAPTER 5

Reactions to Tertiary Time

The dark forces rise like a flood.

— Alto solo from Sir Michael Tippett, *A Child of Our Time*, 1939–41

It was clear even before the Covid pandemic struck that the tertiary time system was adversely affecting economic well-being, societal management and public health, and exacerbating various forms of inequality. This chapter considers the most pervasive effects, starting with the economic context and governance reforms. The impact of the pandemic is left to the next chapter.

To begin by reiterating a point that continues to distort political discourse: the shifts between labour and work, the growth of work that was previously labour, and labour that was previously recreation, all make the GDP measure of economic growth even more unreliable and misleading. If we work to pay for consumer goods at self-service checkouts rather than rely on the labour of cashiers, GDP growth goes down. If we increase unpaid care rather than pay a carer or home help, GDP goes down. If we shop online, supplying our time to generate advertising revenue for tech companies, our work does not count as work. If we walk our dog rather than pay a walker through an app such as Borrow My Doggy, we lower GDP. It is an absurd, arbitrary system.

In the tertiary time era, Hannah Arendt's dystopian vision of a 'jobholder society' has become reality as economists and politicians make a fetish of jobs. Having a job is even equated to freedom, a position taken by the Nobel Prize-winning economist Amartya Sen.[1] Not having a job is depicted as a denial of 'dignity'. Thus 'Bartleby' in *The Economist* says: 'The idea of dirty work should not obscure the fact that having a job is a source of dignity.'[2] But the claim by affluent commentators that any job, however unpleasant, confers dignity, is offensive. And when the state's institutions make jobholding the badge of citizenship and 'value', this inevitably leads to nonsensical conclusions, such as that not being in a job demonstrates a lack of 'social responsibility' or of the 'reciprocity' demanded for entitlement to state benefits.

Loss of the Future

The cult of neoliberalism declared that today's capitalism was the end of history because, it claimed, other ways of running society and the economy had been shown to fail. There was no alternative. Individuals should sell themselves as entrepreneurs of the self to maximize income, wealth and consumption. Whatever was in the past was passé, and not as good as Today. There was no Future, in the sense of a vision of a system radically different from Today's.

Utopian dreams and blueprints, so they reasoned, had been discredited by socialistic delusions of the twentieth century. The philosophical tradition of post-modernism, opposed to grand narratives and suspicious of ideologies, helped cement this paradigm, even though post-modernist guru Jacques Derrida (1930–2004) stated towards the end of his life, 'I refuse to renounce the great classical discourse of emancipation.'[3]

Tertiary time, in the context of rentier capitalism, creates a straitjacket that further impedes thinking of another Future – or as the Greek economist Yanis Varoufakis imagines it, 'another now'.[4] This creates a conservative, reactionary and profoundly pessimistic psychosis, leading many progressive thinkers and politicians to press the minimize button and couch their opposition to the status quo in timid non-conflictual terms and platitudes. Good people become grey people, testifying to the triumph of the neoliberal model.

In essence, there has been a reversal of the presumption of the industrial time era. We expect natural and social regress, not progress. Perversely, for many Today is not as good as Yesterday, and Tomorrow will be worse than Today. We should reject this pessimism but can only do so if we understand what is happening to our time and its effects.

Inequalities of Time

The most transparent flaws of the tertiary time era are the inequality in access to quality time and the varying demands placed on different groups. The elite and salariat have considerable control over their time, the precariat very little.

In all forms of labour and work, there are regressive tendencies. Take work-for-self-management. The affluent can hire an expert to handle their financial affairs instead of spending time doing the work themselves. The precariat cannot afford to hire experts. The potential cost of mistakes, given their scarce financial resources, means they should take more time to understand the intricacies, yet they cannot, as other forms of work and labour crowd out the time and energy needed to do so.

Today, even low-income workers must make financial decisions that are far more complex than in the past. For example, as a *Financial Times* article pointed out, 'The average modern worker in a rich country must now take full responsibility for ensuring they have enough resources to pay their way through old age.'[5] Very low interest rates on savings in recent years made financial investments relatively more attractive, and a source of growing inequality, as you need access to expert advice and enough time to make sensible investments. It is all very well for specialist academics to call for more 'financial literacy education'. The precariat does not have the time for that, or the means to pay for it.

Unlike the affluent, who can buy the time of intermediaries, the precariat must also spend a lot of time in work-for-the-state, dealing in person with diverse government bureaucracies, often as a supplicant, obliged to wait around or queue as a form of disciplinary subordination. The 'transaction costs' of work that the state imposes on the precariat are ignored in analyses of work. Their time is given no respect. Every utilitarian government wants to reform the minority; today's governments are deploying behavioural conditionality to force benefit claimants to do mostly futile, time-consuming unremunerated work. It is a cruel form of inequality.

Work-in-waiting and work-as-job-seeking are also sources of inequality. The precariat is forced to do much more of this than other people. One underappreciated aspect of casual and short-term jobs is the necessary use of time in the intervals between them, looking or waiting for them. That extra time reflects an inequality and intensifies income inequality. Those in and out of short-term jobs, in the concierge economy, in variable-hours contracts, and so on, are either required or directed to perform extra tasks in seeking jobs to satisfy the whims of bureaucrats or to wait around at the beck and call of employers or potential clients. Characterizing all time outside labour as 'leisure' ignores that devouring of time.

Another aspect of tertiary time arrangements is the time unit used to determine labour earnings. In a strange inbuilt inequality, the highest earners gain most of their money annually (dividends, bonuses, and so on), the salariat mostly monthly (although an increasing amount is gained annually), the proletariat mainly weekly, the precariat mainly by the hour or piece rates. But the shorter the period for which payment is made, the greater the volatility and unpredictability and the greater the income insecurity. Almost 60 per cent of the US labour force is paid by the hour, just one suggestive indicator of the growth of the precariat.[6] Unstable volatile earnings intensify stress and have adverse health consequences, both at the time and later in life.

Inequality is also built into the system of training-for-labour. The salariat is likely to have it paid for and to be able to do it in paid labour time, whereas the precariat is likely to have to pay for it themselves and to do it in their own free time. Intensifying this inequality, the precariat has a lower expected return to any training, while perversely being under greater pressure to do more of it. Someone in the salariat, with a structured career path, can do training with a high probability of increasing income and status. By contrast, someone moving in and out of dissimilar jobs (or expecting to do so) will have to decide what type of training to go for, if any, when all options have an uncertain return.

Inequality in time control has also been accentuated by occupational licensing. The transition from guild regulation, where control over time was limited by cultural traditions as well as guild rules, to state regulation, where competitiveness is the main rule of regulatory boards and the financial interests behind them, has put more pressure on those in the lower rungs to labour more. It has also contributed to the restructuring of occupational communities, with a growing precariat that has little control over tasks or job descriptions.

Then there is the inequality of play or recreation. The frenzy of labourism in the neoliberal era encroached on more active forms of recreation. In the USA – the only rich country without mandatory paid vacations – people have been taking fewer and shorter holidays. In the quarter century to 2000, the average American worker took more than twenty days' vacation each year; in 2015 that was down to sixteen days.[7]

Half of those whose jobs entitled them to paid holiday, usually 10–20 days depending on length of job tenure, did not take all their permitted days. And a quarter of all private-sector employees, many in the precariat, have no entitlement to paid holiday at all. They usually cannot afford to take an unpaid vacation either, especially as they may have to give up a job to do so, involving a decision that puts at risk any therapeutic value a holiday may have. Holiday entitlements are a concealed form of inequality.

A similar pattern has existed in Britain, despite mandatory

paid holiday of twenty-eight days a year for full-time employees. At least before the pandemic, two in five employees took only half or less of their holiday entitlement.[8] One reason was fear of coming back to a backlog of tasks, another was fear of losing a job, inducing more presenteeism.

Holidays have the potential to replenish energy, to strengthen personal and family relationships, to recover psychological distance from labour and to give a broader social perspective. Shrinking holidays worsen health. The US Centers for Disease Control and Prevention found that women who rarely took holidays were eight times more likely to develop coronary heart disease or have a heart attack than those who took at least two vacations a year.[9] A study of more than 12,000 men with a high risk of heart disease found that those who did not take annual vacations had a 21 per cent higher risk of death from all causes and a 32 per cent higher risk of dying from a heart attack than those who did.[10]

The salariat and elite can indulge in a lot of recreation-as-labour. They can take recreation time – empty labour – in what is statistically labour time. Veblen's notion of conspicuous consumption by 'the leisure class' has been transferred to the workplace. A well-publicized example is the conspicuous consumption of recreation in labour time in Google's planned UK headquarters in London's King's Cross district, which features a rooftop garden, a twenty-five-metre swimming pool and a multi-use games area for basketball, five-a-side football or tennis.[11]

Such perks reflect a form of unmeasured income inequality, and an unappreciated form of time inequality. Just as you cannot measure work by time in the office, or by contractual hours of labour, so you cannot measure leisure by time out of the office!

One uncharted aspect of tertiary time is that much empty labour is taken by managers and executives, who thereby surrender any moral right to control workers' time. This includes long lunches, sloping off for a game of golf, and having a romantic afternoon fling. There is even a study showing that firms in which the chief executive takes time off to play golf perform worse than others.[12] Besides being a form of inequality, this empty labour mocks the labour time system in general.

The loss of a sense of the future, of believing that society is making progress and that the future is likely to be better than the past or present, afflicts the precariat most. It faces a profoundly different societal prospect than was offered to the old proletariat. The latter largely accepted a social bargain that, in return for disciplined labour, employers (capital) and the state would provide medium-term time security. If you lost a job, had an accident or illness, had a child or reached pensionable age, you would be protected. You could have some secure time, paid in compensatory cash if you had made contributions or had them paid for you, in which to plan a longer-term response. This was memorably described by William Beveridge, in his 1942 report for the British government on reform of welfare after the war, as a temporary 'interruption' of earning power.[13]

By contrast, the precariat is forced to live constantly in the present, without the prospect of control over the short-term future, let alone over the longer term. The future is viewed with foreboding. This is a form of inequality. Having time now that is yours is a valuable asset. Having a feeling of secure future time is psychologically vital. Although it is impossible to put a monetary value on a state of mind of anticipated freedom to be able to fill one's time as one wishes in the future, that feeling is surely worth a lot to most of us.

There are also sharper differences between the salariat and precariat than previously between the salariat and proletariat. The salariat today receives considerable rental income and perks, such as shares and share options, occupational pensions, and paid sick and parental leave, all of which mean less exposure to uncertainty and greater material capacity to have control over time. The precariat is typically denied any of these and must instead adjust to volatile and uncertain income.

Compounding the inequality is that the salariat and elite, with plenty of collateral, have access to low-interest credit or debt with which to strengthen longer-term security and control of time, whereas the precariat is practically forced into building up high-interest, short-term debt that prevents any long-term security or time control. Moreover, the state often subsidizes the debt of the salariat, through tax relief or loan support schemes. In addition, low-interest policies pursued by governments and central banks in the wake of the 2008 financial crisis inflated the price of housing and other assets held by the plutocracy, elite and salariat, increasing wealth inequality.

Meanwhile, those in the precariat have experienced real wage stagnation, prompting them to try to maintain their standard of living by borrowing, including for essential spending on food, medical care, housing, transport and schooling. And with few assets, they have faced higher debt costs than higher-income groups.

A differentiated financial market has thus added to the

growth of inequality and to the dissipation of what few assets the precariat possesses. This cumulative inequality and the accompanying insecurities for the precariat make the overall economy more fragile. Some think the only way out of the impasse is 'a reprioritisation of full employment as the prime target of macro policy'.[14] A more effective escape would be to increase the incomes of the precariat without focusing on jobs per se.

Time inequalities in general make it misleading to measure inequality solely in terms of money incomes. This ignores the volatility and uncertainty that lower the worth of the income received by the precariat, as well as the state subsidies and forms of security given to those owning property, which substantially increase their money income and wealth.

From Black Swans to Chronic Uncertainty

An aphorism attributed to Confucius states that 'insecurity is worse than poverty'. This surely reflects worry and anxiety about making wrong decisions or being hit by a shock that could threaten survival or undermine human dignity. But there is another tradition, drawing from Aristotle, that maintains that only the insecure man is free. Confucius and Aristotle must surely have been considering different degrees of insecurity.

We as humans need basic security in order to function, to reason and to act rationally. But if we had total security, we would become care-less and lose the motivation to try to improve our lot. Basic security is a type of public good, since, unlike a private commodity, someone having it does not deprive others of having it too, in principle. Indeed, basic security is a superior public good, since its value to any individual increases as more people possess it as well.

In the era of tertiary time, millions of people have lost psychological control of their own time because they experience multiple forms of insecurity. In the industrial time era, the state responded to the main forms of insecurity by creating an edifice of measures to generate industrial citizenship, providing labour-based security for those who conformed and who were in stable labour or relationally attached to someone who was. Today, that has withered.

To recall the forms of security on offer in the industrial time era outlined in Chapter 4, they comprised labour market security, employment security, job security, skill reproduction security, work security (occupational health and safety), income security and representation security. None of these are anything like as strong or widespread today and are hard to discern in a tertiary time system.

Most economists make no distinction between the various forms, especially in conflating employment insecurity and job insecurity. The distinction is important. Someone could have a secure employment contract but no job security within a firm, required to shift to a different type of labour if demanded by the employer, while others could have weak employment security but expect to find a similar job elsewhere if necessary.

There is also a difference between subjective and objective security. Someone may have a word-of-mouth arrangement with an employer, meaning that legally they have no employment security, but they may be confident that the employer will maintain the relationship. By contrast, someone may have a written employment contract, but fear it could be terminated at any time. Moreover, the subjective feeling may reflect other factors altogether. If a person has savings or a partner earning well, they may not worry about losing employment, even if objectively they have no employment security. And if deep insecurity is seen as a norm, levels of employment insecurity that would previously have been perceived as such might now be regarded as quite secure!

More generally, insecurity consists of a mix of risks and uncertainty. Risks can be split into contingency and entrepreneurial risks. The former are 'shocks', such as loss of employment or an accident or illness, and 'hazards' that arise from normal, mostly life-cycle events such as marriage, the birth of a child or a decision to go to university. By contrast, entrepreneurial risk is the deliberate decision to invest or speculate in some way. Neoliberalism, the dominant ethos of the past four decades, wants everybody to become a self-entrepreneur, a risk taker.

Three sets of considerations apply to contingency risks: the probability of being hit by an adverse event; of being able to cope if hit; and of being able to recover. The precariat suffers from a high probability of being hit by an adverse event and a lower probability of being able to cope or to recover from it. It lacks robustness – the ability to avoid or resist the potentially harmful effects of shocks and hazards. And it lacks resilience to cope with and recover from adversity.

A dynamic society needs disruption, with inherent shocks and hazards, which the Austrian-born economist Joseph Schumpeter, in his book *Capitalism, Socialism and Democracy* (1942), called 'creative destruction'. Some shocks and hazards have positive as well as negative effects, but this depends on robustness and resilience. Many people have neither.

Alongside risks, there is uncertainty, a special form of insecurity, which has grown as a consequence of globalization, the information technology revolution and the effects of climate change and pollution. Uncertainty is about 'unknown unknowns' – that is, events that have an unknown probability of happening and an unknown probability of what effects they would have, and whether and to what extent people could cope with and recover from them.

In a widely quoted book, *The Black Swan* (2007), Nassim Nicholas Taleb coined the term 'black swan' to denote an event that is rare, has a devastating impact, and is predictable in retrospect, but not in prospect.[15] Since then, the black swan analogy has been weakened by the fact that uncertain, unpredictable and damaging events are no longer rare. This highlights another concept developed by Taleb – the need for societies and individuals to be 'antifragile'.[16]

Just as with risks, we should not aim to avoid uncertainty altogether, even if that were possible. The emphasis should be on building robustness and resilience. In life we confront many unexpected events and changes, the effects of most of which are easily absorbed. These are white swans. Every now and then, a black swan comes along. But in our current era, most of us are confronted not by the occasional black swan but by a bevy of them. And there are not only more black swans, but many are also more devastating, in terms of their effects and how many people are hurt.

Humanity is psychologically and physically ill-prepared to deal with uncertainty. Think of how uncertainty permeated society during the Covid-19 pandemic. One physician dealing with public-health responses to epidemics has pointed out the multiple layers of uncertainty. There is the uncertainty of being exposed and contracting the virus; the uncertainty of whether your body will exhibit minor symptoms or life-threatening ones; uncertainty about the threat to those you love or value; uncertainty over access to support; uncertainty about employment; uncertainty about the prospect of treatment and vaccines; uncertainty about the impact on the community and national economy; uncertainty about what you are producing; uncertainty about loss of credit; uncertainty about what the future holds; and uncertainty about the longer-term impact on mental and physical health.[17]

The precariat is not only more exposed to contingency risks but also to more uncertainty. They lack robustness and are vulnerable to adverse events, societal and personal. Bad things happen to them more often than to others. And they experience more hazards, notably changes in personal and work-related relationships, that bring new risks and uncertainty, and intensify feelings of fragility.

They also lack resilience in coping with shocks or hazards. Trying to do so takes up considerable time, the costs of the effort are higher, the sources of support during the period are fewer. The precariat typically has low, volatile and uncertain wages, no non-wage benefits, no rights-based state benefits, no reliable community or family benefits, and no savings to give short-term security. As a result, they have inadequate time to summon the resources, financial and psychological, to bear the trauma and manage the costs of adaptation and recovery.

To the extent the precariat has access to benefits at all,

the means-tested targeted benefits that are available are themselves multiple sources of uncertainty: whether individuals will be entitled to benefits; whether they will receive them and whether they will continue to do so; whether being in receipt of benefits will be stigmatizing, then and subsequently, or be on records that could be used to deny credit or impede future employment. And, being on the edge of unsustainable debt, the precariat will be uncertain whether they risk being sucked into a vortex of loss of resourcefulness. All this time-consuming uncertainty saps the spirit of resilience and plunges people deeper into precarity, feeling like supplicants, anomic and abject.

This insecurity extends to an inability to recover from shocks. Instead, shocks are typically accompanied by a downward bump in the labour market, often under pressure from so-called welfare agencies, and loss of networks of support. Insecurity also erodes a person's capacity for compassion, altruism and tolerance, and lowers self-esteem and aspirations, for themselves and other people.

People who are insecure suffer a diminution of their 'mental bandwidth', making it hard to focus on decisions beyond the day-to-day. This, coupled with chronic uncertainty, leads to curtailed planning and compressed time horizons. It engenders frustrated aspirations and, among the more vulnerable, feelings of abjection and dejection. This can fan atavistic sentiments, wanting yesterday back – sentiments on which populist politicians can play. At the extreme, chronic uncertainty can induce anomic anger directed inwards, leading to self-harm and suicidal tendencies.

Perhaps the worst uncertainty is linked to the refusal of

politicians to combat global warming and the resultant natural disasters that are growing in number and intensity. In
2021, in its grim sixth assessment report, the Intergovernmental Panel on Climate Change reached a little-noticed
conclusion, that the rarer the type of event in the past, the
higher the likelihood it would become more frequent.[18] In
other words, black swans are becoming more common. Uncertainty is chronic. And, as argued below, it leads to pressure on how we use our time.

The Panopticon State: Nudging Time Use

Another tool of the tertiary time regime is invading our
existence – the algorithm. Permeating all spheres of human
activity, algorithms are a hidden way of changing our allocation of time. This is a dystopia reminiscent of George Orwell's
Nineteen Eighty-Four, published in 1949. Big Brother is out of
control. With the spread of artificial intelligence and machine
learning, algorithms are becoming 'black boxes', making their
own rules, unknown even to their developers, on which to
base decisions.

An algorithm's decision-making criteria reflect a series
of interacting probabilities calculated from reams of data
used to train it. These data often contain implicit biases,
because they are drawn from biased samples. For example,
facial-recognition technology initially worked well for white
male faces but not for black faces or for women, because
the algorithms were trained on the faces of the developers,
overwhelmingly white and male. But algorithmic biases may
be more subtle, such as labelling certain postcode areas as
crime-ridden or subject to high levels of debt default. So, for

instance, a person may be denied a loan or a job because the algorithm determines that the information about them suggests they would be a bad risk. Yet the person has no idea what information has triggered the refusal or whether it is true or false. And they usually have no means of contesting it.

Consider the System Risk Indication, a risk-profiling method used by the Dutch government that aimed to detect individuals supposedly likely to commit welfare, tax and other types of fraud by pooling information about citizens from different government agencies. It came dangerously close to criminalizing people before they had committed any crime, or without evidence that they would commit any. In 2016, use of this system, which had targeted people in poor neighbourhoods, was blocked on privacy grounds. But similar tools are being tested and applied around the world.

The algorithmic black box has an early philosophical foundation. In 1787, the philosopher Jeremy Bentham (1748–1832), while visiting his brother who was working in Russia for the tsarina Catherine the Great (she of many lovers), responded to his brother's request to advise on prison design in a series of letters published in 1791 as *Panopticon; or, The Inspection-House.*

Basing his design on the concept of the panopticon – derived from the Greek words *pan* and *optikon*, 'all-seeing' – Bentham envisaged a circular complex with all the prisoners in cells facing a central watchtower. The guard in the watchtower could see the prisoners but they could not see the guard. And as a prisoner would not know when he was being watched, he would have to assume he was under constant surveillance. Bentham described the prison design as 'an

architecture of choice'. The prisoners were not physically coerced. But if a prisoner did not make 'the right choice', which
was to labour as hard as he could, he would be left to 'eat his
bad bread and drink his water, without a soul to speak to'.

Bentham also recognized a point well understood by
late twentieth-century neoliberals, that prisoners should be
isolated to prevent them forming 'a concert among minds'.
Collective agency would endanger the panopticon project.

Bentham was so enthusiastic about his design that he recommended it for hospitals, mental asylums, schools, factories,
the workhouse and all social institutions. Although no true
panopticon has been constructed, the radial design has been
copied in many places around the world in the past two centuries, including Wandsworth Prison in London and the Presid-
io Modelo (Model Prison) in Cuba, which is now a museum.
Bentham's concept was later used by French philosopher
Michel Foucault in developing his theory of social control.

Behavioural economics is a modern version of the panopticon way of thinking. In an extraordinarily influential book,
*Nudge: Improving Decisions about Health, Wealth and Happi-
ness*, published in 2008, the economist Richard Thaler and
the legal scholar Cass Sunstein proposed that people should
be encouraged to make the right choices such as requiring
people to opt out, rather than opt in, to pension schemes or
organ donation.[19] Without citing Bentham, they used the language of his panopticon papers, even referring to the 'architecture of choice', though the benign intentions highlighted
in *Nudge* would have been exposed as treacherous, or at least
one-sided, had explicit reference been made to its Bentham-
ite precursor.

When Barack Obama became US president, he appointed Cass Sunstein to head the Office of Information and Regulatory Affairs, based in the White House. David Cameron, on becoming UK prime minister in 2010, appointed Richard Thaler as adviser to a new Behavioural Insights Team, based in Downing Street. Soon known as 'the Nudge Unit', its mandate was to prompt people to make 'better decisions' in the interest of 'society'.

Later, the Nudge Unit was privatized and is now a very profitable company, exporting its expertise all over the world. About 400 behavioural insights teams have been established in public- and private-sector organizations globally. Meanwhile, in 2017, Richard Thaler received the Nobel Prize in Economics, epitomizing the contradiction inherent in mainstream economics, which supposedly espouses free-market principles. These assume that people have the necessary information and are free to make up their own minds, whereas 'nudges' aim to guide choices on the assumption that people do not have the necessary information or will not make the decisions the policymakers think are the right ones.

While there is little reliable evidence that nudge theory works in the ways claimed by its proponents, its use continues to spread.[20] The implications are disturbing for the use of time. Consider Amazon, the retail leviathan that is the primary income source of Jeff Bezos, one of the richest men in the world. Amazon has operated a labour-intensification scheme that certainly accords with inducing its white-collar workers to 'make the right choice' as far as the company is concerned. Among the tactics, staff are sent late-night emails that must be answered promptly, and workers are required to attend frequent performance meetings in which they must prove they have performed as expected, answering lengthy questionnaires, on pain of losing pay or even their job. The company has also operated what it coyly calls the Collaborative Anytime Feedback Tool, enabling employees to give 'secret feedback' on fellow workers. The whole ethos of control refined by Bezos was devastatingly revealed in 2015.[21] It appears to have changed little since then.

In the tertiary time regime, the precariat is not only subject to panopticon surveillance, including ubiquitous CCTV cameras in public spaces to spot petty rule breaking. It is also subject to the 'banopticon', which Byung-Chul Han defines as a device that identifies what is deemed undesirable and then excludes those who are alien or hostile to the system.[22] In the UK, for instance, the banopticon state is growing, tightening and multiplying regulations to make this structure more transparent, particularly in the sphere of social policy, including 'anti-social behaviour orders' that offend basic principles of Magna Carta, such as due process.

The banopticon is about exclusion from the community, or exclusion from being a full citizen, to be traumatized, stigmatized or branded metaphorically as lazy, a no-gooder, a grifter or shirker. It is the complement to the panopticon – the latter is surveillance of the many by a central eye, the former the surveillance of the few by a dispersed multitude of little eyes. The prying, ever-intrusive bureaucrats, eager to deny benefit supplicants entry to society, steer them to use time in ways they would not wish to, or expel them for not doing so. The banopticon part of the control society is the governance instrument of exclusion.

Life may not be like a 'social factory', as claimed in an influential book, *Empire* (2000), by Michael Hardt and Antonio Negri.[23] But the panopticon–banopticon state means that actions anywhere can be communicated everywhere, including to current and prospective bosses, landlords and lending agencies. Social record keeping is a defining disciplinary device for tertiary time, pressuring the precariat to behave in 'responsible' ways and to avoid behaviour, or even expression of opinions, that might provoke disapproval. Thus, membership of a trade union or of an activist environmental group may not be advisable on a CV or on a profile that a prospective employer or some government authority might obtain. The salariat is also affected by panopticon trends. Take job assessments or performance reviews that feed into an employee's electronic record. The person being assessed is likely to adjust their behaviour to please the assessor, not because they believe it is correct. As Taleb noted: 'People whose survival depends on qualitative "job assessments" by someone of higher rank in an organization cannot be trusted for critical decisions.'[24]

The array of tools for tracking what people do with their labour, work and private time is growing rapidly. 'Bossware', part of intensified efforts by employers to monitor and quantify employee productivity, not only checks how much time the worker is online but includes software that records computer keystrokes and mouse movements, takes screenshots, identifies which websites are visited and when, activates webcams and microphones, and takes pictures at regular or irregular intervals without the person knowing.[25] A company called Prodoscore, founded in 2016, provides software that monitors the volume of emails, messages, database inputs, and so on, by individual workers to compute a daily productivity score. This is sent to managers and to the worker, who will see their ranking relative to others.

Another monitoring technology, Veriato, assigns workers a daily risk score, indicating whether they could pose a security risk to the employer, for instance, by accidentally or deliberately leaking sensitive information. Among other inputs is the analysis by artificial intelligence of the text of a worker's emails and chats to determine 'sentiment'. Hire-Vue ranks job applicants by barely perceptible changes in posture, facial expression, vocal tone and word choice in the course of online interviews. Other algorithms purport to predict whether individuals will quit a job, become pregnant or try to form a union. Most of these technologies are untested or unknown to the public.[26]

Thus, in the tertiary time system, societal control is exercised by a combination of chronic uncertainty as the main form of insecurity and a mixture of panopticon and banopticon devices. As a result, we are subject to control by two types of fear – fear of shocks and hazards without having the robustness and resilience to overcome them, and fear of surveillance of our activities and attitudes. These have psychological and behavioural consequences, constraining what we do with our time and inducing feelings of loss of control and loss of potential freedom.

The Precariatized Mind

In tertiary society, all time is invaded. The new norm is for people to face a barrage of demands on their time at any moment. The pressure to combine tasks, often different in character, leads to situations of 'unbounded rationality', having too many options.[27] This makes for what should be called the precariatized mind. What is the optimal use of time, or the appropriate amount of time one should allocate to specific actions and types of activity? Should I do more of that, or that, or that, and less of this?

Modern technologies and ways of working make us think we can and should do more in the same time slot. This leads not only to suboptimal decisions on time, but also a constant sense of being superficial and inadequate. Rather than some sort of heroic achievement, multitasking is really a euphemism for being out of control of one's time.

Human brains cannot manage multiple activities at once; multitasking involves quickly switching between activities, which results in poorer performance all round. At its extreme, it deprives us of the capacity to use time proficiently in any way. The situation is more intractable than when Bertrand Russell wrote 'In Praise of Idleness' (1932) or when the anarchist philosopher Ivan Illich (1926–2002) later worried about 'busyness'.[28]

Heavy multitaskers perform much worse on a range of tasks.[29] One study found that being distracted by numerous calls and emails resulted in a drop in IQ by ten percentage points.[30] Another found that multitasking impairs empathy while causing stress, anxiety and fatigue.[31] And, contrary to the popular stereotype, women are no better at multitasking than men; that stereotype no doubt reflects the fact that they tend to face more diverse demands on their time, combining a job with more domestic responsibilities than do men.[32]

Time filling is also a feature of the tertiary time regime.

People are under pressure to be doing something all the time. We are under pressure to be active and to make decisions on a range of demands upon our time, flitting between tasks until exhaustion takes over. The poet Theodore Roethke caught the point well in his poem 'Infirmity': 'A mind too active is no mind at all.'[33] Perversely, another feature of tertiary time and the precariatized mind is mindless passivity, constantly checking for notifications, keeping up the appearance of being always on, available, but often merely afraid of missing out, of losing hold of some tenuous job or being excluded from some unknown activity.

This is intensified by what some have called capitalism's imperative of creativity, reflecting the dictate of the new. People are judged on their 'creativity', their ability to turn the latest thinking into outputs. Information technology has produced a world of speed permeated with anxiety and permanent non-fulfilment. Information, misinformation, fake news, all flash through a shrinking time space. As Herbert Simon, a Nobel Prize-winning economist, once quipped, 'What information consumes is rather obvious. It consumes the attention of its recipients. Hence a wealth of information creates a poverty of attention.'[34]

Moreover, modern information technology disrupts the architecture of conversation, or as Czech novelist Milan Kundera put it in *La Lenteur* (1995), it enfeebles the capacity of conversation to organize time. And by its incessant interruptive power, it disrupts the capacity to use conversation to build and sustain strong relationships. Contact through the mobile phone takes precedence over physical contact; the one interrupts, the other is put on hold. More generally, intensified connectivity has been shown to reduce the depth and intensity of personal and work relationships.[35]

It is scarcely an exaggeration to describe society as afflicted by collective attention-deficit disorder. Tertiary time chips away at the space needed for sustained concentration. We may devote a period of time to something that intrinsically requires continuity of attention, such as care or studying, but are bombarded by demands to use time on other tasks, invading the set-aside space to the detriment of the quality of care or studying. We become used to skipping between undemanding activities rather than delving into something in depth, so that when we are faced with a task or activity that is mentally challenging, it is emotionally easier to switch to something facile. That makes us 'happy'.

The behavioural psychologists and utilitarians who dominate social policy say that being happy is what living should be all about. But the precariatized mind is a diminished mind, readily co-opted by subliminal advertising, by commodified politics and by politicians peddling platitudes that are easy to digest because they make no demands on the mind. The precariatized mind is enervating and ultimately depressing because it is out of control.

The tertiary time regime also affects what might be called network time. In economics, network goods are objects that increase in value as more people have them. Time is a network good, because its value depends in part on whether others, such as family and friends, have a similar schedule. The standard workweek has been much criticized for lack of time to share with valued others.[36] But tertiary time actually involves an increase in the scheduling constraint, reducing the ability to coordinate time with others. Thus a demand for reduced hours of labour may not achieve much improvement in time shared with others if they cannot reallocate time in the same way.

It is sometimes argued that the unemployed have more free time than the employed and also have similar scheduled time, because both can interact socially with others at the weekend. However, in Britain at least, the state has imposed a double penalty on the time of the unemployed. To gain means-tested benefits, such as Universal Credit, they must engage in time-consuming activities such as fruitless job seeking that they would not otherwise wish to do, or would prefer to do at a more convenient time. Unemployed claimants may even have less free time during the week than those in jobs. And they are likely to have less scheduled time at weekends, because they have a more limited social network and less money to spend on social activities.

In thinking about the value of specific blocks of time, there are also *negative* network effects: too many people wanting to do the same activity at the same time; using more time doing an activity than you would wish because other people are doing it; or having your time ignored by service providers faced with high demand. The result is a frustrating mix of queuing and waiting. Most people in rich countries will have the experience of being left to hang on the phone for many minutes or even hours when trying to make an appointment with a doctor, contact an official or register a complaint. Unsurprisingly, high levels of inequality have given rise to an informal labour market in which the elite and salariat, for whom the value of scheduled time is greater, pay someone to queue for tickets to the theatre, new iPhone releases, and the like. In New York, this is a lucrative activity.[37]

The precariatized mind also contributes to feelings of being a supplicant. This is acute in the artistic community, most of whom are in the precariat, relying on applications to funding bodies for projects. Applications and the whole process turn artists into supplicants, petitioning the cultural bureaucracies to fulfil their fleeting dreams and hopes, many of which were sold to them rather than having emerged intrinsically.[38] Bureaucratic funding bodies shape the time and health of a growing artistic precariat, who consume time in making applications, waiting for outcomes, handling rejections, refining profiles. Their only right is the right to make applications.

Stress and Deaths of Despair

The tertiary time system is inherently stressful. This is linked to the personality traits central to neoliberalism – competitiveness and self-entrepreneurship. Philosopher Byung-Chul Han argues that in the twenty-first century we are living in an achievement society, in which everybody is under intense pressure to devote time to achieve more – an Unlimited Can.[39] As Dawn Foster pointed out in her book *Lean Out* (2016), for workers, especially the precariat, always being in competition with others acts as a disciplinary tool: 'Every colleague is competition. As a result, you are constantly on edge, aware that the tiniest slip of the tongue or careless mistake could mean a fall from grace and attendant loss of income. In such circumstances, it is almost impossible to organise collectively. No one employed so precariously dare step out of line first, knowing the inevitable consequences.'[40]

A related pressure is the exhortation to be engaged in your job. While engagement has benefits, high engagement can also generate high levels of stress. In a survey of over 1,000 US employees, two in five reported a high level of engagement and a low level of burnout. However, one out of five reported both high levels of engagement and burnout. These engaged/exhausted workers were passionate about their work but had intensely mixed feelings about it, reporting high levels of interest, stress and frustration. They also had the highest intention to change jobs, even higher than the unengaged group.[41]

Similarly, those in the precariat who must sell themselves through projects and applications suffer from normalized insecurity and feel they have to stay constantly connected and available, leading to mental and physical exhaustion and 'a pathology of precariousness'.[42] As stress lengthens, ill-health beckons from further down the road.

Recall that as the industrial time regime solidified in the late nineteenth century, it led to an epidemic of 'nerves', growing use of opioids and a rising incidence of suicides. History is being repeated. Today, the insecurities and loss of control over time have fuelled an epidemic of stress, and what have been dubbed 'deaths of despair'. In the USA, excess deaths among the young and middle-aged have led to it being called 'land of the dying'.[43]

Psychologists have found a strong relationship between labour-related stress, income insecurity and mental illness. They have argued that the lack of 'free' time is a cause and have criticized the tendency to reframe dissatisfaction with working life as a medical problem, in which the symptoms rather than the sources of mental illness are addressed.[44] One in four British adults (one in five in the USA) is prescribed antidepressants or other psychotropic drugs each year, a ratio that has risen steadily.[45] Since the 1980s, mental-health disability rates in the UK have almost trebled and the prevalence of mental-health problems has risen fourfold, despite growth of public spending on mental-health services.[46]

Enforced underemployment in a jobholder society also causes psychological distress.[47] Similarly, the intensification of time in combinations of labour and work-for-labour is a major stressor. And children of chronically stressed parents tend to suffer more illness in adulthood, both mental and physical.[48]

In a chilling article, a Chinese freelancer in Beijing has described the extreme evolution of the meritocratic tertiary time regime as it is being played out in China, captured by the word 'involution'.[49] The idea comes from a book by American anthropologist Clifford Geertz, *Agricultural Involution* (1963), which describes how more and more labour was expended in Javanese farming for less and less output. In China, the term for involution is *neijuan*, signalling 'an endless cycle of self-flagellation', working ever harder in pursuit of progress towards an unknown destination, without real purpose.

The result is incredible stress and chronic hyperactivity, for which the Chinese precariat has come up with the memes '996' (referring to those labouring from nine in the morning to nine in the evening for six days a week) and '007' (working online twenty-four hours a day, seven days a week). Predictably, the time pressure has led to suicides and mental breakdowns. But it has also led to a movement of passive resistance, through subversive memes and a 'lying flat' campaign on social media encouraging young people to opt out of stressful jobs. This has alarmed the government. In the words of an official spokesman in August 2021: 'In this turbulent era, there is no such thing as lying flat and waiting for prosperity. There is only the splendour of struggle and endeavour. Young people, come on!'[50]

The quiet rebellion against the culture of intense labourism has taken several directions, including a refusal to do overtime and a willingness to boast about being lazy. This has gone under the odd name of 'touching fish', drawing on a Chinese proverb that states, 'Muddy water makes it easy to catch fish' – that is, it is possible to use a crisis or period of chaos for personal benefit. One practitioner of 'touching fish' told a blog, 'We are not willing to try our best to do our work. Instead, we spare time and energy to do our by-work. Isn't it better than spending all your efforts at work?'[51]

This attitude may be taken to extremes in China, but it is a global trend in a global economy. If everybody is competing with everybody else, there will be many losers. And if the gains from winning keep rising, as they do under rentier capitalism, while the costs of losing also keep rising, partly because the cost of trying to win goes up, the toxic combination is a prescription for mass stress and depression. This is today's reality.

Shift labour, rotating shifts and unpredictable schedules, all characteristic of tertiary time, are associated with stress, health problems and family break-up. They interfere with self-care time, family routines and the maintenance of regular friendships. Studies show that 20 to 30 per cent of shift workers suffer from insomnia or other sleep problems, which have adverse effects on mental and physical health.[52]

Unpredictable labour time also leads to unpredictable and volatile income, and a general lack of income security, causing more anxiety, loss of sleep and bodily stress. A US study found that workers with the least stable labour schedules were more than twice as likely to report psychological distress as those with the most stable schedules.[53] And parents with unstable labour schedules tend to have inadequate care arrangements for their children, which has adverse effects on their development independent of the impact of parental stress.[54] Moreover, low-income people are more likely to experience schedule instability, further entrenching lifetime inequality in health disparities that grow over time.[55]

Han's book *Burnout Society* (2010) characterized the twentieth century as an 'immunological era', in which infections by viruses and bacteria were the main causes of disease and death, largely conquered by vaccinations and antibiotics. By contrast, the twenty-first century is a 'neuronal' era of neuro-psychiatric diseases, such as depression, attention-deficit hyperactivity disorder, burnout syndrome and borderline personality disorder. Since these are not infections, but are baked into 'the performance society', no immunological technique can combat them.

The coronavirus pandemic that struck in early 2020 undermined that simplistic model. But so too does history. Pandemics, as well as widespread mental and psychological collapse, appear to become more frequent and worse at the end of periods of rising inequality and the breakdown of the dominant economic paradigm. What we have seen in the early twenty-first century is largely a socio-political reaction to a crisis of stress and mental ill-health linked to changes in the economy, society and personal relationships.

Tertiary Time's Adjustment Occupations

In a period of socio-economic transition and crisis, a large amount of time is spent dealing with mental pressures and disorders. And in such periods, new 'adjustment occupations' emerge to soothe emotional turmoil and persuade people to internalize the new order in time use. It might be described as work-for-reproduction, as the underlying objective is often to adjust to being a functioning member of the new productive system.

Looking back to the late nineteenth century, the expanding adjustment occupations included religious practitioners and also new quasi-medical occupations offering an array of unfamiliar remedies. The stress caused by the disruption to economic, social and family relations legitimized neurology, whose practitioners prescribed sedatives, hypnotics and stimulants for the nervous symptoms of insomnia and sleep disturbances, 'sporadic elation', chronic headaches, anxiety and depression. Psychiatry emerged as an invasive occupation affecting other occupations, such as policing and the religious professions. Its approach presumed that stressed, insecure individuals needed to adjust to the new demands on their time, not the other way round.

Which adjustment occupations have flourished in the tertiary time crisis? At the most benign level, corporations are creating fancy new job titles for executives, such as chief listening officer, chief growth officer, chief sustainability officer, chief medical officer, chief talent officer, and even chief remote officer, responsible for designing and disseminating best practices for home working.[56]

However, new social-control occupations are of greater concern. The stresses that multiplied as the tertiary time regime took hold have given renewed opportunities for psychiatrists – medical practitioners who deal with recuperative and remedial adjustments – and psychologists, who offer preventative adjustment. Both have been part of the paternalistic apparatus of control, which extends to social work, policing and prisons.

In the early twenty-first century, perhaps the most powerful adjustment mechanism to emerge was cognitive behavioural therapy (CBT), a form of treatment developed in the USA. In 2008, the UK's New Labour government, urged on by its 'happiness tsar' Lord (Richard) Layard, launched a national scheme entitled 'Improving Access to Psychological Therapies', based on training a workforce of cognitive therapists to aid anxious citizens. It was formally adopted in the guidelines of the UK's National Institute for Health and Care Excellence and was also included in the Australian Medicare system.

While CBT seems to reduce anxiety and depression in some people, the experts are not sure how or why. It aims to correct 'cognitive distortions', 'negative automatic thoughts' and 'faulty reasoning'.[57] It sits comfortably with behavioural economics' nudge theory. But we all do our share of faulty reasoning. We snatch at quick decisions, because we lack the time – or believe we do – to make more considered choices. That is stressful in itself. Ironically, it seems people with depression are more likely to understand that they do not have control over their time, whereas so-called mentally healthy people feel they have more control than in fact they do. This surely leads us to think the desirable response is to find ways of increasing control over our time.

In any case, the happiness agenda has had limited success. The neoliberal emphasis on positivity, on self-entrepreneurship, on hyperactivity in pursuit of achievement, leaves too many behind. A review of studies of CBT between 1977 and 2014 found that its effectiveness wears off.[58] But now psychiatrists have come up with ACT, the acronym for Acceptance and Commitment Therapy. This represents a refinement of the neoliberal perspective, as the words suggest. Just learn to accept you are no good! Just commit to being better! Of course, it is more sophisticated than that, and it is comforting to know that a review of studies of ACT in the professional journal *Psychotherapy and Psychosomatics* concluded that it was better than a placebo for anxiety disorders and depression.[59] That is hardly setting the bar very high.

Like CBT, ACT seems yet another adjustment tool distracting attention from the structural causes of widespread mental distress – inequality, insecurity, uncertainty and the stresses that come with tertiary time.

The Erosion of Leisure

While induced to do more labour, work-for-labour and work-for-reproduction by materialist pressures, we consume goods, services and entertainment insatiably in the belief that this is the goal of labour and work. So we use our limited 'free time' for recreation, because we need to recuperate and unwind and because commercial interests want us to do so. But passification follows.

When Bertrand Russell said it was good for a child to be bored, he surely did not mean it would be good for a child to be bored most of the time. But he was surely right that being constantly entertained dulls the imagination. A person who is feeling bored is soon likely to find their mind filling with thoughts and ideas. Being permanently glued to screens or earphones is to have the imagination truncated and distorted by creators of those images or sounds. Such passification erodes real leisure.

No powerful interest wants us to spend time on leisure in the Greek sense of *schole*. Reflection, debate, creative and regenerative idleness, all are disparaged or seen as time wasting. A result is the thinning of democracy, shown in declining turnouts in elections, declining membership of political parties and declining activity inside them.

The Greek idea of a citizen was someone with the status and capacity to participate in the *polis*. Although put into effect in a sexist, inegalitarian way, it recognized that deliberative democracy required both time in participation and time to acquire and sustain the capacity to participate effectively. It required civic education and exposure to the arts to reinforce empathy, activities necessarily using up time. Today, that has been sacrificed in the pursuit of 'human capital'. Civic knowledge encourages higher voter turnout and a higher probability of electing individuals attuned to local communities and the values of truthfulness and knowledge. Loss of civics leads to support for charlatans.

Civic knowledge and participation in political life were considered vital by the founding fathers of the USA, where, as Thomas Jefferson stated, the impetus for public schooling was to teach people how to be citizens. Not any more. The annual Civic Health Index compiled by the US National Conference on Citizenship documents a steady decline in civic knowledge and engagement, and in time spent in voluntary community activity. Despite a jump in political engagement following the election of Donald Trump as president in 2016, turnout in the 2020 presidential election was still only 67 per cent of the voting-age population, low by international standards (though as it happens the same as the UK in the 2019 general election). And partisanship has stifled serious political debate.

Loss of control over time has gone with a loss of energy for opposing commodifying trends. Commodification closes the pores of the whole day, not just the pores of time in labour, the objective perceived by Marx as inherent to capitalism. A result is the erosion of *schole*.

The Enfeeblement of Liberal Freedom

In thinking of time, we should not give in to the cynicism of Macbeth, reacting to the sudden death of Lady Macbeth:

Life's but a walking shadow, a poor player
That struts and frets his hour upon the stage
And then is heard no more. It is a tale
Told by an idiot, full of sound and fury,
Signifying nothing.[60]

This suggests that the way we use our time does not matter in the end; it has all been an elaborate game. It leads, if not to the extreme opportunism of a murderous schemer, at least to the amoral levity of politicians who say whatever they think will help them succeed. Refined by increasingly sophisticated public relations and social media, this has been a successful tactic in an era of information overload and a perceived lack of time to check the veracity of what we hear or read. The unprincipled politician knows they can get away with telling lies, as long as it is done with aplomb.

Philosophers and theologians have pondered over free will since at least the ancient Greeks. But two later philosophical traditions – liberal freedom and republican freedom – are relevant in considering control of time. We will come to republican freedom later; it is freedom from potential domination. Liberal freedom is the freedom to be moral, to act in a certain way because we believe that is the moral way of behaving. It is a freedom that is nurtured within the family and community, or alternatively corroded by society. If your time is controlled by others, or by a machine or device, you cannot be moral, because being moral requires space and time itself to make moral decisions.

We can say that Macbeth had liberal freedom, even though his morality was pernicious and easily poisoned by the sweet words of Lady Macbeth. But suppose you are on an assembly line, doing repetitive tasks at high speed, as so memorably portrayed by Charlie Chaplin in the 1936 film *Modern Times*. At least until you clock off and exit the factory, you cannot exercise liberal freedom; you cannot make moral decisions. Your mind and body are preoccupied. It is Taylorism in the extreme. Somebody subject to such labour intensification can be lured into false consciousness, inclined to think in particular ways and to lose the ability to think in other ways. On that assembly line, Chaplin goes temporarily insane and is taken away by men in white coats. The physical control over his time extends to loss of control over his mind.

The Amazon warehouse is the twenty-first-century equivalent. Workers are set demanding targets for picking and packing goods, continuously monitored through their handheld scanning devices, and are given neoliberal incentives – financial rewards for above-norm achievements and penalties for underperforming or for petty infractions of the rules of labour. The panopticon labour process is far advanced. And one difference between the twenty-first-century variant and Chaplin's is the extent of societal controls, including 'nudging', that are invading space and time away from workplaces and outside labour time.

Workers in general seem to be labouring more intensely than two decades ago. In UK government surveys, the proportion of employees 'strongly agreeing' that their job required them to work very hard rose from 30 per cent in 1992 to 46 per cent in 2017. The proportion reporting that they had to work to tight deadlines for most of their time increased from 53 to 60 per cent. And the proportion saying they worked at very high speed had risen from 23 to 45 per cent.[61] Labour intensification has occurred among managers, nurses, aerospace workers, schoolteachers, information technology staff and carers. There is also evidence of labour intensification elsewhere in Europe and in the USA. And labouring with high intensity causes stress, depression and burnout, and presenteeism when sick.

Digital labour is similarly micromanaged time. Algorithms controlled by a modern form of labour broker, extracting rental income from every transaction, also act as monitoring devices, a virtual form of supervisor. They intensify uncertainty, which exerts control over the precariat – the uncertainty of not knowing to what extent the panopticon machinery is operating, and the uncertainty of not knowing the consequences of being detected not doing what is required or doing what is not required.

The Precarity Trap

We now turn to the implications of the ways in which the state controls the time of people on the lower rungs of society. For a start, in remorselessly tightening conditional welfare, the state has made it more costly and time-consuming to seek and retain benefits. Means testing – long favoured by mainstream politicians – has consistently been shown to produce severe poverty traps, where moving to a low-paid job results in loss of benefits, leaving the person little better off, if at all. The poverty trap has worsened as flexible labour markets have resulted in falling wages and shrinking entitlement to non-wage benefits.

Even if benefit withdrawal is spread over several months

or tax credits are used, international evidence shows that those at the edge of the labour market often face an effective marginal tax rate on income of over 80 per cent. This means there is a huge disincentive to take a low-wage job, especially bearing in mind the costs in time, commuting, away-from-home meals, appropriate clothing, and so on. In October 2021, the taper for Universal Credit in the UK (benefit lost for each extra pound of earned income) was reduced from 63 per cent to a nominal 55 per cent, in recognition of this disincentive, though income tax and National Insurance contributions push the effective marginal rate much higher.

Now picture the situation from the perspective of someone in the precariat. After losing a job, she (or he) must apply for benefits. This starts a time-consuming process, in which she must fill out intimidating forms – with supporting documentation at the ready – and answer intrusive questions designed to determine eligibility, including household arrangements and other personal information. If she needs to apply in person, she faces a long and expensive trek to queue at the benefits office or help centre. Often, she will find she has the wrong documents, or not enough of them. Back she goes, to do it all again. The process can take months, not just days.[62] Meanwhile, she will exhaust savings, use up friends' goodwill, incur debts and possibly lose housing.

At the end is the precarity trap. Once she has used a lot of time, energy and determination to obtain benefits, bureaucrats will tell her how she must use her time. This may include some form of workfare, and she will have a nagging fear of needing to go through all that time-consuming activity again. If offered a low-paid, short-term job the other side of town, she would not only lose benefits and gain relatively little income. If that job came to an end, she would go more months without income while re-applying for benefits. The combined precarity and poverty traps mean that someone in the precariat has a strong disincentive to take the sort of low-wage job on offer. Thus new forms of work and labour are intensifying insecurity, while using time in destructive ways.

The Time Cruelty of Universal Credit

Over the past four decades, utilitarian paternalistic politicians have built a state-benefits system designed to control the time and activity of those falling into dependency on it. Being told what to do and what not to do, under threat of punishment, is a denial of liberal freedom. It is also a denial of republican freedom, obliging millions of people to become supplicants to those in positions of unaccountable authority.

Welfare policy has always consumed the time and affected the health of those gaining benefits, those trying to do so, those who could do so but do not apply for them out of ignorance, fear or shame, and those around them in their lives. The UK government's flagship reform of 2013 that introduced Universal Credit has had huge repercussions. While there is little to suggest it has increased employment, ostensibly a primary aim, it has resulted in distress and hardship for millions of people. The amount paid is not enough to live on; the five-week waiting period for benefits forces many into debt and destitution; the conditions claimants must comply with are onerous; and the sanctions regime is punitive and denies due process. The work-for-the-state done by claimants does not count for anything.

One independent study, covering 52,000 adults over the period 2009 to 2018, found that the introduction of Universal Credit was associated with a 6.6 per cent increase in the prevalence of psychological distress among claimants, including a sharp rise in clinical depression.[63] Other studies have shown the claim process itself, and the hovering threat of sanctions, exacerbate long-term health problems. Doctors' organizations have reported increased visits to GPs (general practitioners), adding to their overburdened workload, and costing time for both doctor and patient in treating avoidable health problems.[64]

There are other time-related injustices built into the UK welfare system. For instance, paternalistic discrimination in paying for childcare favours 'jobholders'. All families in England with three- or four-year-old children can claim fifteen hours a week of free, government-funded childcare or nursery, but in 2017 this was doubled to thirty hours if both parents (or the single parent) are in a job. Those not in a job are likely to be poorer on average and need more financial help. Indeed, 70 per cent of the families eligible for thirty hours of subsidy had higher-than-median incomes.[65] While policymakers presume those not in jobs have more time for care, this may not be true. The policy has even led to nurseries withdrawing places for those only entitled to fifteen hours in favour of those entitled to thirty hours, compounding the inequality.

The DWP and its umbrella scheme of Universal Credit are the main form of panopticon–banopticon apparatus impinging on the time and lives of the precariat in Britain and the growing underclass or '*Lumpen*-precariat'. It is a shocking indictment of the politics of time constructed in the neo-liberal era. Yet most of the public who are not enmeshed in the system probably know little or nothing of its meanness or unfairness.

The Charity State

Finally, there is an incidental devourer of time that has emerged in the crisis period of tertiary time, just as it did in the crisis period of industrial time, in the Victorian age. One outcome of the era of neoliberalism and rentier capitalism is the revival of the charity state, as austerity policies have slashed government funding for social benefits, social and community services, and the commons more generally. In the words of Maddy Desforges, chief executive of the National Association for Voluntary and Community Action, whose members support about 200,000 local charities and voluntary groups in Britain, the sector is increasingly 'backfilling' the gaps in government provision, while itself experiencing a squeeze on financial resources.[66]

Andy Haldane claimed in 2020 that 'the social sector is rising to the challenge of supporting the left-behind and left-alone'.[67] He should have asked: 'Is this desirable?' Instead, he argued that the social (aka charity) sector should be provided with financial and volunteer support. In so doing, he forgot the lesson emphasized by the philosopher David Hume (1711–76), that charity is a matter of pity, and pity is akin to contempt. Reducing people to dependency on charity is a denial of citizenship. And it encourages utilitarian thinking by the state and politicians, absolving themselves of responsibility for the minorities left behind.

In the progressive reaction to the industrial time era, there was a consensus that the welfare state would displace reliance on charity by building a system of social rights. But in the twenty-first century, the charity state has emerged as a global system, with the plutocracy at its peak, displaying philanthropy through huge foundations set up to dispense funds as they see fit. At the other end are countless little charities, many of which emerge and disappear like fireworks, many run by volunteers and a poorly paid precariat devoting a lot of time to good causes.

Most people who give time to charitable work are doing so with altruistic motives and deserve respect. It is the system and what it represents that should be questioned. A charity state is paternalistic, moralistic and demeaning. It displaces social solidarity and compassion with pity and that underlying contempt. It turns minorities into supplicants and many into little more than beggars.

From early in the formation of societies, begging has constituted the main use of time for a minority, and in natural or human disasters it has sometimes been the lot of a majority. But for the past century it has been presumed that modern welfare states have relegated begging to a tiny minority of social misfits, drug addicts, alcoholics and rejects.

Sadly, this is a gross delusion. While begging has increased alongside homelessness, it is not only those on the street who must use time begging to survive. Millions more are teetering on the brink, many in full-time jobs but obliged in shame to seek out charitable food banks. In 2021 there were over 1,300 food banks in the Trussell Trust network, the largest food bank charity in Britain, compared to under

100 in 2010, and two relatively new phenomena – clothes banks and hygiene banks (for hygiene items including sanitary products).[68] The Hygiene Bank, a non-profit charity, now has dozens of local operations all over the UK.

Food banks have proliferated across Europe and North America. Meanwhile, in the USA, 'America's unspoken hygiene crisis' has been accentuated by the exclusion of hygiene products from items that can be purchased with the main voucher-based means-tested benefits.[69] For a significant minority of people, seeking out charity and waiting in queues for what might be available accounts for a considerable amount of time. It is part of the inequality of time, something the precariat knows all too well.

Charity is a palliative, a safety valve for rentier capitalism that allows the growth of the class structure and the drift towards authoritarian politics run by and for the affluent. People who are forced by deprivation and insecurity to seek charity are exhorted to feel grateful and to act accordingly. Ultimately, those responsible for the policies that produce their deprivation can turn on the supplicants and deny that they are deserving or honest.

For example, in May 2022, a Conservative MP claimed in the House of Commons that there had not been a 'massive increase in food banks' and that people using them were only doing so because they did not know how to cook, adding for good measure that people could make a meal for 30p a day, 'cooking from scratch'. Ironically, his government had axed the teaching of home economics in schools in 2014, which included lessons in cooking and budgeting.

But his claim was absurd. In 2009–10, just before the

Conservatives came to power, about 409,000 people used food banks run by the Trussell Trust for three days of emergency food in a week. In 2018–19, just before Covid struck, that had risen to nearly 2 million, and during the pandemic it rose to over 2.5 million. Surely cooking skills had not fallen that fast. Much of the increased resort to food banks was due to impoverished claimants subject to sanctions or cuts in benefits.

The MP cited a food bank in his constituency that he favoured. Anybody needing or wanting a free food parcel had to register for a budgeting course and a cooking course. So, they had to use time in trying to obtain the food and then commit to using more time in work for which there was no proven need, let alone remuneration.

What does the new charity state mean for the use of time? Supplicants must trek to places they would otherwise not wish to go to, spend extensive time in queuing and, in many cases, awkward embarrassing form-filling. As supplicants, they dare not complain and, in any case, the frontline suppliers of charity are generally not responsible for the system in which they are operating. Indeed, many volunteers are themselves using time that could otherwise be used to improve their standard of living. It is not an edifying spectacle.

CHAPTER 6

Time in the Eye of Covid

The hours of folly are measur'd by the clock, but of wisdom no clock can measure.

— William Blake, *The Marriage of Heaven and Hell*, 1790

A Shock Foretold

Just as the financial crash of 2008 was predictable and predicted, so was the Covid-19 pandemic of 2020, not in its specifics but as a generic shock. It was already the sixth pandemic of the twenty-first century, following SARS in 2003, H1N1 (swine flu) in 2009, MERS in 2012, Ebola in 2014 and Zika in 2016 – an unprecedented spate of viral outbreaks. It was not a black swan event, in that it was predictable, but the uncertainty existed in the timing, its severity and the responses by states and international bodies. Governments proved wilfully unprepared, then slow to react.

Covid was to have transformational effects on how people used time and on the politics of time. While the comparison was with the Spanish flu of 1918–20, which resulted in 50 million deaths worldwide, the global economy in 2020 was in a more fragile state than back then, when it was emerging from the First World War. Whereas in 1918–20 government and household debt were modest in comparison to national income, in 2020 government debt, corporate debt and household debt globally were all at unprecedentedly high levels. A pandemic or other major shock could be expected to tip millions of people and firms into unsustainable debt and bankruptcy.

There was a lack of robustness and resilience in the face of a systemic shock. And when it came, few political leaders focused on longer-term implications. At best, they reacted with palliatives, not preparation for a transformation of time use amid chronic uncertainty.

Like financial crises, which have also become more frequent, pandemics increase the incidence of absolute poverty, the intensity of poverty, and the severity of income and wealth inequality.[1] In today's rentier capitalist economy, this manifests itself in increased returns to ownership of all types of property, which has been accentuated by the policy responses of governments and central banks. Property owners did extremely well during the pandemic, aided by government handouts in the form of tax breaks.[2]

Financial capital thrived. And Blackstone, the biggest private-equity firm, became the world's largest property manager, mopping up inflated wealth. Just as policies in response to the financial crisis of 2008 boosted the income and wealth of financial capital, so the policies in response to the pandemic boosted the plutocracy, bolstered the salariat and left the precariat deeper in debt and insecurity.

Time suddenly mattered in seemingly new ways and led to a surge in interest in how we could and should use it better. One immediate consequence was a disruption to the rhythms of the standard seven-day week, as society quickly drifted into what some called an interminable present. People joked that Monday had been replaced by Noneday, Thursday by Blursday. As the pandemic dragged on, the return of the old notions of the workweek became increasingly doubtful. Lockdowns and working from home generated new jargon, such as 'poly-working' and 'side hustling', to mean doing more than one job from home, or 'Zoombies' and 'Teambies', referring to people exhausted and debilitated by the plethora of on-screen meetings and conferences held on Zoom or Microsoft Teams. But there were wider challenges for a new politics of time, from the daunting to the more parochial.

The Morbid Symptoms

Pandemics leave a legacy of higher morbidity, with a higher incidence of nervous disorders for years afterwards. This was the case following the Russian flu of the 1890s as well as the more devastating Spanish flu. Millions of people who survived subsequently suffered from stress, depression, chronic lethargy or debilitation.

Covid was to be no different. An international survey in 2021 identified over 200 symptoms of post-Covid syndrome (PCS), or long Covid. In Britain in early 2023 an estimated 1.8 million people were reporting PCS symptoms lasting over three months after they had or suspected they had Covid. Of these, 1.2 million had been suffering PCS for at least a year and for 690,000 it was over two years, with a particularly high incidence among women and the middle-aged. This was linked to a more generic condition – chronic fatigue syndrome (CFS) – which can result in permanent debilitation.

Three-quarters of sufferers said it affected their day-to-day activities, including ability to work.[3]

Health services, which in Britain were already struggling following cutbacks and privatization in the preceding period of austerity, were overstretched. Millions did not receive treatment for cancer and other life-threatening conditions, resulting in unnecessary deaths and illness. In late 2022, the British Heart Foundation claimed that over 30,000 people had died 'needlessly' from heart disease since the start of the pandemic, amid high numbers of non-Covid excess deaths – that is, more deaths than expected based on previous years.[4]

Not all health effects were negative. During the first lockdown in the UK, about a third of people said they felt better than before, and few wanted to return to old labouring routines and demands on their time.[5] However, Covid accentuated stress among the precariat. Social media and electronic labour reduced social interaction, and increased heteromation normalized more work-for-labour. Social and economic shocks became harder to bear. Mental health deteriorated everywhere, with increases in loneliness, anxiety, depression, insomnia, harmful alcohol and drug use, and self-harm or suicidal behaviour.[6] In the first year of the pandemic, the global prevalence of anxiety and depression increased by 25 per cent, according to the World Health Organization.[7]

Pandemics always increase suicidal tendencies. In the first century AD, the poet Ovid wrote that people hanged themselves during a plague to 'kill the fear of death by death's own hand'.[8] Suicide rates rose during the Spanish flu. And while the impact of long Covid has yet to be fully felt, suicide attempts and deaths rose during the pandemic.[9]

For young people, the additional stress amplified existing trends of heightened anxiety and depression, especially among girls. Jean Twenge, an American psychologist, has attributed rising rates of self-harm and suicide among US teenagers since about 2010, when smartphones started to become ubiquitous, to social isolation resulting from spending too much time online, especially on social media.[10] And studies show that the more time teens spend on social media, the less time they spend meeting up with friends and the worse their mental health is.[11]

In a survey by the US Centers for Disease Control and Prevention in spring 2021, 44 per cent of US teenagers said they had felt sad or hopeless in the previous year. But in 2019, before Covid, that figure was already 37 per cent, against 26 per cent in 2009. The pandemic made a mental-health crisis worse. In the UK, a survey in 2022 found that 44 per cent of teenagers met the threshold for acute psychological distress, up from 23 per cent in 2007. Those with parents in distress were most likely to feel the same.[12] Meanwhile, an NHS-commissioned survey of children and young people in England concluded that one in six children between the ages of seven and sixteen had a probable mental disorder in 2022, compared with one in nine in 2017. For young people aged between seventeen and nineteen, an even more alarming one in four had a probable mental disorder in 2022, compared with one in ten in 2017.[13] Society was in disarray.

The main story was that Covid accelerated an existing upward trend in all forms of morbidity, echoing what had taken place in the crisis era of industrial time at the end of the nineteenth century. A sign was the steadily rising proportion of the population resorting to antidepressant drugs, particularly in the most deprived areas.[14] Mental ill-health reflected multiple insecurities. Such were the waiting times for access to mental-health services that Greater Manchester created a new basic service named Waiting Well, to support people while they waited for treatment. Predictably, time spent waiting was time in which the symptoms worsened, lowering the probability that treatment would work. And it involved yet another form of inequality. Many in the salariat suffering from stress and depression were able to receive assistance from their employers.[15] Those in the precariat had no such help.

Inequality in life expectancy had been increasing steadily prior to the pandemic, while the average number of 'healthy life years' – years of life free of disability or disease – had actually fallen since 2014, with those on low and insecure incomes doing worst of all. The need for a time policy that fosters good health was surely urgent.

The Impact on Reproduction Time

The pandemic also accelerated the shift from shopping in person to shopping online and home delivery. Online shopping has been sold as 'more time living, less time shopping'. But sifting through a range of options eats up time; for some, it became an addictive use of scarce time. While the amount freed is unclear, online shopping does reduce time spent in the social activity of in-person shopping, with adverse psychological effects. Pre-Covid research showed that people value the social aspects of physical shopping, including chatting with sales staff, which boosts emotional well-being and can alleviate loneliness.[16] Consumers also like to touch products and enjoy the sensory stimulation of visiting a shop. None of these attributes can be replicated online.

More positively, there have been signs of retail commoning. Lockdowns encouraged slower, more local and personal modes of shopping.[17] A YouGov survey found that 40 per cent of Britons shopped locally during the lockdowns, most saying they would continue to do so after restrictions were lifted.[18] People like independent shops, as opposed to high-street chains. Such 'real shops' are increasingly recognized as a community resource, as in the revitalization by Shrewsbury Town Council of a market building as a centre for food stalls, cafés and specialist shops.

However, the pandemic also accelerated the conglomeration of companies providing online goods and services, as well as the shift from cash to card payments, which take rentier income from millions of people in brokerage charges. The gorilla in the commercial jungle is Amazon, which has become so ubiquitous that one think tank dubbed this the Amazonia era. The reported wealth of Jeff Bezos, its founder and CEO until 2021, rose by $35 billion in the first three months of the pandemic, when millions of people were losing all their income and drifting further into debt.

The effects on other aspects of reproduction time were mixed. Less time was spent in school travel and recreation on school premises, and more in teaching and learning at home. This was to the pecuniary advantage of nuclear families with one or both parents in the salariat and with spacious properties. However, in the UK parents reported they were doing over three hours a day more on childcare and nearly two hours on home schooling.[19] Many also did their job from home. Parents' mental health suffered, absolutely and relative to others, with women more affected. 'I am clutching at my sanity,' said one harassed mother in a post on Mumsnet, a parenting forum.

Parents also cut back on time used for replenishing knowledge and skills. Time spent on informal studying plummeted from an average of twelve minutes a day to just one minute among British parents (and from sixteen to twelve minutes for those without children). This will have an impact on their labour and work in the future. It was another form of inequality. The salariat were more likely to be offered paid time off during lockdown – 29 per cent of high-income earners with a postgraduate degree in the United States, for example, compared with only 9 per cent of those without a college degree. And one in five highly educated workers received financial help from their employer for childcare or tutoring, against one in twenty without a college degree. Time-related inequalities intensified.

The Pandemic and Automation

When Covid struck, leading economic think tanks, including the US National Bureau of Economic Research and the International Monetary Fund (IMF), predicted that it would accelerate automation of jobs.[20] Joseph Stiglitz, a Nobel Prize-winning economist, claimed that the extra costs of Covid were 'accelerating the development and adoption of new technologies to automate human work'.[21] Numerous studies had previously claimed that artificial intelligence and the ongoing technological revolution would lead to mass joblessness.[22]

There were signs that automation was accelerated by the

pandemic. Robots do not need to socially distance and do not become sick. Pittsburgh International Airport became America's first to use cleaning robots using ultraviolet technology. Stores in the UK and USA experimented with checkout-free technology, where shoppers use their smartphone to scan a QR code on entry, are watched by cameras as they pick goods from shelves, and when they leave are automatically charged.[23] Some stores began to operate with no customer-service staff. Unsurprisingly, the UK's Office for National Statistics (ONS) reckoned supermarket cashier jobs were among the most at risk.

Such developments suggested that the scope for labour-displacing technological change had increased. But a study by *The Economist* found little evidence of this in practice; indeed the pace of automation of routine tasks appeared to have slowed.[24] And both the pandemic and new technologies also raised the prospect of new sources of labour and work. One study of French firms concluded that the effect of automation may be to increase employment in firms adopting it, not to reduce it.[25] That could indicate a tendency for automation to concentrate production and employment in more technologically advanced firms, taking business from less productive companies.

Similar trends have arisen in Japanese and Finnish manufacturing.[26] The results are consistent with growing inequality due to rentier capitalism, in which automation skews rewards towards the top.[27] In fact, automation and artificial intelligence expand alongside growing employment. The biggest challenge lies in finding ways to respond to the maldistribution of the economic gains.

Job Furloughs

In 2020, in response to the pandemic, the UK government introduced an unprecedented measure that was nothing less than a reversal of the long thrust of social policy underpinning capitalism. The job furlough scheme paid people substantial amounts on condition that they did no labour. It was literally a policy of giving something for nothing. Other countries introduced similar measures.[28]

Under the Coronavirus Job Retention Scheme (CJRS), the government subsidized firms to pay employees they put on furlough – that is, kept in employment but required not to do any labour for the firm. The CJRS, and its equivalent for the self-employed, the Self-Employment Income Support Scheme (SEISS), commanded almost universal political support, including from the opposition Labour Party and the Trades Union Congress, which later pressed for the schemes' extension.

After they were wound down in late 2021, the IMF issued a report claiming they had been successful and recommending their renewal if the Omicron variant of Covid spread. Prominent journalists voiced agreement.[29] And the head of the Royal Society of Arts' Programme for the Future of Work lauded the CJRS's 'extraordinary success', adding: 'Even in the long-view history of Britain's welfare state, it is hard to imagine a policy as huge or as effective as "furlough" . . . it is hard to argue against a verdict of "job done".'[30]

This chorus of approval was extraordinary. The policy was uniquely flawed, with multiple faults. Of course, if government throws nearly £100 billion of subsidies to a minority of firms and workers, that will be popular with the recipients. But a scheme should be judged by what it does for the many, not the few, and for its opportunity cost, as well as for its longer-term distortionary effects.

The UK's furlough scheme, which covered over 11 million people during 2020–21, was possibly the most regressive social policy in modern history. It paid 80 per cent of the wage of employees up to £2,500 a month. This meant that somebody earning £3,000 beforehand received £2,400 for doing nothing, whereas somebody who had been earning £800 received £640. So, a high-wage earner received nearly four times as much as a low-wage one. To compound the regressiveness, the loss of £160 a month for a low-income earner may have meant impoverishment, whereas a higher-income earner, probably with savings, was likely to recoup the income loss with lower job-related expenses such as spending on transport.

Under the scheme, people who lost their jobs obtained nothing. People who accepted a wage cut and continued doing labour to keep their firm in business received nothing. Essential workers, such as health or care workers, refuse collectors and many others, obliged to continue in their jobs, also received nothing. Nor did the scheme reach the growing number of people supplying labour through 'umbrella companies', unregulated intermediaries employing half a million workers in 2020–21.[31]

The self-employed scheme was similarly regressive, paying 8 per cent of pre-pandemic profits quarterly up to £7,500. About three-quarters of those registered as full-time self-employed took advantage of the scheme, compared with a third of eligible employees gaining from the job fur-lough scheme. But the SEISS excluded people if their self-employment provided less than half their income, a common category in the precariat. Of those receiving less than half their income from self-employment, a majority had total earnings of less than £25,000 a year.

Adding to the regressive responses, the government in-troduced a gimmick, the Eat Out to Help Out Scheme. This subsidized restaurant meals in August 2020, which benefited those who could afford to eat out. Research soon showed that it was not only a gift to the more affluent but also boost-ed Covid infections.[32]

Double standards applied. Unlike the strict conditions im-posed on benefit claimants, no conditions were imposed on companies claiming furlough payments, other than the re-quirement that the furloughed employees did no labour. Thus Donald Trump's company received over £3 million for fur-loughed staff of his luxury golf resorts in Scotland, although his managers also laid off more than 250 others.[33] Trump, a multi-billionaire, surely could have afforded to cover the wages. But there was no means testing for corporations. Multi-nationals making billions of pounds in profits gained from the furlough and other subsidy schemes, while the destitute had to prove their destitution and more to obtain a pittance.

Even before the CJRS began, the head of Her Majesty's Revenue and Customs predicted widespread abuse.[34] I myself argued that it and the other schemes, including subsidized business loans, were obvious targets for fraudsters, which would worsen the regressive nature of the measures.[35] Sure enough, an early survey found that one in three furloughed employees had been asked or ordered to work, earning revenue for the employer collecting the government handout.[36] In mid 2022, HMRC estimated that nearly 5 per cent or £4.5 billion of payments for the furlough, self-employment and Eat Out to Help Out schemes had been claimed fraudulently or in error, half of which was incorrectly paid to employers claiming furlough payments for staff who continued to work.[37] By October 2022, HMRC had launched 50,000 investigations, the cost of which was a further waste of public resources on what was from the start a patently faulty scheme. It soon became clear that most of the money wrongly paid out would never be recovered.[38]

Though there were egregious cases of fraud – for example, by inventing employees using fake or stolen National Insurance numbers – many fraudulent claims will have gone undetected. They will have added to the regressive character of the scheme, since high-income salaried employees were more likely to be able to do unseen labour at home. And the government deliberately accepted the fraud risk to, in its words, 'get money to those who need it, as fast as possible'. Yet the people who needed financial help the most were not covered by the scheme. And very different rules were applied to those who lost their jobs and were obliged to claim Universal Credit; they had to wait at least five weeks and often longer to obtain meagre benefits. Those on furlough received their money straight away.

The Bounce Back Loan Scheme, for small and medium-sized businesses to survive the pandemic, was equally prone to fraud. One businessman obtained a £50,000 loan that he used to buy class A drugs; a student claimed a £50,000 loan for a used-car dealership that did not exist; an ex-restaurateur obtained the same amount for a restaurant that had already closed.[39] In April 2022, the House of Commons Public Accounts Committee noted that about £5 billion of the £47 billion spent on the scheme may have been lost to fraud, while another £12 billion was lost mainly through businesses collapsing during the pandemic.[40] The National Audit Office (NAO) calculated that 55 per cent (£26 billion) of all spending on the bounce-back scheme might never be recovered due to fraud and involuntary default.[41]

Other countries also suffered huge losses through fraudulent claims for Covid support, though for most there was only anecdotal evidence. The US Secret Service estimated that a whopping $100 billion was stolen from the $2.2 trillion Coronavirus Aid, Relief and Economic Security (CARES) Act, which included an employee retention scheme and low-interest loans to smaller businesses as well as direct payments to individuals.[42]

There were also wider economic effects of furlough. Paying workers only if they do no labour whatsoever encouraged complete economic inactivity rather than reduced production and short-time working. It penalized those who performed labour, and so depressed production by more than would otherwise have occurred. And there was a large deadweight effect, with the government funding furlough payments for employees who would have been or could have been covered by their company in any case.

The scheme also discouraged firms from restructuring during the pandemic, deterred labour mobility and propped up 'zombie' firms that had little chance of survival in normal times. Millions of workers were in empty labour, using time in labour for zombie firms or put on furlough by them. As a result, the rate of bankruptcies was lower than normal during the pandemic recession.[43] But corporate insolvencies soared with the withdrawal of government support in 2022.[44] Voluntary insolvencies – some probably declared to avoid loan repayments – reached their highest level since records began in 1960.

In December 2021, the Treasury said companies in general had 40 per cent more cash in the bank than before the coronavirus crisis, with a £7 billion rise in net deposits. The Covid policies had enabled many firms to gain in net terms, not just to survive, while millions of low-income people were much worse off, with over 2 million forced to turn to food banks. Should that be regarded as success?

The billions of pounds squandered on these fraud-ridden regressive measures could have been used to reduce inequality and chronic insecurity, in ways that would have increased people's control of time. And perversely, instead of retaining workers' attachment to jobs, the furlough schemes may have loosened it. For many people, staying at home began to seem an attractive option.

In early 2022, mass protests erupted in Australia, Belgium, Bulgaria, Canada, France, New Zealand and elsewhere. Centrist politicians reacted by castigating protesters as right-wing extremists. But the truck drivers and other manual workers who led the protests, mostly men, had been among those most penalized by the policies governments had pursued. These had protected finance, corporate capital, property owners and the salariat able to keep on working, quietly earning at home, while manual workers had been required to continue operating essential services, often for less pay than those on furlough. They were manifesting a defensive form of commoning, bonding with others in Occupy-style public action, as in Canberra, the Australian capital.[45] Individuals were finding a sort of community in a society that lacked it.

In sum, the UK government's economic measures in response to Covid were regressive, unfair, distortionary and, predictably from the outset, open to widespread abuse. And millions of people had practice in lying about how they were using their time.

Remote Labour: Working from Home

The extent of working from home had been growing in the two decades to 2020, but it was still very much a minority phenomenon. In the UK and USA, about one in twenty were doing their job mainly from home in 2019.[46] Covid lockdowns prompted a step change.

By the summer of 2020, over 40 per cent of workers in Europe and North America were doing their jobs from home.[47] In the USA, they accounted for about 62 per cent of total labour services and, weighted by earnings, contributed over two-thirds of economic activity.[48] In late 2021, while the figures had fallen after lockdowns ended, 40 per cent of all US labour was still being done remotely and 88 per cent of employers were offering flexible hours, against 27 per cent before the pandemic.[49]

In European Union countries, in mid 2020 on average 48 per cent of employees were doing their jobs from home, partly or exclusively. In Belgium, Denmark and the Netherlands the figure was more than half, and in Finland it was over 60 per cent.[50] In Britain, the proportion doing their jobs at home peaked at 49 per cent in June 2020 but was still over a third at the beginning of 2022.[51]

These figures may well be underestimates; the furlough schemes gave an incentive to conceal home labouring. Of course, not all remote labour was being done inside people's homes, although most was. Some built garden sheds as workplaces.[52] Some hotels and pubs, short of recreational and business visitors, rented out rooms as day workplaces. These developments, facilitated by corporate investment in digital hardware and software, further weakened the old mould of jobs and fixed workplaces. Use of remote-working systems soared. By late 2020, the various platforms had over 300 million users, led by Microsoft Teams, Zoom, Google Meet and Cisco Webex. By 2021, a new networked reality had become global and a dominant source of time use.

So-called hybrid models of labouring proliferated, alongside the 'nowhere office'. Employees might spend part of the workweek in an office (perhaps designated as a co-working space, with hot-desking), part of it working in a public place such as a café, and part at home. It was a reversal of the industrial time regime, when workers were dragged out of the home environment into factories and mines.

One study suggested that after the pandemic about a quarter of all paid labour days would be from home or away from a firm's office or factory, a fivefold increase from the pre-pandemic situation.[53] However, employer attitudes to remote home working were mixed. David Solomon of Goldman Sachs described working from home as 'an aberration'. Jack Dorsey, then head of Twitter, let it be known early in the pandemic that its staff could work from home 'for ever' (a policy immediately reversed when Elon Musk took over in October 2022), whereas the founder of Netflix said home working was a 'pure negative'.[54] Deloitte's 20,000 employees in the UK were told in June 2021 that they could decide 'when, where and how they work', following the perceived success of remote working.[55] Kevin Ellis, chair of consultancy firm PwC with 285,000 employees in 155 countries, said that the firm wanted 'to help enshrine new working patterns so that they outlast the pandemic'.[56]

Among predictable consequences of the shift to remote labour was a reduction in office space kept by corporations. In 2021, Capita, a provider of outsourced services to the UK government, announced that more of its offices would be closed. S4 Capital, a big advertising and marketing firm, terminated various office leases and developed a hybrid office model intended to suit its workers, whom the firm described as 'digital natives'. NatWest said it expected only 13 per cent of its 64,000 staff to work full time in its offices in the future, while a third would be allowed to live and work anywhere in the UK and would have to attend a NatWest office only twice a month.[57]

In England, 18 million square feet of offices were vacated between 2020 and the end of 2021, with one in ten offices predicted to be surplus to requirements post-pandemic.[58] One estate agent told *The Economist*: 'The days of people taking a 74-minute average commute into town to process email, and then 74 minutes back out – they're gone.'[59] A survey of workers in twenty-seven countries showed that working from home saved about two hours per week of commuting time per worker in 2021 and 2022.[60]

Among those doing remote labour, attitudes became increasingly positive as time went on. In a survey of over 30,000 people in thirty-one countries in January 2021, 73 per cent said they wanted remote options to continue.[61] As one commentator put it, workers did not want to go back to 'hard pants'.[62] However, most wanted a hybrid model, mixing home labour with labour at the workplace. A survey of nearly 5,000 employees in the UK in early 2021 found that 40 per cent would prefer to work from home for two or three days a week, 28 per cent for four or more days.[63] In the USA, those doing labour from home reported more satisfaction and happiness, and many said they would like to work (labour) from home nearly half of the time on average, up from 5 per cent before the pandemic.[64] By 2022, managers and workers across industrialized countries seemed in broad agreement that two or three days a week of telework would be ideal, contributing positively to both productivity and employee wellbeing.[65] Some 60 per cent of UK managers surveyed in mid 2022 agreed that home working increased productivity and motivation.[66]

How did the shift to remote labour affect the amount of labour? It certainly engendered greater variability in the allocation of time, with some doing less labour than they reported and many doing a lot of work-for-labour – that is, putting in more hours than they were being paid for. But the general conclusion was that almost everywhere people were working more hours.[67] Thus the commuting-time survey mentioned above found that on average 40 per cent of the time saved was used for extra labour or work-for-labour in jobs, including second jobs or 'side hustles'.

One study based on use of business software found that

employees working from home in the UK, Australia, Canada and the USA were at their computers for an extra two hours a day.[68] British employees increased their working week by nearly a quarter, often working through lunch and logging off around 8 p.m. In another survey, 30 per cent of employees said they worked more hours at home.[69] Across the EU, Eurofound data suggested that remote staff were twice as likely to be exceeding the EU's forty-eight-hour working week.[70]

Remote labour also invaded other areas of time use. A study by the Royal Society of Public Health reported that 56 per cent of employees found it harder to switch off when working remotely.[71] And a co-founder of the flexible work consultancy Timewise commented that the 'working day is at risk of losing its barriers and there will be real impact on mental health and wellbeing'.[72]

Evidence on productivity was mixed. At an economy-wide level, there was little to suggest a boost.[73] Early on in the pandemic, studies suggested that home working had increased labour productivity. A survey by PwC in 2021 found that 52 per cent of American employers thought their employees had become more productive, although only 34 per cent of workers agreed.[74] The divergence may reflect the fact that employers focused on output per employee, including those working more hours whose output per hour may have fallen. That said, another 2021 survey, in the UK, found that 54 per cent of remote workers thought they did more per hour than before.[75]

However, while workers may feel they are doing more, they may not necessarily produce more. A study of 10,000 professionals at a large Asian tech company found that the productivity of those working from home fell by up to a fifth. Many were working more hours but output fell, partly because they were spending more time in meetings. Japan's Research Institute of Economy, Trade and Industry suggested that working from home reduced productivity by almost a third.[76] And another study concluded that working from home may reduce the drive to be ever more productive, with the positive effect of turning people into better friends and partners.[77]

So-called frontline workers, whose jobs required their presence in person, may also have had lower labour productivity due to feelings of resentment or a perceived need to take more precautions. In response, some firms offered such workers more flexible options, such as longer working days in exchange for fewer days a week, and 'worker-first' scheduling that enabled people to adjust schedules according to outside commitments, such as caregiving or doctor's appointments, or to swap shifts or add extra hours. Still, most workers in low-paid insecure jobs continued to have their schedules determined by their employers, unable or fearful to ask for more flexible arrangements to suit their needs.[78] In 2023, the UK government gave all employees the right to ask for part-time work or home working from the first day of a new job, rather than after six months. But employers still had the right to reject such requests and were under no obligation to offer flexible working when recruiting.[79]

The reallocation of time saved from not commuting was also regressive. Those with more education were better able to use time saved to do more labour in their primary job. The ONS found that on average people working from home spent more time in their job than those doing jobs outside their home, and were being paid above-average wages. Many of those working from home also did many unpaid overtime hours, particularly in the evening.[80]

The shift to remote labour further blurred the boundary lines between types of activity. One person, described as a computing and work–life-balance expert, attributed a deterioration in so-called work–life balance to pressure and insecurity created by employers' use of tracking software. 'They feel like there is an expectation to always be on call,' said Anna Cox. 'It has such an impact on workers, particularly those who are not high-status managers.'[81]

The scope to do labour from home obviously depends on the type of service required and on the online capacities of modern technologies. One study concluded that 37 per cent of all existing jobs in the USA could be done entirely from home, including 90 per cent of finance jobs.[82] And higher-paying jobs were typically much better suited to home working than lower-paying ones.[83] In late 2022, some 44 per cent of British workers laboured partly or wholly from home, but home working was far more prevalent among those with high incomes and professional jobs.[84] Jobs from home look set to become one of the modern drivers of income inequality.

For many employers and their workers, a hybrid system combining home working or remote labour with time in the workplace has become the new normal. More than two-thirds of managers in a 2022 survey said employees were not expected to come to the office more than four days a week.[85] The tertiary time system is merging with elements of the pre-industrial time system. Time use will never look the same again.

Offshoring and Digital Nomads

The globalization of the labour process and labour market has been growing steadily for the past two decades. The rising proportion of offshorable jobs means there will be many more trade-offs between remote labour and offshoring, or outsourcing labour. Here is a new reality – the exportability of time, coinciding with the export of labour without the export of workers. This took off in the early 2000s and will surely escalate in an era of pandemics.

Work-from-anywhere – remote working from wherever a person chooses to stay – is becoming a new business model. Companies are emerging to arrange visas and travel for those wishing to do it and finding and renting locations for them. This is another way in which national labour markets are giving way to a globalized one, accentuated by the Covid pandemic.

Harbingers of the transformation include Dropbox, the cloud-storage company, which encourages employees to spend 90 per cent of their labour time away from the office, and Airbnb, which rather aptly allows workers to labour wherever they want in their home countries and in any of 170 countries for up to ninety days a year.[86]

The notion of 'anywhere jobs' is ambiguous, since they are not jobs as such, but non-routine service tasks that can be done online from anywhere. One study estimated that one in five jobs could be converted into anywhere tasks.[87] Since many highly skilled as well as lower-skilled jobs can be converted, this could further reduce the labour share of income in rich countries, as skilled online tasks are taken by workers elsewhere willing to accept lower pay.

In the USA, a PBS TV series, *The Future of Work*, in 2021 documented how many people were moving out of stable nine-to-five jobs into the precariat. Internationally, this has been romanticized in the notion of digital nomads, roaming the world and spending as much time as they can in exotic tropical locations. There is a gushing literature promoting this model of time use.[88]

By mid 2021, it was reckoned that 10 million Americans were digital nomads, unburdened by mortgages or permanent jobs, while 55 million more were in the odd-job economy.[89] A similar growth has taken place in Europe, which includes eight of the top ten countries for digital nomads, referred to by the consultancy Deloitte as 'laptop luggers'.[90] An online marketplace for tax consultants to help such workers has been created, named the Work from Anywhere Team, because, according to Michael Huertas of PwC, 'tax being drawn along national lines is really archaic'.[91]

So far, governments have not shaped social and labour market policies to suit the needs of workers providing labour from outside their country of citizenship or usual residence. But, as of early 2023, over two dozen countries around the world had followed Estonia's example and begun issuing 'digital nomad visas'. These draw in temporary migrant workers for six months or more with tax reliefs and logistical support, without burdening the social-security system. Something similar is happening within other countries: the USA has 'Zoom towns', some offering generous cash incentives to attract remote workers, often referred to as 'amenity migrants'.

Multinationals contemplating work-from-anywhere

schemes for at least some employees have included PwC, Deloitte, Twitter, Google, Siemens and Cisco. This could lead to digital nomads in lower-cost countries gaining a competitive advantage over their peers in the country where they are supplying their labour.

Among the troubling aspects is that so-called digital nomadism will expand the global precariat while weakening their political strength by being scattered and rootless.[92] In fact, some see this nomadic working life as also a rejection of the nation state, claiming that they are expressing a new freedom to spend time without the constraints of any particular state.[93]

So far, the number of such 'world citizens', as they see themselves, is too small to make much impact politically. However, if the number grows and they spend more time in nomadic roaming, they could be disenfranchised everywhere and so be depoliticized, diminishing public participation in the life of the *polis*, in that use of time seen by the ancient Greeks as the most valuable of all.

More Inequalities of Time

The pandemic and government responses resulted in several new regressive developments, besides further enriching the grotesque wealth of the rentier plutocracy and the property-owning salariat. One scarcely noticed trend was the provision by large-scale corporate employers of more non-wage benefits to their salariat, including extra holiday allowance entitlement and ultra-flexible labour schedules.

Netflix, the global streaming service, improved its practice of unlimited holiday allowance and flexible labour options. Other big corporations have followed.[94] There was also a shift from office to off-workplace perks.[95] Firms emerged to develop 'bespoke' perk packages for employers to use, including wellness apps and virtual exercise classes.

Bonding sessions for the salariat have become more prominent in big corporations in the absence or reduction of daily contact in workplaces. This is another source of inequality that has involved a further growth in empty labour for the salariat in the form of 'bleisure', a combination of business and leisure. Salesforce, a major multinational, has created a resort, Trailblazer Ranch, in California, where employees congregate for nominal training and immersion in the company's culture. The company offers what it describes as 'tactile experiences like guided nature walks, restorative yoga, garden tours, group cooking classes, art journaling and meditation'.[96] This could be termed the corporatization of leisure because, although it is partly 'recreational' and partly empty labour, it also has a quasi-political function, encouraging support for a privileged form of capitalism.

The pandemic also increased more conventional forms of labour market inequality. Across the OECD, low-paid workers (derisively referred to as 'low-skilled') were more likely to lose their jobs, while high-skilled (for which, read 'high-paid') workers were more likely to have their working time reduced.[97] And more low-paid workers in jobs were required to continue to labour, often exposed to health risks, while higher-paid members of the salariat were put on furlough and able to stay at home in comfort.

It is unclear whether the shift to remote labour will affect the bargaining power of workers in general. It may reduce it, by reducing the workplace community and sense of common time demands and solidarity. It could also be an isolating factor. Those doing concierge labour or tasking online are likely to see their bargaining power further eroded. And a new systemic form of wage differential may emerge between employees doing similar labour and work in large enterprises, with pay determined by where they are usually living. In a video to Meta (Facebook) staff, Mark Zuckerberg announced: 'We'll adjust salary to location . . . There'll be severe ramifications for people who are not honest about this.'[98]

White-collar employees will probably have more flexibility in their use of time, while the precariat will have flexibility imposed on them through zero-hours contracts and on-call apps. Meanwhile, for the salariat, remote labour offers the prospect of more choice and autonomy, albeit compromised by increased employer surveillance, as we shall see. But for many in the precariat, home labour is also a route to more intensive exploitation and self-exploitation. Excessive output levels may be enforced on insecure isolated 'outworkers', leading to more burnout. This was the main reason why such labour was banned in the USA in the 1930s, when mass unemployment weakened the ability of millions of people to reject such conditions. The state stepped in to overcome a market failure.

The spread of home labour has been both a new source of inequality and inequity and a reflection of them. If masses of people are to be partial or full-time home workers, those who have access to good facilities and means of production will have an advantage over those who do not. A basic requirement is adequate space within the home, to do the labour and to keep personal living separate. In England, owner-occupiers are far more likely to have a spare room that could be used for home labour than people living in rented accommodation, who are more likely to be in the precariat and on lower incomes.[99] Many people simply are unable to conform to this new labour system.

One source of inequity is labour-induced disability. Pre-pandemic surveys had found that those labouring from home were more likely to suffer from neck ache, wrist pain, nerve damage and sleep deprivation.[100] Although many were glad to avoid commuting, many also said that home labour was more stressful. One reason for physical and emotional problems was that people did not have ergonomic equipment at home. And insecure people may work too intensely for their own good, a form of self-exploitation.

Home labour has also increased the reversal of a defining feature of industrial capitalism, described by Karl Marx as workers being free of the means of production. In the industrial time era, capitalists owned these and workers were denied them. Now, increasingly, workers themselves are required to possess means of production to be employable, so resource-poor workers are at a structural disadvantage. Those with poor housing and shortage of funds for buying equipment may find there is a new barrier to employment. Some may come under pressure to accept jobs at lower wages if they accept use of means of production supplied by employers.

Another aspect is the effect on intra-household relationships. If more than one person is competing for limited labour space and online bandwidth, who has priority? This may lead to a new form of gender-based inequality, especially if a man's labour has a higher rate of return than a woman's. But it will in any case intensify inequities in households.

Some warned of a 'she-cession', because women dropped out of the labour force during the pandemic at higher rates than men or were forced to cut back time spent doing their jobs, hurting promotion and career prospects.[101] By contrast, others expected women's need and demand for more flexibility to redefine the labour market for all.[102] This presumes that most people have career jobs, which is hardly the case. And the pandemic probably accelerated the long-term trend towards the double feminization of the labour market – that is, towards the sort of labour relations for all that are typical of women's jobs, as well as both the relative and absolute substitution of women for men in jobs, which has been a global phenomenon.[103]

But in perhaps the most important structural outcome of the enforced growth of distance working, major companies will accelerate the contracting-out of jobs. Outsourcing will mean more offshoring of labour. It happened in manufacturing earlier this century as China and other Asian countries emerged with the infrastructure and productive capacity. Now it is happening to services. Among the predictable consequences will be a shrinking salariat in high-income countries and a further enlargement of the precariat.

Presenteeism as the Scourge of Jobism

Presenteeism was accentuated by home labour during the pandemic. Employers had a commercial interest in dissuading employees from going to their workplace if they had an infectious disease or illness, since they could bring down others, lowering production and productivity. But this concern is largely absent when labour is being done from home.

Will that lead to less willingness to provide health insurance or paid sick leave? The ONS reported that, on average, those doing labour from home took half as much sick leave as those doing labour in offices or factories.[104] This suggests they were losing out on sick pay (income) and endangering themselves and their families, maybe because they were trying to do their jobs when ill.[105] The ONS speculated that people might feel well enough to work from home while sick but not fit enough to travel.[106] However, there may also be an unwritten expectation that a mildly sick person should continue to labour and perhaps a less forgiving attitude towards those who fall sick. People may fear that not delivering when sick will lead to loss of income, as a form of retribution or simple commercial calculation. This may have led to a new form of presenteeism – in the home.

Most low-income workers cannot afford to take time off, not just because of lost earnings but also because many lack statutory or occupational sick pay or entitlement to adequate state benefits. In the UK, during the first two years of Covid, statutory sick pay was just £96 a week, hardly enough to encourage people to take sick leave if they could avoid it. But nearly 2 million employees – clearly part of the precariat – did not qualify for sick pay at all, for the perverse reason that they did not earn enough to be entitled to it – that is, to be earning at least £120 a week.

In implicit recognition of this inequity, the government set up a fund to pay up to £500 to cover a period of enforced self-isolation. However, nearly two-thirds of those who applied for this failed to obtain it, seemingly because the local bodies were not given the money to pay it. So, a large number of people were barred from obtaining compensation if they took time off due to sickness. A result was that they had a financial incentive to stay 'employed' even if sick, potentially exposing colleagues to infection, if they went to their workplace, and family members if they stayed at home 'working'. More likely, many would have pretended to continue to labour.

The dysfunctional system did not stop there. A further 5 million people did not qualify for statutory sick pay because they were classified as self-employed.[107] Many migrants were ineligible. And more than 647,000 seasonal workers over the New Year festival season of 2021–2 also did not qualify.[108] Whatever the form of presenteeism, it leads to a higher probability of future sickness and worse ill-health, not only for the person, but also for family members and colleagues.[109]

The pandemic may also have accelerated the demise of the standard seven-day week. Under the lockdowns and with mass home working, all days blur into one another. In response, companies wanting to keep going 24/7 moved to create labour schedules that enabled them to do so more easily. Arup, a design and engineering company, typifies this. It set up a labour system known as Work Unbound, allowing everybody in its large workforce to spread their core hours over seven days a week rather than the old system of Monday to Friday.[110] Many choose to spend part of their labour time during weekends. The scheme seems popular with employees, but it risks inducing some to be constantly tied to labour.

Another expanded form of presenteeism was the unused holiday. Many people were unable to take a conventional holiday in 2020 because of lockdowns and restrictions on travel. This produced another inequity worth quite a lot of income. Under Britain's working-time regulations, employees were previously entitled to carry eight days of leave over to the following year. The rule was amended in 2020, allowing employees to carry over a further four weeks into 2021 and 2022, if the employer agreed. Employees in large corporations or in the salariat were far more likely to have been allowed to carry over all or part of their paid holiday entitlement. Those in the precariat were most unlikely to have been given such a privilege.

Overemployment

Overemployment is spreading, a practice of deceptively holding two, three or even four full-time jobs at the same time, without the knowledge of any employer.[111] This partly stems from the prevalence of empty labour in many jobs and could be described as a new norm among borderline proficians with salariat status. The typical profile is an IT employee able to coast in a full-time job. Indeed, some of what they produce could simply be duplicated for a second employer.

In Britain, overemployment was brought to public attention during the pandemic by the revelation that Sir Geoffrey Cox, a former attorney general, in addition to his full-time job as a Conservative MP, serving the interests of his constituents and participating in parliamentary shaping of legislation, was spending much of his time in a luxury beach villa in the British Virgin Islands, where he was defending the BVI government in an enquiry into government corruption.

It emerged that earlier he had made rich pickings advising companies in the Cayman Islands, another tax haven, later lobbying against tougher financial regulations for the British territory. Sir Geoffrey, who earned over £6 million from his side hustle, skipping votes in the House of Commons to do it, was only one of many Conservative MPs holding lucrative second jobs.[112] While MPs must declare outside financial interests, which do not strictly count as deceptive over-employment, the scandal sparked interest in the phenomenon more generally.

Advocates claim that overemployment is not over-work, but just a way of capitalizing on empty time. A growing online community, overemployed.com, gives advice on how to manage two full-time jobs without either employer knowing, and how to manage taxation. The practice as such is not illegal, provided earnings are declared for tax purposes. However, it could violate employment contracts and non-compete agreements stipulating that the person cannot work for a competitor. There are also known examples where people have subcontracted an additional job to friends or relatives, a clear breach of the labour contract and unlikely to be recorded in official labour market statistics.

Defenders of overemployment argue that, if employers are satisfied, no harm is done and that, just as companies can fire people whenever they wish, employees are justified in exploiting overemployment opportunities. One finance worker in his mid-twenties told a reporter that it is 'a way for workers to take control of their lives and not need to be

subservient. The nine-to-five is officially dead. Companies
can accept this and give us freedom.'[113] Perhaps the premise is valid, but the way of taking the freedom is surely not.

Moreover, overemployment is possible mainly for already
well-paid remote workers. Low-wage manual workers, who
may nevertheless be cobbling together two or three jobs to
make ends meet, are unlikely to have that opportunity. It
is another small way in which labour market inequality is
growing.

Tightening of the Panopticon State

Many of those doing jobs from home laboured more, partly
because of the difficulty of separating home and labour life,
but also perhaps because their labour was being monitored
more strictly.[114] Algorithmic monitoring of employees accelerated during the pandemic.[115] A survey in Britain in early
2022 found that a third of workers were being monitored,
against a quarter in mid 2021. The use of camera monitoring
in people's homes rose from 5 per cent to 13 per cent over
the period.[116]

In recent years, many large firms employing manual service workers have monitored them and set complex performance tasks through algorithms, such as queue monitoring in
supermarkets and deliveries-per-hour guidelines for delivery drivers. Amazon has notoriously policed toilet breaks.
But the pandemic led to a huge growth in monitoring home
labour and the development of ever more sophisticated techniques for doing so.

Firms selling the technologies and software say the aim is
to protect consumers, investors and employees from abuse.

However, they are hardly benign. One company, Remote-Desk, initially said its employee-monitoring software was aimed at producing 'work-from-home obedience'.[117] When that created public alarm, the company hastily changed the language. But the intention was clear. It boasted that its software created 'an office-like environment through continuous webcam monitoring to secure employee identity and ensure productivity in a remote workspace'.[118] It does not take much imagination to see the invasion of privacy in that.

A US study found that monitoring software was linked to more employee tension and less job satisfaction, causing higher staff turnover.[119] Most disliked by employees, according to research by Britain's Trades Union Congress, were facial recognition software and mood monitoring (76 per cent against), monitoring of social media accounts outside work (69 per cent), recording location on portable devices (67 per cent) and monitoring of keyboard strokes (57 per cent).[120] In 2021, the UK All-Party Parliamentary Group on the Future of Work recommended stricter regulation of labour surveillance, including an Accountability for Algorithm Act. According to its report, *The New Frontier: Artificial Intelligence at Work*: 'Pervasive monitoring and target-setting technologies, in particular, are associated with pronounced negative impacts on mental and physical wellbeing as workers experience the extreme pressure of constant, real-time micro-management and automated assessment.'[121]

A French multinational call centre company, Teleperformance, employing 380,000 people in thirty-four countries, with UK companies and government departments as clients, told employees: 'If the system detects no keyboard stroke and mouse click, it will show you as idle for that particular duration, and it will be reported to your supervisor.'[122] Another company told its employees labouring from home to keep a video conference call open all day so that a manager could watch what they were doing.[123]

While some firms have held back from introducing the most intrusive forms of monitoring because of employee concerns, others are pressing ahead in the absence of regulation. And even tighter regulation is unlikely to arrest the spread of the panopticon state in seeking to control how people use their time. The costs of surveillance are falling, the potential commercial gains from deploying it are rising, and once a few firms set the tone, others will feel it is the normal action to take.

Tightening of the Banopticon State

Covid led to a tightening of the banopticon state – that is, a tendency to deny people entitlement to social rights, benefits and services, in the process imposing demands on some people's time to an onerous degree. To the regressive character of the furlough schemes must be added the mean-spiritedness of the benefit system. As *The Economist* warned in 2020, 'Better to raise taxes to finance an adequate welfare state than to lay poverty traps and distort incentives with poorly designed eligibility rules.'[124] Instead, the government gave just an extra £20 a week to the 6 million receiving Universal Credit and nothing to the 2.6 million dependent on legacy benefits in areas of the country where Universal Credit had not been rolled out.

When the government removed the extra £20 from

Universal Credit in late 2021, Prime Minister Boris Johnson claimed this was in everybody's best interest. He added: 'The best way forward is to get people into higher-wage, higher-skilled jobs, and if you ask me to make a choice between more welfare or better, higher-paid jobs, I'm going to go for better, higher-paid jobs.'[125]

This was class politics. There was no such choice. If better-paying jobs were available, people would not need the welfare. And it was hardly in the interest of someone on a low income to have their income reduced. This amounted to £1,040 a year, the biggest-ever cut to benefits, pushing half a million more people into absolute poverty, many in jobs.[126]

Overall, over a third of Universal Credit recipients were in jobs, paid so little that they qualified for benefits. Another 20 per cent were not required to take a job, due to illness, disability or maternity. And the basic benefit was miserably low to start with, at less than £100 a week or 20 per cent of average previous income, much lower than in every other European country.[127] Britain also had higher childcare costs than other OECD countries except Switzerland. So, swapping benefits for a low-wage job would have left a low-income mother seriously worse off.

A survey of so-called key workers during the pandemic – care workers, supermarket employees, education and emergency-service workers, all relatively low-paid – found that many were in an economic security trap, forced to choose between protecting their income or their health. Many were in a poverty trap set by Universal Credit; the more they laboured the less benefit they obtained, making gains from extra earnings minimal.[128]

Internationally, the pandemic sparked a wave of experiments with cash grants. Many were described as basic incomes, despite being given only to a random sample of residents of a community or to low-income people, or both. Nevertheless, they marked a signal break with the previous, and still predominant, trend of giving benefits only to those deemed to be the *deserving* poor.

Income support during the pandemic enabled people to stay safer. Those who were denied support, or given inadequate support, were unfairly put at greater risk. Obliged to go to jobs to gain income, many people not only risked Covid infection but put others at risk by potentially acting as spreaders. It would have been a form of general social protection to have given everybody adequate income support, to enable all to stay at home if they felt at risk or were a risk to others. A basic income for all would have been a public-safety measure.

A cross-national study of travel patterns found that, in low-income communities, there was much less reduction in people's movements for labour and work than in higher-income communities. But it also showed that movement was lower in areas where there was income support for low-income groups, helping them comply with public-health rules and thus helping control the spread and persistence of Covid.[129]

By contrast, one trend during the pandemic was a rise in the numbers reduced to seeking food packages from food banks. This visible hardship prompted the British government to launch yet another ad hoc measure, rather than confront the causes. It set up a Household Support Fund, giving local authorities a very modest amount to provide one-off sums to applicants who were on low incomes. The Department for Work and Pensions suggested local authorities should use food banks as delivery partners. The charity state was strengthening the culture of supplication.

The DWP also dished out vouchers instead of cash to some claimants, claiming paternalistically that cash had a risk of fraud because recipients might use it to buy items outside 'the policy intent' of food. This policy used up the time of supplicants and of people volunteering at food banks. It contrasted with the job furlough scheme, where there was large-scale fraud but no requirement that recipients had to use the money in particular ways.

In mid 2021, a group calling itself the Independent Food Aid Network designed a small-scale study to look at the economic and psychological impact of providing cash instead of food packages. Families were given cash equivalent to the value of a typical food package. Recipients appreciated the increased flexibility in how they used their time and in being able to allocate the money to their most pressing needs at any particular moment. Rachel Tribe, a clinical psychologist working on the study, made the obvious points: 'We know that visiting a food bank can be a humiliating experience; often, accessing food banks involves queuing and answering questions about why help is needed, which can make the process stressful and undignified. Cash allowed people to shop around and cater for specific needs, such as allergy-safe or culturally appropriate foods.'[130] And, of course, it gave them more autonomy and dignity, which the affluent who form and back the government take for granted for themselves.

Perhaps the most inexcusable part of social policy was the systematic delay in giving claimants what they were fully entitled to receive. Time spent waiting for benefits was a denial of social rights. For instance, in mid 2022, new claimants for disability benefits, some 300,000 people, were having to wait on average for four months.[131] The lengthy waiting time was a reflection of official disdain and obviously impoverishing a vulnerable part of the population.

It wilfully abused due process. Almost half of all those applying for independent payments for disability were initially refused. But after waiting for months, 68 per cent of those who appealed were eventually successful. Not only should the benefits have been back paid but the appellants should have been compensated for the unmerited period of unjustified economic insecurity.

The sanctions regime operated for Universal Credit – which reduces or withdraws payments if claimants fail to comply fully with strict conditions – is also an egregious abuse of due process. The number of Universal Credit sanctions in late 2022 was more than double what it had been in the comparable pre-Covid period. And, although half the appeals against sanctions are successful, those who appealed to the DWP's Independent Case Examiner had to wait fifty-three weeks before their case was even allocated to an investigator. By contrast, sanctions were imposed immediately.

In other words, many of the poorest in the land were languishing for many months, denied money that would have given them subsistence. This was surely indefensible. People's time was being inexcusably abused, without penalties for the abusers or compensation for the abused.

Way-to-Work: Vindictive Madness?

Unemployed claimants for Universal Credit were not allowed to refuse temporary jobs, creating the precarity trap described earlier. They could not refuse zero-hours contracts. If someone left a job voluntarily to take another that did not last, they lost benefits for having left the first job voluntarily. Another twist came in 2022 when the DWP introduced the Way to Work scheme, obliging job seekers to accept jobs below their occupational level from the fourth week of receiving benefits, rather than after three months as previously. Refusal could lead to sanctions.

After two years of cosseting the salariat by paying them not to do jobs, the government was telling the unemployed they must take a low-level job after four weeks, even though taking a job below one's occupational level lowers lifetime expected income and the probability of obtaining a job suitable to their qualifications. It further disadvantaged the poor since those with savings or family support could avoid recourse to Universal Credit and an enforced drop into a lower-level job. The government's claim that the Way to Work scheme would help tackle labour shortages and propel 500,000 claimants into jobs within six months was nonsensical. At the time, among the 433,000 people who had been on Universal Credit for less than three months, there were only 179,000 job seekers.[132]

The tight labour market instead reflected shrinking labour supply, due partly to a reduction in migrant labour, partly to early retirement by older people as a preferred option to low pay and health risks in available jobs. With the exception of financial and business services, real wages were falling, despite low unemployment.

Already, the basic unemployment benefit was one of the lowest in the OECD, at £325 a month, well below the official estimate of absolute poverty. The deliberate squeeze on benefits forced people to take jobs they did not want or that were ill-suited to their capabilities or needs, while sanctions led some to drop out of the labour force altogether.

The NAO found that, after being sanctioned, people were just as likely to stop claiming benefits without finding a job as they were to move into employment.[133] According to a Swedish study, after a sanction people were more likely to take jobs that were low-wage, part-time and below their occupational level.[134] And a survey in the UK and Denmark found that most employers disliked welfare conditionality because the fear of losing benefits led many unsuitable people to apply for vacancies.[135]

Separately, the DWP further tightened the rules to require more people with disabilities to attend weekly face-to-face meetings with staff in jobcentres, even though this was already causing widely reported mental distress.[136] Many claimants must attend these weekly meetings for months while awaiting a Work Capability Assessment that could rule them unfit to be pushed into jobs. And the government's proposal in March 2023 to scrap the flawed assessment, which regularly categorizes sick and disabled people as 'fit for work', appears to be aimed at pushing even more of those with disabilities into jobs. In effect, it will deem all but the most severely sick and disabled potentially 'fit for work' and reduce their financial support, a move that will especially hit people with short-term or fluctuating illnesses.[137] The DWP's treatment of disabled people, especially those with mental disabilities such as severe depression or agoraphobia, has been linked to hundreds of suicides and thousands of other deaths during the decades of welfare reform.[138] It is a flagrant abuse of people's time, with hideous consequences.

Evidence from the United States paints a similar picture. Labour requirements in means-tested welfare schemes lead to fewer receiving benefits but not to any increase in the employment rate of claimants.[139] And sanctions are associated with poorer school performance by the children of those sanctioned, as well as more child abuse and greater likelihood of family break-up.[140]

None of the evidence affected the punitive thrust of British government policy. In November 2022, the chancellor announced that 600,000 people on Universal Credit would be 'coached' to increase their labour supply. One could guess that if someone did not wish to be coached, sanctions would follow. Their time was not their own.

In summary, during and after the pandemic, the government made life tougher for the precariat, and induced them to do more work-for-labour and work-for-the-state, with, it is no exaggeration to say, life-threatening consequences.

The Great Resignation

The year 2021 was meant to mark the Great Return. As lockdowns and furlough schemes ended, employees were expected to flock back to their jobs in offices and on factory floors to restore old norms of labour. Instead, as the economy began to recover, firms in countries as different as the UK,

France, Greece, the USA and Israel grumbled about labour shortage.[141] Echoing the aftermath of the Spanish flu pandemic in 1919, many people did not want to go back to their former workplaces and let it be known that old, tolerated ways were no longer tolerable.

In the USA, President Joe Biden's economic advisers attributed labour shortages to workers' stronger bargaining position, enabling them to move to higher-paying jobs with better conditions. The political right blamed the temporary cash benefits during the pandemic, which Republican-controlled states refused to extend. But reluctance to return to jobs may have been prompted by other factors, such as lack of affordable childcare, disruption to childcare arrangements, fears that more workplace interactions would lead to more infection from the virus, and anticipation of more stress due to understaffing coupled with increasing demand for labour from existing employees.

A more interesting story, dubbed the Great Resignation, suggested that Covid prompted a transformational change in the way many people wished to use their time, with millions quitting jobs in the search for a better way of living. Record numbers of American workers quit jobs in 2021, notably in hospitality and catering, where burnout was widespread due to stressful working conditions and uncertain, volatile schedules.[142]

In the UK, job quitting rose sharply from late 2020, continuing at a high rate through 2021. In one survey, 41 per cent of employees across the world said they would consider leaving their job within the following year.[143] Another survey of over 16,000 employees in sixteen countries found that 54 per cent were prepared to change jobs unless afforded some flexibility in when and where they could work.[144] One in four UK employees surveyed by the Randstad employment agency in late 2021 said they were planning to change employers.[145]

However, job quitting had been on an upward trend long before Covid.[146] In the USA, the quitting rate rose steadily in the decade to 2019, after a sharp fall following the financial crash of 2008. A drop in 2020 gave way to a sharp increase in 2021. The Chief Knowledge Officer of the American Society for Human Resource Management attributed the Great Resignation to 'Covid clarity', as people looked to do something less onerous or more satisfying. As one twenty-seven-year-old woman, previously a doctor's assistant, told a journalist: 'People keep talking about how this is a generation that keeps switching jobs. It's because no one allows themselves to be bullied or be undervalued. And you know what? That's absolutely right. Our parents taught us that you should stick with it, stay at a job, but why?'[147]

Some commentators waxed lyrical about what was happening. But the evidence suggested that, except for the over-fifties, quitting was mainly to change job. Changes did not appear to lead to a higher or lower occupational level, although many job movers did obtain higher wages. But the Great Resignation did not improve career paths, and tailed off in late 2021, with less quitting and lower wage growth.[148]

One aspect was a reversal of the previous trend towards rising labour-force participation by people in their fifties, sixties and seventies as a consequence of better health, more flexible labour options, increases in the statutory retirement age and diminished pensions. In the USA, more than 3 million 'excess retirements' accounted for over half the 5.25 million people who left the labour market from the start of the pandemic to mid 2021. In the UK, by late 2021 over 300,000 fewer older people were in the labour market than if pre-pandemic trends had continued, accounting for nearly a third of the million fewer people overall.[149] By mid 2022, younger people had mostly rejoined the labour force, while early retirement by those in their fifties and sixties accounted for most of the post-pandemic rise of half a million in the number of working-age adults not in jobs or looking for one.[150]

One reason seems to have been rising morbidity associated not just with the pandemic, which hit older people disproportionately, but with the neglect of healthcare for other illnesses due to overstretched health services. The number of people in Britain claiming disability benefits doubled in the year to mid 2022.[151] In the USA, there were similar indications of prevalent ill-health, with 1.6 million people every month off sick for at least a week in 2022 compared with 1 million before Covid.[152] And older people, especially those with no options to do jobs remotely, may have preferred a cut in income to the heightened health risk of being in jobs and in commuting to and from them. Before Covid, they could take low-wage service jobs because they could complement inadequate wages with a pension or savings. Others benefited from the rise in value of their property and savings, giving them a financial cushion and a greater ability to retire. The withdrawal from jobs by those in their sixties, in particular, may be part of the Great Withdrawal, not just the Great Resignation.

Predictably, mainstream commentators lamented the shrinkage of the labour force. As the director of the Institute for Employment Studies observed: 'Labour supply just cannot keep up with labour demand, and the problem appears to be getting worse.'[153] But unless you know why people are not labouring or looking to labour, you cannot say it is a 'problem'. Some may have turned to unpaid care activities, some may have gone back into education, some may have decided to retire fully rather than dabble in the labour market. And the 'problem' could produce two desirable reactions: higher wages and an increase in automation of low-productivity, unattractive and dangerous jobs. To presume it is a problem is labourist prejudice.

Perhaps supporting the more sanguine view, after the pandemic receded there was a spurt in the number of people setting up as 'self-employed' or establishing own-account businesses. This happened alongside the deluge of bankruptcies of zombie businesses that had been propped up during the pandemic. A million new firms sprang up across OECD countries between the first lockdowns and the end of 2021.[154] This may have been due in part to the increase in savings by people who had gained from furlough schemes, as well as a desire to change lifestyle and reduce exposure to infection by the virus in large-scale workplaces. Did it also reflect a view that formal jobs were to be avoided if possible?

In the USA in 2020, as the Covid-19 virus spread and employment fell, over 4.4 million new businesses were registered with the Internal Revenue Service, a 24 per cent increase over the previous year. In 2021, new business applications rose by a further 23 per cent to 5.4 million for the year, the biggest number since 2004 when the US government started collecting such data.

This was a 'great de-jobbing' rather than a Great Resignation, and mostly reflected people setting up as self-employed. Nearly a third of new entrepreneurs came from the unemployed; one survey found that over 50 per cent of new businesses had been started because of economic need.[155] However, as the economy started to recover in 2021, new business applications were still being filed at twice the pre-pandemic rate. More people were prepared to take advantage of low interest rates, the growing availability of online tools, a desire for remote working, and a growing conviction that labouring in large-scale firms and offices was not just unpleasant but dangerous to health.

In the UK, the experience was rather different. Before the pandemic, there had been a big increase in self-employment, from about 8 per cent in 1975 to about 14 per cent in 2019, most of whom were sole traders. But in 2020 the number of self-employed fell from 5 million to 4.2 million and bounced around that level in 2021 and 2022. Some, mostly the higher-paid, who were paying themselves through their company to gain tax advantages, may have reclassified themselves as employees to benefit from the job furlough scheme or as a result of a government crackdown on bogus self-employment. But many appear to have withdrawn from the labour market because of illness or early retirement.[156]

Of course, trends can quickly reverse. Just as the Great Resignation was exercising the commentariat, a counter trend was identified, dubbed the Great Unretirement. Prompted by the spurt in price inflation, the number of people aged sixty-five and over in the UK labour force jumped by 173,000 in mid 2022.[157] This was linked to the rise in the age of pension entitlement, lower personal contributions to pension funds and rising debt. Above all, it was a new pattern of ageing, so that more of the salariat in their fifties were opting out of labour while more people on a low income in their sixties and seventies were opting back in, from necessity.

Anti-Work as Anti-Labour

The Great Resignation or Withdrawal prompted claims of a mass rejection of work, which one commentator called the largest disruption since the Second World War.[158] It was more an acceleration of a long-term trend of rejection of labour. Some commentators denied there had been any change at all.[159] But there was one potential harbinger. A US study found that the post-pandemic labour-force participation rate understated the tightening of the labour market, because the number of hours of labour people wished to provide had not only declined during the pandemic but had also not rebounded.[160]

There was a subversive reaction towards labour unleashed by the pandemic. Reddit's Antiwork message board, described as 'a magnet for the overworked and underappreciated employees of America', had 1.6 million subscribers by early 2022.[161] One popular post was by someone wanting to give up his dead-end job to spend time woodworking.

The people behind Antiwork have encouraged workers to strike passively – for example, calling for a boycott of Amazon on Black Friday, the day after Thanksgiving when

Amazon and other companies offer big consumer discounts. Some psychologists are convinced that the culture of work changed as a result of the system break that the pandemic achieved.[162] We shall see.

The anti-work sentiment gelled with deliberate shirking on the job. More people are trying to become what the writer Nilanjana Roy calls 'time millionaires', clawing back time from employment to spend on their own pursuits. And remote working has given more opportunity for empty labour. One serial time millionaire told a journalist, 'I could not be happier. My boss is happy with the work I'm doing. Or more accurately, the work he thinks I'm doing.'[163] One author, in savaging labouring, urged people to 'do nothing' instead.[164] But that leaves out the societal need for *schole* and the human condition of wanting to work, not labour.

Finally, a new term entered the lexicon of labour, 'quiet quitting'. Some dismissed the idea. However, there was anecdotal evidence of a downward shift in the effort bargain, in labouring to rule, rather than being slavishly attached to jobs. Was this a sign of emancipation from labour? It certainly posed awkward questions for those asserting from a position of comfort that a job gives a person dignity and freedom.

Job Options: Labourist Endgames?

There has been a strange convergence in political policy stances in reaction to the growth of the precariat and the collapsing model of labourism. The rhetoric has differed but essentially both social democrats, on the left, and neoliberals and libertarians, on the political right, have taken a similar posture. The right has said people must take jobs; social democrats have said that everybody must have job opportunities. The right has said they will make sure people take jobs; the left that they will make sure everybody has a job. In reality, they have both preached some variant of workfare.

The fetish of jobs has permeated the consciousness of most commentators. In a serious article, a politically left-leaning journalist said she had hesitated to acquire an app enabling her to scan the price of items picked from supermarket shelves and produce a total to be charged at checkout because she thought widespread use of the app would lead to job losses for checkout workers.[1] So, she did not use a time-saving device, in the interest of preserving a tedious, undemanding, boring and badly paid job.

Surely in a society that respected the time of everybody, with an income-distribution system that shared the benefits of labour time saved, such technology would be welcomed.

The well-meaning conscience of the journalist reflects a loss of human perspective. We should delight in all prospects of removing the need for stultifying jobs. Can we imagine a future where an objective of job minimization replaces job maximization?

Wage Subsidies: Third Way Endgame

In the 1990s, when globalization and other factors were driving down real wages in OECD countries, a group of social democrat leaders formulated a strategy known as the Third Way. Among their policies were in-work benefits in the form of tax credits – that is, top-ups to low wages aimed at ensuring people in jobs did not fall below a subsistence standard of living. The biggest such scheme was the US Earned Income Tax Credit; in Britain too New Labour adopted this approach with gusto.

Tax credits function much like the wage subsidy underpinning the Speenhamland system at the end of the eighteenth century. They are state-financed wage top-ups that are only paid if the person continues in the low-wage job. By the time of Covid, 58 per cent of British households with at least one wage earner were receiving the Working Tax Credit or the Universal Credit equivalent. Britain's furlough scheme during Covid, discussed in Chapter 6, was also a wage subsidy.

As the Speenhamland system demonstrated, wage subsidies have well-established defects. Indeed, they can act to depress the wages and living standards of those on the lower rungs of the labour market and impede productivity growth and technological innovation.

Suppose the government says it will top up wages below a certain amount. Employers can profit by paying a lower wage than otherwise, knowing that the state will make up the difference. As for the impact on productivity and technological innovation, depressed wages due to tax credits mean that employers can still profit from low-productivity employees, and will be under less pressure from labour costs to raise their productivity. More generally, artificially cheap labour reduces 'dynamic efficiency': there is less pressure to introduce technological innovations to raise productivity and, potentially, to reduce the need for labour through automation.

So, tax credits tend to depress wages and subsidize low-wage jobs. In addition, wage subsidies to create or maintain jobs, whether direct or as tax credits, have large deadweight effects (the jobs would have been created anyway) and substitution effects (subsidized jobs displace non-subsidized jobs). They are mainly a subsidy to employers. Yet the British and other governments continue to use them.

In 2020, the UK government launched the £1.9 billion Kickstart job creation scheme, promising to create 250,000 high-quality jobs for young people under the age of twenty-four who were on Universal Credit and deemed to be at risk of long-term unemployment. These jobs would pay a minimum wage for twenty-five hours a week for six months. How paying just the minimum wage for twenty-five hours a week could create high-quality jobs was never explained.

There is a long record of failed youth wage schemes in the UK and elsewhere, which should have been enough to prevent another costly gesture. Sure enough, in November 2021, the National Audit Office concluded that Kickstart was most unlikely to deliver value for money. The Department for Work and Pensions, in its initial cost–benefit analysis, had already assumed that only 50 per cent of jobs would be additional, but in the event most job placements coincided with a strong post-lockdown recovery in labour demand, implying an even higher deadweight effect.[2] The actual cost of each extra job created was thus at least twice the nominal subsidy, estimated at £7,000 per job, and perhaps much more. By late 2021 Kickstart had notionally created 96,700 jobs, instead of the targeted 250,000, but that was merely the number for which the subsidy was paid.

The NAO pointed out that the DWP was not monitoring whether the jobs were high quality or offered training or were given to people for whom they were intended. It was yet another smokescreen act of labourism, amounting to a subsidy to capital that raised profits by lowering labour costs. This is bound to happen if the overriding objective is to preserve or generate jobs. Yet, despite the evidence of its failings, Kickstart was extended to March 2022, while its partner scheme for unemployed adults, the Job Entry Targeted Support scheme, was extended to September 2022.

Tax credits and wage subsidies have been a way to hold up labourism, based on the premise that maximizing the number of individuals using a lot of time in labour is the optimum way for people to live.

Conditional Welfare: The Libertarians' Endgame

Meanwhile, those on the political right (along with some on the left) have taken another route to maintaining labourism at a time of declining real wages and job fragmentation. They have set out to make access to state benefits increasingly conditional on performing or preparing for work as labour. This amounts to little more than obliging more disadvantaged people to use up time in what is a mostly pointless use of it.

In the UK, the DWP has explicitly stated that being on Universal Credit should be as close as possible to being in a job: 'Deliberately mirroring a contract of employment, the Claimant Commitment makes clear that welfare is no different from work itself. Just as those in work have obligations to their employer, so too claimants have a responsibility to the taxpayer: in return for support, as some in jobcentres now say, claimants are "in work to find work".'[3]

As Neil Couling, head of Universal Credit, told two parliamentary committees in March 2021: 'The system does require the 2.5 million people on universal credit [in the 'work-related activity group'] to engage with work search as a condition of receiving universal credit . . . You are not going to get a job unless you look for one.'[4]

There is moralistic insanity behind such statements.[5] The implications for both personal time use and wellbeing are enormous. The posture presumes there are suitable available jobs out there, that the unemployed are all capable of searching for jobs in the way the DWP specifies, and that the DWP knows what is best for them. Suppose, to be generous to the DWP, that there was a 60 per cent probability that each of those presumptions was true. That would mean that it would be fair on fewer than one in every five claimants.

To recall, Universal Credit is a form of social discipline aimed at inculcating docility in those already resigned to the stigmatization of applying for state benefits. It is a regime of time control imposed by a vast street-level bureaucracy, operating a life-threatening system of sanctions that are grossly disproportionate to the alleged offences.

At the heart of the strategy is control of time of those in the lower reaches of the labour market, the precariat. It is a system that pays no respect to the value of the time of the millions who are claimants at any one point, and to many millions more who could become involved. And most labourists seem oblivious to the depressing effect on wages from the treatment of those in the margins of the labour market.

The 'Job Guarantee': A Social Democrat Endgame

Meanwhile, many social democrats yearn for a form of industrial time, derived from a labourist perspective that the main objective of economic policy should be full employment. Their proposals, which include the populist policy of a guaranteed job for all, amount to various forms of workfare.

Although most proponents do not say what would happen if someone offered a guaranteed job declined to take it, some have said they would lose benefits. In the UK general election campaign in 2015, Ed Miliband, then Labour Party leader, proposed that all 18–24-year-olds out of employment for a year or more would be offered a job, with those who refused losing benefits. This is the essence of workfare.

The job-guarantee proposal should be seen in the context of the historical debate around the right to work. This evolved from the right to work to the right to labour and then the duty to labour at the peak of the industrial time era after the Second World War. This was the period of industrial citizenship, when a growing range of social rights were made dependent on the performance of labour and willingness to perform labour in the so-called standard employment relationship, which applied to men in stable full-time jobs. Social democrats and other labourists still hark back to this supposed golden age while advocating policies based on the implicit view that workers have a duty to labour.

Advocacy of a job guarantee for everyone able to work gathered momentum after the financial crisis of 2008 and during the subsequent decade of austerity. In the US presidential election in 2020, prominent Democrat senators and presidential candidates came out in support, including Kamala Harris, who became vice-president.

In Britain, Lord Layard, Tony Blair's happiness tsar, pushed for a job guarantee during the New Labour government.[6] He also said that youth should be forced to take jobs. But if jobs make you happy, as he claimed, why do people need to be forced to take them? Still, in early 2020, as Covid struck, the Resolution Foundation, a centrist think tank, proposed that a guaranteed job should be provided to all school leavers and graduates.

For a while the idea was all the rage. Many commentators claimed a job guarantee would be politically popular. Much was made of a US poll that asked people whether they would support a scheme to guarantee a job for anybody 'who can't find employment in the private sector', if paid from a 5 per cent tax on those earning over $200,000 a year. The result was 52 per cent in favour. Supporters thought this was 'stunning'.[7] With such a loaded question, one should be stunned by the bare-majority support. After all, most respondents were being told they would not have to pay, and that there were no alternative jobs available – an unlikely scenario.

Distinguished voices have persisted. In their 2021 proposal for a 'public job programme' guaranteeing a full-time public-sector job paying at least the minimum wage, Robert Skidelsky and Simone Gasperin said the scheme should aim for full employment, adding: 'Definition of full employment can be made quite precise and uncomplicated: it exists *where all who are ready, willing and able to work are gainfully employed at a given base wage.* This corresponds to the absence of "involuntary" or "unwanted" unemployment.'[8]

That 'uncomplicated' definition would be hard to translate into practical rules. Determining whether a person is voluntarily or involuntarily unemployed is notoriously arbitrary, and it does not help that the authors state that 'involuntary unemployment includes forced underemployment: those in work for less hours than they would wish'.[9]

This implies the scheme would guarantee a full-time job to every underemployed person who wished to be in one. Given extensive underemployment in a tertiary labour market, with many such workers in jobs that pay at or below the minimum hourly wage (2 million people in the UK in 2020), the number of guaranteed public-sector jobs to be provided could be much greater than the existing number of registered unemployed.

In a paper co-written with Rachel Kay, Skidelsky recognized that 'there is not always a clear line between voluntary and involuntary part-time working, since government policies, including the availability of in-work benefits, shape choices'.[10] In that case, how would policymakers restrict job guarantees only to the involuntarily underemployed and unemployed?

If you become unemployed, it is likely that, initially at least, you would seek a job paying as close as possible to your past earnings or to what you think is appropriate for someone with your level of education or training or with your occupational background. That is likely to be above the minimum wage offered in a guaranteed job. Surely, you should not be described as voluntarily unemployed in these circumstances. And if you were obliged to take that guaranteed job, you might jeopardize your chances of obtaining a job better suited to your needs and aspirations.

Similarly, what happens to those considered to have left a job voluntarily, perhaps because they disliked their working conditions or erratic labour schedule? If they decline a minimum-wage job in the hope of finding something better, it would be unfair to call them voluntarily unemployed. Most people in labour markets have what can be called an aspiration wage and a reservation, or lowest acceptable, wage. The first is higher, but usually falls as the spell of job-seeking unemployment lengthens. Would job quitters also be guaranteed a job? Most job-guarantee proposals imply that all unemployed would qualify, however they came to be so, if they met the scheme conditions.

Defining what is meant by 'able to work' is also problematic. Most people probably have some sort of constraint, if not a disability, but whether they are able to work depends on the type of job on offer, the duration of labour, the availability of appropriate facilities, and their personality. Those with periodic disabilities, such as depression, can sometimes do a job they are qualified to do, sometimes not.

A job-guarantee scheme would thus spring a familiar trap – the arbitrary distinction between those who can work, who would thus be eligible for a job, and those who cannot work.[11] In Britain, this distinction has led to demeaning and stigmatizing capacity-to-work and availability-for-work tests to determine eligibility for benefits, resulting in discriminatory action against disabled and vulnerable people, and those with care responsibilities.

What, then, would happen to somebody who declined to accept the guaranteed job? One advocate, the American economist Pavlina Tcherneva, has painted a comforting picture of voluntary choice: 'If you go into the unemployment office, you can collect unemployment insurance. But what if we had a policy where you were provided a choice: either you take unemployment insurance, or if you're looking for a job, we can guarantee you a basic employment opportunity at a minimum living wage with some benefits.'[12]

This is surely not what would happen. Many of the unemployed do not have (or no longer have) unemployment insurance, but at most a meagre means-tested, conditional benefit, which they may or may not obtain, and may or may not retain. And it is unlikely that the employment office would allow real choices. The menu of jobs would almost certainly be sparse. And in the aftermath of Covid, if over a third of jobs can now be done at home, would people have the choice to take a job at home or away from home? If yes, how would home-based jobholders be monitored?

Another claim is that a job-guarantee scheme would act

as a macroeconomic stabilizer, expanding and contracting automatically with the business cycle, analogous to an unemployment insurance fund. Its success in doing this would depend on whether the government allocated extra funds in a timely manner, and how speedily the newly unemployed and underemployed could be selected, interviewed and allocated to job vacancies. Any attempt to speed up the process would generate a high degree of make-work or low-productivity activities.

From the 1960s to 1980s, Sweden pursued an economic model that deliberately used monetary and fiscal policy to keep the economy running below the full employment level to control inflationary pressure, alongside active labour market policies to put all the unemployed into jobs or training. But over the years the model operated, the economic return to those jobs fell to zero.[13]

Who would be eligible for a guaranteed job? Many proposals have been vague. Skidelsky and Gasperin provide one of the most comprehensive, stating that 'the government would guarantee a job to anyone who cannot find work in the private sector, at a fixed hourly rate which would not be lower than the national minimum wage rate'.[14] But how would the government know if a person cannot find work? Presumably, it would have to allow for some period of job searching and evidence that this has taken place, as well as judge what would count as acceptable work. All this would require an intrusive process in which street-level bureaucrats would determine whether someone could find a job.

There is also an issue of labour market efficiency. A market economy requires some frictional unemployment, as people search for what they think might suit their needs, capabilities and aspirations, and as firms search for suitable candidates for jobs they want done. But if a job is guaranteed, some of the unemployed will ask whether it makes sense to search for a job for long. After all, searching is personally costly and often demoralizing. They may be persuaded to abandon the effort and take whatever is on offer. A guarantee scheme could thereby reduce labour market efficiency, leading to less suitable matching of workers and jobs. Ultimately, a job guarantee would risk putting the economy in gridlock.

That is why some advocate that guaranteed jobs be provided only for the long-term unemployed, usually defined as those registered as jobless and job seeking for twelve months or more. This raises another problem. Almost by definition, the long-term unemployed will be among the least employable and are likely to lack the required skills. The jobs they could be expected to perform adequately would be menial, low-productivity ones. This would mean abandoning any pretence that jobs to be guaranteed would be 'high quality' and career oriented.

Some advocates, particularly in the United States, suggest such jobs should be in the private sector. However, most recognize the absurdity of requiring private firms to guarantee everybody a job. The usual proposal is for the public sector, government and its agencies, to act as employer of last resort.

Hyman Minsky, the first prominent economist to advocate a job guarantee, and subsequent proponents have nevertheless failed to demonstrate how one or other of Tocqueville's scenarios outlined in Chapter 3 would not follow.

Either the state would absorb more and more workers into low-productivity jobs – as happened during the 1960s in countries pursuing Keynesian policies – or the state would direct more firms to take on workers they would otherwise not wish to employ, holding down wages and impeding improvements in working conditions.

Advocates of a job guarantee often cite the success of the New Deal policies in the 1930s pursued by Franklin D. Roosevelt when US president.[15] They certainly expanded jobs in the construction of infrastructure, such as roads and bridges, and even in the planting of 3 billion trees. But while unemployment did come down, the rate never fell below 15 per cent, and in the recession of 1938–9 it rose to above 17 per cent.

Skidelsky and Gasperin do not state what type of public-sector job would be guaranteed under their proposal. But in the UK and many other countries, the range of public-sector jobs is more restrictive these days, due to extensive privatization. In a 2018 editorial, the *Guardian* argued that a job guarantee 'would only offer employment under-supplied by the private sector', singling out jobs in 'environmental clean-up' and 'social care'.[16] These may sound appealing on paper but represent a narrow, unattractive range of jobs on offer. Indeed, proponents hardly ever suggest that guaranteed jobs would match people's skills and qualifications, instead falling back on low-skill, low-wage jobs they would not dream of for themselves or for their children.

It is all very well to say a job guarantee would be part of a Green New Deal and involve only green jobs. But green jobs can be dirty and dangerous, such as mining for the minerals needed for clean energy technologies and many jobs in the waste and recycling sector. As the European Agency for Safety and Health at Work noted, 'We tend to associate the word "green" with safety – but what is good for the environment is not necessarily good for the safety and health of workers who are employed in green jobs.'[17] And if they were not menial manual jobs, those placed in them would need training and supervision. That would have implications for the duration of the jobs. But most advocates propose only temporary jobs, lasting from three to six months.

In any case, identifying jobs to be provided and administering the process would be a bureaucratic nightmare, as shown by the shambles of many community payback schemes for offenders convicted of minor misdemeanours, even though they are on a small scale and the labour they offer is free. And if the guaranteed jobs are providing desired services or goods, and are subsidized, what happens to others already doing such jobs? The risk is that they would be displaced or obliged to take a pay cut if they were paid more than those in the guaranteed jobs.

The potential substitution effects would probably be large if the jobs were in firms operating as outsourced providers of government-funded services, as is most likely in modern Britain, where so many services that used to be provided by public agencies are now provided by private firms. Would the government guarantee the jobs of existing employees as well, with no decline in wages? There would also be dead-weight effects – subsidizing jobs that would have been created anyway.

Then there is the issue of how much those in guaranteed jobs should be paid. Paying only the national minimum hourly wage may result in earnings below subsistence. As the London Good Work Commission concluded in 2018, it was 'simply not possible to survive, let alone live' on that wage in London.[18] Conversely, anybody paid less than the minimum wage or working fewer than the guaranteed hours would have an incentive to quit their current job for a guaranteed alternative. This would mean better-paying jobs for more of the underemployed and the precariat. But the fiscal cost would be daunting.

For example, in the UK in 2021, 17 per cent of those in jobs (about 5 million people) were paid below the living wage, which was £9.90 an hour (£11.05 in London). And 1.4 million of the low-paid were also wanting extra hours. In addition, 1.6 million self-employed, not covered by minimum-wage legislation, had low hourly earnings.[19] In the USA, the situation was as bad. Nearly a third of its 163 million workers were earning less than the $15-an-hour, minimum-wage target supported by Democrats, trade unions and civil society groups.[20] Imagine if a large proportion of those quit in hope of obtaining a guaranteed better-paying job!

If all unemployed were eligible, regardless of how they came to be unemployed, it is hard to accept the claim that a job-guarantee scheme in a recession 'would largely pay for itself by minimising the fall in government revenues'.[21] Rather, the increase in public spending would simply create a proliferation of jobs paying less than the tax-paying threshold. Public spending would increase, tax revenue would not.

Guaranteed jobs may also be inflationary. If wages at the bottom are raised, wages above would rise to preserve differentials. And there would be nothing to stop wage-push inflation, simply because workers would have a stronger bargaining position, with less fear of unemployment. The only restraining factors would be fear of automation and fear of more offshoring. But it would hardly be fear, as a job would be guaranteed anyway!

A public-job guarantee could put upward pressure on private-sector wages, which could lower private-sector labour demand, resulting in fewer jobs. But if jobs were guaranteed for everybody wanting them, the upward pressure on wages would persist. Public works have been shown to have this effect.[22] If private-sector jobs shrink due to higher prospective wages, the government would have to guarantee even more jobs. It is also possible that a public-job guarantee would generate a variant of the Great Resignation from private-sector jobs witnessed during 2021.

Another claim is that a job guarantee would maintain employability better, the claim apparently strengthened by the presumption that 'the comparison is not between a PJP [public job programme] and a "good" job, but between a PJP job and no job'.[23] It is a presumption that being in any job is better than waiting and searching for something closer to what one wants, and it is a presumption that taking a job improves employability and income in the longer term. As mentioned earlier, there is considerable evidence that taking a job below one's skills and qualifications reduces a person's employability in their main sphere of competence and can also lower their long-term income prospects.

A job-guarantee scheme would be paternalistic. It presumes the government knows what is best for individuals. Suppose someone was pressed to take a guaranteed job on a construction site (infrastructure, a favoured area for guaranteed jobs) and suffered an injury due to incompetence or lack of training and experience. Would the job-guarantee agency be held responsible and obliged to pay compensation? It should, since it put the person in that exposed position. And would proponents really like their elderly relatives to be given social care by untrained and probably resentful people obliged to take a guaranteed job or lose benefits?

Guaranteed jobs would be a recipe for perpetuating low productivity. This was a fatal flaw of the Soviet system as it unravelled in the 1980s. If you are guaranteed a job, especially if it is only temporary and low-paid, why bother to work hard? And if you are an employer and are given a subsidy to pay employees guaranteed a job, why bother to use labour efficiently? The labour is almost free, as far as you are concerned. A worker would only need to produce a little more value than the cost to the employer to make the guaranteed job profitable. This would cheapen low-productivity jobs relative to others and reduce the incentive to invest in labour-displacing technology that would boost productivity.

Another claim by Skidelsky and Kay is that a guarantee programme 'would be a powerful lever to push down the average number of hours worked'. If more people were in jobs, and the guarantee were extended to the underemployed (labouring fewer hours than desired), that would imply more hours, averaged over the total labour force. But the authors imply this would be more than offset by dynamic effects.

First, they claim a job guarantee 'would weaken employers' control over the employment contract'. There is no reason to presume this, since the prospect of a job guarantee instead of their current job would only appeal to those in low-wage jobs and those doing fewer labour hours than they want. Second, 'by eliminating cyclical unemployment . . . it would substitute an upward for downward pressure on wages'. However, in recent decades the positive association between employment growth and average wages has ceased to hold.

Third, 'by reducing fear of technological unemployment it would reduce opposition to automation'. But as shown in Chapter 4, in a tertiary economy automation is linked to heteromation – that is, technical change induces more work even if less labour. Finally, it 'would maintain total spending and total investment'.[24] It is not clear why that should reduce labour time.

The policy would also reinforce labourism, by failing to make the distinction between work and labour. Those who back guaranteed jobs typically ignore all forms of work that are not paid labour. A job is a means to an end, not an end in itself. Economists tend to be inconsistent in this respect. In textbooks, labour has disutility; it is negative for the worker. Yet many economists who use or write these textbooks then advocate putting everybody in jobs. The emphasis on jobs is also non-ecological, since it is tied to pursuit of GDP growth. Would it not be better to encourage other forms of work that are not jobs?

Many forms of work that are not labour are more rewarding psychologically and socially than the jobs most people are likely to obtain. A regime of putting everybody into jobs – that is, in unchosen activities – would be state-orchestrated alienation. Surely a progressive should want to minimize the time we spend in stultifying and subordinated jobs, so that we can increase the time and energy for forms of work and leisure that are self-chosen and oriented to personal and community development.

Ironically, a job guarantee could inadvertently reduce the amount of work and time devoted to useful productive activities. For instance, one scarcely noticed outcome of the Finnish basic-income experiment of 2017–18, in which 2,000 randomly selected unemployed people were given an unconditional cash payment instead of a conditional benefit requiring them to look for a job, was that many started forms of work that were not jobs.[25] That work would not have taken place had they been obliged to take a guaranteed job.

The jobs-guarantee route would not challenge capitalism as a system, merely prop it up through making up to some extent for macroeconomic market failure. The implicit premise is that a jobholder society is worthy of being preserved. All the practical detailed schemes have indicated that jobs to be guaranteed would be conventional – minimum wage, at fixed workplaces, full-time labour, away from home, reporting to bosses. Yet since Covid, most people in office jobs say they want a hybrid model of work from home and labour in offices, while others want a task-based or project-based labour market, rather than old-style jobs.

If we accept that much of the work done in society that is not labour has more use value and imputed market value than many jobs, then what is the economic or social sense in wanting to put as many people in jobs as possible? Guaranteed jobs do not imply, as Minsky claimed, that meaningful work will be available for anyone who wants it.[26]

To sum up, the practical objections to a job guarantee become evident as soon as the details are considered: what jobs, who would be responsible for providing them, who would qualify to be offered them, what would the jobs pay and for how many hours, who would pay, how much would it cost to supervise participants and to police compliance with a job's requirements, and what would be the effects on other workers and on the wider economy?

Moreover, the job-guarantee proposal fails to recognize that today's crisis is structural and requires *transformative* policies. It would barely touch the precariat's existential in-security that is at the heart of the social and economic crisis, let alone address the aspirations of the progressive part of the precariat for an ecologically grounded Good Society.[27]

The Four-Day Week

Another popular policy proposal, advocated mainly by social democrats, is a statutory limit on labour time in the form of a four-day week. Already adopted by a small but growing number of companies around the world, a move to a four-day week was advocated by Britain's Labour Party in its 2019 election manifesto and favoured as an option by several governments, including Ireland, Spain, Scotland, New Zealand and Japan. A much-reported trial in Iceland from 2015 to 2019 has been followed by trials in Ireland, the USA, Canada and the UK, where a six-month trial involving around sixty companies with nearly 3,000 employees was launched in mid 2022.[28] Spain and Scotland started trials soon after.

Perhaps the best argument for moving to a four-day week is that it would be a way of compensating people for the restraint on economic growth needed to combat global warming. As one proponent said: 'Instead of more stuff, governments need to offer people more time.'[29] But most advocates argue the business case that a shift to four-day weeks can boost labour productivity with no loss of output, or even an increase in output. As a tool for degrowth, therefore, it is not promising.

Firms that have moved to a four-day week claim success.[30] Thus Perpetual Guardian, a New Zealand estate-planning firm, found it increased productivity and reduced employee fatigue; Pursuit Marketing, a telephone and digital marketing company in Glasgow, reported a productivity increase of 30 per cent; and Microsoft Japan, which gave employees Fridays off in August 2019, said productivity had jumped 40 per cent.[31] The UK trial in 2022 was also deemed a success, with almost all the companies deciding to continue with the new arrangements. Four in ten employees said they felt less stressed and nearly three-quarters reported reduced levels of burnout.[32]

Less reported were the downsides. A study of the change to a four-day week by Perpetual Guardian found not only labour intensification, as employees struggled to complete the same workload in fewer hours, but also increased managerial pressures via performance measurement and monitoring. Employees took shorter breaks and spent less time socializing with colleagues in order to resume their measurable tasks. While some workers thrived, others felt the urgency and pressure were causing heightened stress levels, leaving them in need of the additional day off to recover.[33]

Similarly, US fintech start-up Bolt found that although most of its employees wanted its four-day-week experiment to continue, 40 per cent reported more stress as a result. Many took their job home and used Fridays as a day to do

labour uninterrupted by meetings or encounters with colleagues.[34] Other research shows that people with more intensive workloads tend to think more about their jobs outside
labour hours and cannot switch off until they have resolved
work-related problems. Others stay connected because they
need to check what is going on in order to feel in control.[35]

Microsoft Japan did not extend its month-long experiment. Other companies have simply extended the length of
the normal working day, reducing the cut in hours to well
below a day's worth. The four-day working week introduced
by Atom, a UK internet bank, cut hours from 37.5 to 34, less
than a full day.

Moving to a four-day week would also reduce the UK's
minimum legal paid holiday allowance from 28 to 22.5 days
a year, adjusted pro rata for the lower number of days worked.
As for the Iceland trial, this was not actually an experiment
with a four-day week, as widely reported, but a reduction
for some public-sector workers from forty to thirty-five or
thirty-six hours a week.[36] The UK trial too asked companies to cut employee hours by 20 per cent, not necessarily
to move to a four-day week. So although some firms gave
all staff Friday off, others let them work 80 per cent of their
previous hours on a flexible basis.[37]

None of the evidence suggests that a four-day week
should be imposed as a general model. It cannot work well
in the context of tertiary time. With more people working
online or outside formal jobs, it seems a crude policy. As the
above examples suggest, it may have the perverse effect of
increasing the amount of work people are required or induced to do, in absolute terms and relative to labour. It may

also make it harder to adjust labour and work time to different life stages. Someone might want to labour more in their youth so as to take time out later for other activities, or vice versa. Anything that made that choice harder would restrict their freedom rather than liberate them from labour.

In 2018, full-time employees in the UK put in on average 42.5 hours a week (excluding sickness and holiday leave), well above the EU average, and labour hours had declined only modestly over the previous half century. More than 17 per cent of employees, and 26 per cent of self-employed, did over forty-five hours.[38] Would a statutory measure to implement a four-day week radically change that? In an industrial-time production system, it would have done, because labour time was relatively well defined. But in the tertiary time regime, cuts in labour time are likely to result in more unpaid work-for-labour. For example, Hutch, a London-based games designer taking part in the UK trial, found that 43 per cent of employees worked more than their contracted hours, while at Stellar Asset Management, a financial services firm, many staff took important calls or Zoom meetings on their day off.[39] And the self-employed, accounting for 13 per cent of the labour force in 2022, would not be covered by a statutory four-day week.

Unsurprisingly, in opinion polls most British workers say they would like to reduce their working time, by which they mean labour time.[40] But most have not done so, while there has been a peculiar reversal of the historical pattern. Higher-income earners in the salariat on average labour and work for longer than lower-paid employees, who would probably be more affected by a statutory four-day week. Those on a low wage, in the precariat, could see reduced earnings and an increase in the ratio of unpaid work to paid labour, as they would be less able to resist employer pressure to do extra work above the hours paid for the four days.

France provides the best-documented experiment in statutory cuts to labour time in the modern era. In 1998, the *Réduction du temps de travail* law introduced a thirty-five-hour standard workweek for the private sector with no reduction in wages. The government paid a social-security rebate to companies if they negotiated a cut in hours with unions and increased employment. Many companies reacted by negotiating a wage freeze or slowdown with unions, as well as agreements to labour more than thirty-five hours at busy times, fewer hours at other times. This was permitted by the law, which required thirty-five hours as an annual average.

Workers in general welcomed the move. However, as employers adapted, workers complained of labour intensification and increased demands for flexibility. There was a marked increase in stress from labour. And after falling for several years, weekly hours started to rise as rules on overtime were weakened. So, the outcome was mixed.[41] In Germany, where shorter labour hours have resulted mainly from collective bargaining, the results are more encouraging. But the reduction in hours slowed in the 1990s, and much of the decline was linked to concession bargaining as unions tried to slow the remorseless outsourcing of jobs.

Most proposals for four-day weeks also do not consider scheduled time, time for sharing with family and friends or for social activities. A salutary lesson comes from a remarkable historical reform intended to shorten working time while maximizing production and productivity. In 1929, in what was known as the Red Calendar, the Soviet Union introduced a rotating seven-day workweek, in which everybody had a schedule of labour for five days out of the seven, randomly decided by their factories. On each day one-fifth of the workers had the day off.

This increased the continuous operation of factories while also increasing the number of days off from labour to seventy-three days a year from the previous fifty-two (the norm in industrial countries at that time). But to many people's surprise, the experiment flopped after just two years, mostly because workers hated it.[42] The main reason was the loss of scheduled time – that is, time shared socially with those they valued, especially family members.

Extra time off labour is of less value if it does not coincide with similar time off by those close and dear to you. Without a standard workweek, the probability, P, that your day off will coincide with that of N others is proportional to P^N. With two days off per week of seven days, each person has a P = 0.28 chance of being off on any given day. Thus the chance of two friends being off on the same day is 0.28^2, or 8 per cent, which is once every twelve days. The probability of three friends having the same day off is just 2 per cent (once every forty-five days), and for four friends merely 0.5 per cent (once every 162 days or twice a year).[43] So, unless the reduced working week is the same four days for everybody, or employers are required to allow requests for specific days off, the scheduling time constraint will be psychologically and socially unwelcome.

While it might seem contradictory to propose a job-guarantee programme and a systemic cut in labour hours, the four-day week could be seen as labour sharing. But if workers want a workweek of thirty-six hours or more because of low wages, legislating a four-day week would lead to what happened in France when it introduced its thirty-five-hour week; the average went up to thirty-seven hours.[44] As the guaranteed public jobs would pay the minimum hourly wage, workers put in those jobs would not want a four-day week either.

'Labour-Time Rights'

One other form of labourist response is worth mentioning. During the tertiary time regime, growth of flexible labour relations has led to interest by trade unions and governments in what have been called 'time rights', or what should be called 'labour-time rights', since they apply only to labour, not to other forms of work.

Such rights include a right to reduce labour hours, for example, to care for young children, and then return to longer hours. This is enshrined in French and German legislation, though not in the UK's.[45] But even in those countries, it applies only to those employed in larger firms, with more than fifty employees in France and forty-five in Germany. As such, it is a form of concealed inequality, between those employed in big firms and those employed in small ones, and between those in big firms and those doing other forms of work.

If it deserves to be called a right, it surely should apply to everybody doing any form of work. An equitable policy would be one that enabled everybody equally to alter their hours of work. But there is no prospect that policy pushed by unions will go in that direction.

One group given inadequate labour protection are

workers who labour during the night. This form of labour has grown during the tertiary time era, and in Britain now accounts for one in every nine people in jobs, the highest proportion since records began.[46] Time rights for them would no doubt be very welcome.

Paying People to Spend on Time-Using Activities

The Covid-19 pandemic spawned some creative policy ideas, often lacking coherent ethical values, but motivated by political considerations. One almost amusing idea was to pay people to go on holiday, or at least to offer them financial incentives (subsidies) to do so.[47] The main idea was to revive tourism, regarded as a hard-hit sector. An irony was that before Covid there was concern about the adverse effects of mass tourism, linked to carbon emissions from aircraft, pollution from cruise ships and wear-and-tear of favoured tourist destinations such as Venice, Barcelona and Athens. Indeed, Venice, having erected turnstiles to control the influx of the 40 million tourists coming into the city each year, announced plans to charge an entry fee of €10 a day.

The pandemic changed that mentality. On top of direct payments to airlines and airports and lower VAT rates for hotels and restaurants, some governments introduced payments to tourists themselves. In 2020, Italy launched a holiday bonus scheme costing €2.4 billion, under which low-income Italian families – defined as having an annual income below €40,000 – could receive up to €500 to help pay for any domestic holiday. Sicily went even further.

It seems churlish to criticize such schemes, which many

of us would welcome if we were beneficiaries. But they are regressive. The people least able or likely to take holidays were in the precariat or wallowing in abject poverty. They received no such largesse.

Concluding Reflections on the Jobs Fetish

In May 2020, 3,000 academics signed an open letter calling on governments to 'democratise work', 'decommodify work' and introduce a 'job guarantee'.[48] It was a classic end-of-era social democratic manifesto. I insisted that my name be withdrawn from the proposed list of signatories, having three objections.

First, work was defined only as paid labour, thus excluding all work that is already decommodified such as unpaid care work, done by more people for more time than any other form of work. Second, the letter did not define a 'commodity', which is something bought and sold, with a price. So, labour must be a commodity, unless the academics were proposing that labour be unpaid. Third, for all the reasons given earlier, a job guarantee would be a road to workfare. The letter should have been about decommodifying people, not their labour.

The jobs fetish has been a gospel of the left. Of course, advocates of more jobs would bridle at the suggestion that they are in favour of putting more people in alienated, subordinated positions. Presumably, they would claim that to be in a job is the only way to obtain an income and be a productive member of society. They should ask themselves if they or their friends would wish to be doing jobs of the type millions are expected to take. They might retort that they would wish people were in decent jobs, with good pay and working conditions. But they could not escape the fact that many jobs are inherently banal, dull and dulling, using up the time of those pushed or lured into doing them, and then kept in them by fear of material deprivation.

Where is their progressive imagination? Could they not imagine a Good Society in which time spent in jobs was reduced as much as possible, for everyone? The only way to move the politics of time in that direction is to topple jobs from their ideological pedestal. That is not only because many jobs are 'bullshit' jobs, as the anthropologist and activist David Graeber famously described them, that make no contribution to society.[49] It is recognizing that putting as many people as possible in labour, in jobs, is scarcely a progressive vision.

Imagine for a moment a future in which automation and degrowth (or whatever it may be called) meant that the number of jobs had been substantially reduced, deliberately and with good intentions, with revenue being shared among those in and out of jobs. Imagine politicians going on TV or video and boasting, 'We have cut the number of jobs by 10 per cent in the past two years, freeing people of 15 per cent of labour time.' The opposition might jump up and say, 'Had our policies been pursued, the number of jobs could have been cut by 15 per cent and labour time by over 20 per cent.' A public debate couched in those terms would be very different from the labourist one that has prevailed over the past century.

That nirvana could only come about if job minimization was accompanied by development of a new income-distribution system. The twentieth-century distribution system has collapsed, accelerated into terminal decline by a decade of austerity and then by the pandemic slump. It is not labour time that has withered, but the social income linked to labour. The returns to property or assets have risen steadily, leaving less to go to those using time to labour. Expanding the number of jobs is a feeble response. That would merely spread labour more thinly, expand the precariat and increase the number of low-productivity, low-paying jobs.

The answer lies in tackling the income-distribution system, by dismantling rentier capitalism, taking back and recycling to everybody the rentier income currently taken by the plutocracy, elite and salariat. Among the benefits, we could then devote more time to work, rather than labour, and to leisure as well as recuperation and recreation. Statutory reductions in labour time would not achieve much in the contemporary context of rentier capitalism.

The final chapter moves from the recent past to an imagined but realizable future, emboldened by revisiting a rather more substantive vision outlined in reaction to the breakdown of industrial time in the late nineteenth century. William Morris wrote *News from Nowhere* (1890) partly in response to a gradualist road to socialism depicted in another utopian novel published two years earlier, Edward Bellamy's *Looking Backward* (1888). By contrast, Morris foresaw a rupture with the capitalism of his day, a transformation into a society of conviviality and gentler human nature. In a review of Bellamy's book, he concluded: 'In short, a machine life is the best which Bellamy can imagine for us on all sides; it is not to be wondered at then that his only idea of making labour tolerable is to decrease the amount of it by means of fresh and ever fresh developments of machinery.'[50]

This was not good enough for Morris. And so he did what all progressives should do from time to time, which is to imagine a Good Society of the future. And at the end of *News from Nowhere*, he rounds off with a flourish: 'Yes, surely! And if others can see it as I have seen it, then it may be called a vision rather than a dream.'

The Emancipation of Time

Nothing is ours, except time.

— Seneca, *Letters from a Stoic, c.* AD 65

We are now in the 2030s . . . The 2020s, about ten years ago, marked the crisis point of what could be called the Global Transformation, analogous in global terms to Karl Polanyi's Great Transformation of national economies in his 1944 book of the same name. Just as Polanyi recognized that developments in the 1930s and early 1940s threatened the annihilation of civilization, a juncture when society could have gone in either direction – towards a very dark night for humanity or a new progressive transformation – so the early 2020s marked such a moment. It is essential to recall how dangerous a time it was, not just for the UK but for many countries around the world.

Some prominent commentators blamed elites for the crisis, claiming that fundamentally the capitalism of the time was not the problem.[1] History has not borne out their analysis. The following focuses on what happened in Britain, recognizing that other countries faced similar crises, with varying reactions.

The Morning Before

Looking back, it is clear that the years from 2010 to the early 2020s were a traumatizing period, in which the hubristic neoliberal ideology forged in the 1980s finally met its nemesis. The prescribed treatment for the economy and society resembled medieval quackery. Applying the leeches by rolling back protective regulations, curbing social protection and liberalizing finance had not unleashed the promised economic growth. So the applied remedy was more bleeding, yet more of the same. Society withered as inequalities and insecurity grew. By the end, a majority were muttering, 'Enough is enough.'

Some said public fatigue after three years of battering by the Covid pandemic, and the rising tide of mental and physical illness during that time and afterwards, created fertile ground for radical change. Some added that it was partly because of anger that deaths and illness had been made worse by the running down and creeping privatization of the National Health Service during the preceding decade of austerity. Many were also shocked by the neglect of care homes, having lost elderly relatives or fearing having to enter one themselves in due course.

Some lamented the proliferation of food banks – over 2,500 in 2022, almost double the number of McDonald's restaurants.[2] As distressing was the growing number of 'hygiene banks' providing toiletries and sanitary products, and 'warm banks' (also called 'heat hubs') that mushroomed during the winter of 2022–3.

Many were disgusted by the 'Partygate' scandal, a series of boozy parties in 10 Downing Street and elsewhere, when

Prime Minister Boris Johnson, Chancellor of the Exchequer Rishi Sunak and other highly paid officials broke lockdown laws they themselves had devised. Despite lying to parliament and the public about their involvement, they were allowed to continue in their positions. And there were revelations of other reprehensible behaviour involving figures in the governing party, including the award of Covid-related contracts for hundreds of millions of pounds to party donors and associates.

After Johnson was forced to resign, an unedifying scramble to become his successor resulted in the selection of Liz Truss, a strident libertarian who had joined the free-market Hayek Society as a student at Oxford. Her disastrous 'dash for growth' with unfunded tax cuts ended in a humiliating exit as the shortest-serving British prime minister in history. Rishi Sunak, her replacement, a former hedge-fund manager groomed by Goldman Sachs and wealthier even than the new king, calmed the financial markets with a new dose of austerity, worsening inequality and the deterioration of public services.

Millions faced penury in a 'cost of living crisis' as prices for basic goods and services soared, energy costs rocketed following Russia's unprovoked invasion of Ukraine, and interest rates were hiked to combat inflation, which was attributed by the media and the government to the war, supply-chain disruption and wage pressures. In reality, it was as much due to the fattening of profit margins by monopolistic corporations and predatory financial speculation.[3] Meanwhile, supermarkets ran out of lettuce and tomatoes, and food prices rose at the fastest rate in over forty years, up by nearly 20 per cent in 2022.

At the same time, the government, encouraged by the

Bank of England, was forcing down the real (inflation-adjusted) wages of nurses, junior doctors, teachers and train operatives. To give just one example, university staff were offered a derisory 5 per cent pay rise in early 2023, which amounted to a 15 per cent real wage cut from 2021 and a 25 per cent cut since 2009.[4] Meanwhile, bankers' bonuses were allowed to soar and Sunak revealed that, in the three years dating back to when he was Chancellor of the Exchequer, he had income and capital gains of nearly £5 million and paid a lower rate of tax overall than people reliant on wages and salaries.[5] Resentment simmered.

More people came to understand the economic ideology that had steered Britain into an era of rentier capitalism, in which more of the income was going to the owners of property, while successive governments kowtowed to financial interests and the plutocratic elite. Above all, the precariat had grown enormous amid generalized anxiety fed by chronic uncertainty and insecurity, buttressed by obscene levels of inequality.

The neoliberal economists and their political offspring had long preached that inequality did not matter. Indeed, in 2003 Chicago-based Robert Lucas, a high priest of the neoliberal revolution who received the Nobel Prize in Economics in 1995, stated unashamedly, 'Of the tendencies that are harmful to sound economics . . . the most poisonous is to focus on questions of distribution.'[6] But the tide was turning. In 2021, Chinese president Xi Jinping quoted on more than sixty occasions a saying attributed to Confucius, 'A wise leader worries not about poverty but about inequality.'[7]

The corrosive effects of inequality were plain to see. The

pandemic showed that high and rising inequality was a killer: countries with high levels of inequality had much higher death rates from Covid-19.[8] But the lethal effects of inequality had already been demonstrated in the decline of overall life expectancy in Britain in the preceding decade. For all age groups, the mortality of the poor had gone up, while that of the rich had continued to fall. The record was far worse than for other European countries, with 700,000 more deaths between 2010 and 2022 than would have occurred had the previous long-term trend continued. *The Economist* concluded its review of the evidence with the chilling statement that some '10m years of life have been lost in Britain over the past decade, compared with what might have been expected in 2011. That grim total keeps ticking up.'[9] That time lost reflected the cynical policy of austerity and the devastation of public services.

And the incidence of mental and physical ill-health mounted. Some 2 million people reported suffering the effects of long Covid in early 2023,[10] and nearly 400,000 were waiting over a year for hospital treatment.[11] Millions were in need of mental-health services, which were desperately under-resourced.[12] But while it is well established that mental health deteriorates not only during but after stressful events, and that post-traumatic stress disorder spreads after pandemics, there is also an opposite effect, known as post-traumatic growth, in which living through stressful circumstances induces positive psychological change.[13] After experiencing chronic stress, anger directed at a dysfunctional economic system that failed to protect them can spur people into wanting to transform the existing order. This is what happened in the UK in the post-Covid period.

Ecological decay deepened the social and economic malaise. Almost every day brought stories of natural disasters
linked to climate change, loss of species, degraded ecosystems, pollution and destruction of the natural environment
on land and in the sea. Yet governments were failing to act.
Worse, in response to soaring fossil-fuel costs in 2022, the
British and other governments increased energy subsidies
to keep consumer prices down, dampening the price incentive to reduce consumption.[14] They actually stepped up production and use of oil, gas and coal. These measures were
the reverse of what was needed to combat global warming,
sparking angry protests across the world.

Thus, a unique combination of circumstances created a
moment of progressive opportunity, personified by Kairos,
one of the ancient Greek gods of time. The pandemic had
been the equivalent of a war: millions of people had been
seriously ill, with nearly a quarter of a million deaths in the
UK alone; lockdowns were seen as lost segments of life; yet
an elite were able to escape into their bubbles of privilege,
epitomized by 'Partygate'. And young people suffered particularly severely during the pandemic and cost-of-living
crisis. The Royal Society of Arts found that only two-fifths of
young people believed they would ever own a home, only half
thought they would ever earn enough to support a family,
and half thought they would never be able to retire in comfort. 'Generation precariat', as the RSA dubbed them, had
had enough.[15] All this helped create a public mood in favour
of transformational change.

A transformative politics requires a combination of class-
based anger directed at a common antagonist, widespread

grievance about the loss of something of value, and articulation of a vision of a better future. Anger stems from a perception of injustice and illegitimate inequalities. But that awareness must be articulated in order to lead to political action. Some injustices are not easily spotted but become part of popular discontent once people are informed. This is relevant for the inequality in access to quality time. Why should some have a lot of control over their time, and others have little or none?

The challenge in such moments is to convert anger from being anomic – that is, passive and self-pitying – into active opposition to its underlying causes. People need not only to understand those causes but to want to right the injustice, which requires empathy and compassion. Here was the biggest challenge in the early 2020s. Public attitudes had been shaped by utilitarian politics and by the fraudulent claim that Britain was truly a meritocratic society in which success was due to individual talent and hard work and was thus 'deserved', while lack of success reflected individual failings rather than circumstance.

To combat these attitudes, political leaders came to realize they needed a politics of time. Commentators recalled the words of William Beveridge in his 1942 report: 'It is a time for revolutions, not for patching.'[16] He was scarcely a revolutionary, being a staid Edwardian with a civil service mentality and deportment. But his radical proposals caught the mood of the moment.

During the Covid pandemic, there were plenty of indicators that the public, if not mainstream politicians, were ready for a revolutionary transformation. For example, in surveys conducted in Britain and the USA in 2021, people were asked to choose between four alternative scenarios for the post-pandemic future: back to normal, with strong government; back to normal, with more individual autonomy; progressive (that is, reduced inequality), with strong government; and progressive, with more individual autonomy. In each survey, a majority preferred the progressive options, with more preferring the alternative that prioritized individual autonomy.

Nevertheless, a majority expected a return-to-normal scenario, reflecting a pessimism born of decades of disappointment. In a demonstration of 'pluralistic ignorance', participants thought they were unlikely to obtain the future they wanted, falsely believing they were in a minority. Once they came to realize they were in fact in the majority, their motivation to support a progressive agenda grew dramatically.

Overall, it was evident that people were eager for change and a better future. Some of the surveys' incidental findings bear reflection. One respondent recalled his pre-pandemic lifestyle: 'The constant, constant pressure and anxiety. I was always – from the time I woke up to the time I went to bed – calculating what needed to be done next, how quickly it needed to be done, and how many different things can I do at the same time to make sure it ALL gets done? After this, I hope I never go back to that. I want to forget that ever was my life.'

Another told the researchers: 'This [the pandemic] forced everyone to slow down and appreciate the smaller things in life. I won't miss overlooking all of the little things – I now have more appreciation for all the things we considered standard in life pre-covid.'[17]

Recalling Beveridge's moment, there was that mood again

as countries emerged from the pandemic. It was a time for revolutions, not for patching. Even the elite were troubled. In winter 2021–2, just before the Russian invasion of Ukraine, a survey of business leaders who participate in the World Economic Forum's annual jamboree in the Swiss mountain resort of Davos found that just 16 per cent were 'positive' or optimistic about the global outlook; the rest were 'worried' or 'concerned'. Four-fifths expected the future to be consistently volatile. The issues worrying them were environmental decay, 'social cohesion erosion', 'livelihood crises' and 'mental health deterioration'.[18] The clouds were gathering.

In Britain, the groundwork for transformation began in 2023. But it started badly. The main opposition party set out a very conservative agenda that could easily have been a Conservative manifesto. Sir Keir Starmer, the Labour leader, listed five 'missions' for his government if elected. In order, these were to secure the highest sustained growth in the G7 (UK, USA, Canada, Italy, France, Japan and Germany); build an NHS fit for the future; make Britain's streets safe; break down the barriers to opportunity at every stage; and make Britain a clean-energy superpower.[19] There was nothing there to inspire the precariat. Nor did the chronic inequalities and economic insecurity affecting millions of people merit a 'mission'. For the first time ever, the progressive political party did not make reducing poverty and inequality one of its top priorities.

Unsurprisingly, the first general election in the post-Covid era was a messy affair. Faced with a discredited political 'right' and an uninspiring 'left', many in the electorate stayed at home while others opted for smaller parties such as the Liberal Democrats, the Greens and, in Scotland, the

Scottish National Party. The result was a dysfunctional government, with deep ideological and personal divisions that, in one form or another, also permeated the opposition parties. In addition, more people could see through the pretence that dealing with the ecological crisis was compatible with pursuing rapid GDP growth, prompting mounting protests and direct street action. A fresh general election was soon seen as inevitable.

And then a political miracle happened. Determined to prevent another period of Conservative government, the leaders of the main opposition parties made an electoral pact. They agreed not to split the anti-Tory vote, instead uniting behind a single opposition candidate in key parliamentary constituencies, presenting voters with a one-time, single-election manifesto based on a core set of transformational policies, including a commitment to electoral reform within the next parliamentary term.

The rationale for such a pact had long been clear. Those wanting change were split between parties, whereas those opposing it were concentrated in one party. Under the first-past-the-post electoral system, it was hard for any progressive party to win on its own. Yet the Labour leadership had spurned reform, putting party before progressive politics. In 2019, the Conservatives won a landslide election victory despite mustering the votes of just 29 per cent of the electorate.

Despite the obvious unfairness of the election result, even sympathetic commentators said the chances of a progressive alliance were close to zero.[20] It took political courage for the compact to take shape, albeit helped by the public mood of disgust and the desire for transformational change. In the end, the alliance was confronted by a tired Conservative Party, the equivalent of what Benjamin Disraeli in 1872 called 'a range of exhausted volcanoes; not a flame flickers on a pallid crest'.[21] In the ensuing election, the alliance swept into office, becoming the Progressive Alliance Government or PAG.

The Morning After

Food comes first, morals later on.
— Bertolt Brecht, *The Threepenny Opera*, 1928

Some called the reforms by the new government 'rentier socialism' because its signature measure aimed to capture rentier income gained by owners of private property in the preceding era of rentier capitalism and recycle it to everybody. It was also referred to as 'community capitalism', a term coined in 2021 by Andy Haldane that had the virtue of disarming critics who feared loss of what they misleadingly called the free market.[22] Neither term seemed quite right.

Whatever the suggested labels, it was the transformation that mattered. First was the need to reverse the tendency for rentier capitalism to generate further inequality. The PAG repeatedly reminded the public that the Bank of England, like all central banks in rich countries, had reacted to the pandemic with measures that automatically increased the share of income going to finance capital. By pumping money into financial markets, they inflated asset prices, enabling asset holders to increase their wealth without doing anything to 'deserve' it. This had to be corrected. Meanwhile, the PAG transformation strategy needed to respond to another related issue – catastrophic indebtedness.

Debt: Eye of the Storm

In 2023, debt globally was higher than at any time in history. Rising debt was inevitable in an era dominated by finance.[23] And higher interest rates engineered by the US Federal Reserve, the Bank of England and other central banks with the intention of curbing inflation merely pushed more firms, banks and households into bankruptcy. Debt's mirror image was rising savings inequality. In the USA, Europe and China, most household savings since the 1980s had been accumulated by the rich, while there had been precipitous dissaving (running down savings and going into debt) by those in the bottom half of the income distribution.[24] Household debt across Europe rose from 80 per cent of GDP in the 1970s to about 170 per cent by the time of the pandemic; the increase was even greater in China, Japan and the USA.

In Britain, credit-card debt jumped to record levels as lower-income households tried desperately to maintain living standards, even paying for essentials, in the face of rising prices, stagnating wages and declining state benefits.[25] Average real wages were below their level in 2008 and were expected to remain so until at least 2026, the longest squeeze on worker incomes for two hundred years. And the problems had been worsened by the Brexit own-goal, which had cost Britain 4 per cent of GDP and lost the Exchequer at least £30 billion a year, equal to the tax rises imposed in 2022.[26] Political mismanagement further ensured that the UK suffered the largest Covid-induced economic contraction of all G7 nations and was the only G7 economy not to have recovered to pre-pandemic levels by the end of 2022.[27]

The PAG realized that one of its immediate priority 'missions' was to free people from the web of debt spun by finance over several decades. It understood that chronic debt breeds political decay. As Aristotle recognized 2,400 years ago, a democracy with privatized finance always morphs into an undemocratic oligarchy. Any financialized economy drifts towards the concentration of economic and political power in the hands of financial representatives. This happened to an extreme degree under rentier capitalism.

The PAG needed to devise a strategy for breaking the power of the financial oligarchy, which had captured the state. Finance thrived by pushing people into debt. Chronic indebtedness determined how a majority used their time, labouring in jobs for longer, negotiating with creditors or queuing for charity, and intensifying stress and mental illness.

In Aristotle's time and for many centuries before and after, the usual result of unsupportable debt accumulation was a debt jubilee, when the ruler wrote off debt so as to weaken the power of moneylenders. However, the PAG foresaw no consensus on what types of debt should be forgiven (student debt, mortgage debt, unsecured debt, and so on). There was also concern about unfairness. Some people would have forgone spending to avoid debt, whereas others would not. And debt relief implied a moral hazard, benefiting those who may have been reckless rather than the prudent. But since paying down debt was vital both for society and the indebted, the PAG came up with an ingenious solution. Instead of a blanket debt jubilee, it would make sure everybody had the wherewithal to reduce debts and avoid incurring more. We will see later what they did. First, though, we should recall the second immediate 'mission' set by the PAG – reducing the economic uncertainty felt by a majority of the population.

Understanding Uncertainty

In the era of rentier capitalism, thousands of unforeseen economic shocks and financial crises required stabilizing measures that invariably bailed out the financiers and increased inequalities. The economic system was riddled with uncertainty. An analysis by *The Economist* found that the International Monetary Fund, global overseer of stabilization policies, had failed to predict any of the 220 country recessions between 1999 and 2014.[28] Even economists who had made their reputation with elaborate predictive models had to admit that the world economy was chronically unpredictable.[29]

A word of the year in 2022 was 'permacrisis'. Another term that captured the situation well was 'polycrisis', as a string of natural disasters and man-made crises blended into each other and made them worse. And economic uncertainty linked to a constant expectation of impending crises had inclined more people to vote for populist and often authoritarian reactionaries.[30]

The world was living in an age of 'predictable unpredictability', as *The Economist* put it.[31] Besides more economic shocks, it was evident that there would be more devastating natural disasters as climate change worsened, as well as more pandemics and more technological disruption as the pace of change accelerated. Morbidity was also a rising threat. Germs thrive in an age of international travel and crowded cities.

The age of uncertainty was playing havoc with people's sense of control over their time. Thus the PAG won plaudits for making reducing the impact or threat associated with economic uncertainty one of its primary 'missions'.

Most people crave more control of their time. Control means being able to choose what to do or not do and for how long, with reasonably predictable outcomes, as if playing a perpetual game of chess. Most of us would be limited chess players because our minds cannot string together a long sequence of moves and counter moves. A similar limitation applies to control of time. Our time will never be fully ours, especially when we must respond to unforeseen circumstances. However, we can push for policies to limit the unwanted control of our time by others, particularly others in positions of unaccountable authority. That is a negation of our freedom. So, we should aspire to achieve what Hegel called 'the negation of the negation', erosion of the power of uncertainty.

In philosophical terms, the challenge could be conceived as ontological – that is, constantly unfolding, with no end point, the opposite of a teleological 'perfect'. We will never have total control, but we can aim to have more. The imperative is to identify unwanted controls of time that are illegitimate or unnecessary, and focus on combating them, then move on to what comes next.

Humanity has always operated with constraints imposed on rationality by uncertainty. As noted in Chapter 5, economists and psychologists agree that uncertainty is a form of insecurity that differs from risk. For risks, one can make an estimate of the probability of an adverse outcome and devise a risk-pooling insurance scheme to give people a measure of resilience.

An example was unemployment insurance. In an industrial society, in which male workers typically slotted into full-time jobs, then lost them, then returned to similar jobs when demand picked up, an unemployment insurance system worked reasonably well. But it broke down as a mechanism for income security in a production system in which the probability of recovering from a job loss was low and uncertain. And it provided less control over the perceived future. This failure had become steadily worse since the 1980s because the value of unemployment benefits had shrivelled, in real terms and relative to average wages, and fewer people had any such benefits at all.

So, the PAG was confronted with a transformational question: how could government respond to a combination of uncertainty and loss of control of time by helping people to become more robust and resilient? The immediate challenge was to reduce the power of uncertainty. This required *ex ante* safeguards and forms of security, to prevent or moderate the adverse impact of shocks and hazards, rather than the *ex post* compensation supposedly provided by insurance schemes. The appropriate analogy is preventative medicine, which is surely better both for the individual and for society than more costly treatment after the ailment has taken hold.

While most people had long accepted the efficacy of vaccines to protect against illness, society had not carried that principle into the economic domain.[32] People, particularly in the precariat, needed the social equivalent of vaccination. Many of the wealthy elite and salariat, who had their 'vaccination' in the form of savings and property, traditionally frowned on the idea that others should have social vaccination, in case it made them lazy. The PAG, determined to repudiate this class-based hypocrisy, saw the potential of basic income as a social vaccination, of which more shortly. But first consider two of the PAG's constitutional initiatives.

The Growth Transformation Commission

GDP measures everything, in short, except that which makes life worthwhile.
— Robert Kennedy, 1968

In the general election campaign, the Progressive Alliance pledged to establish two independent commissions to draw up policies to which it was committed in principle. The first was to seek a replacement for GDP, the conventional measure of economic growth. Devised by Simon Kuznets in the 1930s and later refined by Richard Stone, both of whom went on to receive a Nobel Prize in Economics, it was known from the start that GDP was not a good measure of economic progress. The GDP index gave equal weight to the production of guns and butter, failed to account for environmental degradation and ignored all work that was not labour, including unpaid care, volunteering and commoning. But early critics were ignored.[33]

Indeed, in mid 2022, Labour's Sir Keir Starmer said his top priority in government would be 'growth, growth and growth', while Prime Minister Liz Truss, in her speech to the Conservative Party Conference in September 2022, declared, 'I have three priorities for our economy: growth, growth and growth.' Neither Truss nor Starmer questioned GDP as the measure of that growth.

An effort to devise an alternative to GDP, launched

in 2009 with much fanfare by French president Nicolas Sarkozy, fizzled and faded.[34] In the 2020s, the timing was more propitious. It was boosted by a survey showing that GDP growth was the least-understood economic concept among the public.[35]

The PAG directed the first commission to build a narrative around 'eco-growth', rather than GDP growth. It wanted to avoid the term 'degrowth' because it could be misinterpreted as reducing living standards. The Greens and ecological economists had long advocated degrowth. But there were several possible meanings, including de-emphasized growth – just deciding not to make GDP growth a target. After all, some growth, even of GDP, cannot be stopped since it reflects people's economic activities. People keep on inventing, supplying new services, producing more food and so on. Governments cannot stop that.

What governments can do is recalibrate what is meant by growth. Interest flared in subjective ideas. But concepts such as wellbeing and happiness were utilitarian. The happiness of a majority could be gained at the expense of the unhappiness of a minority. A more promising measure was use of time. If an economic value were imputed to care, for instance, then an increase in care would imply an increase in growth. If an economic value were imputed to participating in education, an increase in time in education would increase growth. And certain activities could be given negative economic value. That might apply to jobs that those in them regard as not contributing any economic value, which could be a third of all jobs.[36]

The Growth Transformation Commission was inspired by several international reports, including one in 2022 by

McKinsey Global, the world's most prominent consultancy to governments and corporations, which stated that a fundamental transformation of the global economy was vital if the world was to have a realistic chance of reaching net-zero climate emissions by 2050.[37]

The commission was also tasked with taking account of inequality, research having shown that growing inequality had resulted in £240 billion of welfare losses.[38] This led it to consider variants of the Genuine Progress Indicator, derived from the Index of Sustainable Economic Welfare first suggested in 1989, which had tried to take account of environmental, social and financial factors.[39]

Under rentier capitalism, an unsustainably high rate of GDP growth was needed to raise the living standard of the majority, because most of the additional income went to the plutocracy and elite. Very little trickled down to the precariat. So the commission reasoned that the emphasis should not be on economic growth, for the ecological reasons people finally understood, but on finding other ways to raise and measure living standards.

One way was to incorporate measures of non-market activities that people were doing and valued. Take gardening, for example. Before Covid, and bearing in mind that one in eight British households had no garden, on average every adult gardened for ten minutes a day, with those over the age of sixty-five doing twenty-six minutes a day.[40] If they had been paid wages for doing that work, GDP would have been substantially higher, and would have been boosted during the pandemic when people spent more time gardening.

More important was unpaid care work, ignored in

measures of economic growth for over a century but whose value was brought into sharp relief during the pandemic. It was ridiculous that unpaid care had been excluded from national income statistics and given a value of zero, even though statisticians had ways of imputing value to non-market activities. Imputed values had long been used in measures of GDP, including imputed rent for owner-occupied housing. Without this, a country with 100 per cent home ownership would, other things being equal, appear much poorer than one where all housing was rented.

That statisticians and their political masters had not incorporated unpaid care into measures of GDP testified to sexism, since most was done by women. It also highlighted the ideological bias underpinning GDP statistics. It began as a measure of resources available for mobilization for the Second World War. Women doing housework were regarded as not 'mobilizable'. This reasoning by male statisticians was prejudiced and was promptly proven wrong by the surge of women entering the labour force in the war effort.

In the twenty-first century – finally – separate estimates were made of the economic value of housework and unpaid care work, though they were put in separate satellite accounts. For the USA, one estimate based on time-use data and average hourly wage rates for housekeepers put the market value of childcare, cooking, cleaning, washing, gardening, driving, and such like, at $3.8 trillion in 2010, adding 26 per cent to GDP.[41]

Apparently, fewer hours were spent on those activities in 2010 than in 1965, when household work was estimated to account for an extra 39 per cent of GDP. But, whereas women had reduced their time by 7.3 hours a week, men had on average increased theirs by 4.9 hours. For both men and women, there was a decline in time spent cooking and, on average, about an hour a week more time spent shopping, suggesting increased commercialization of time.

In the UK, the Office for National Statistics had been estimating satellite accounts for household activity since 2002.[42] Its approach was to put a money value on household output, such as number of meals cooked and number of children cared for. This took no account of quality. The methodology divided household work into six categories – shelter (including do-it-yourself maintenance), transport, nutrition (cooking), laundry, childcare, care for the elderly and disabled, and volunteering.

For the year 2000, the ONS estimated that total unpaid household work was worth £877 billion, about 45 per cent of all economic activity for the year. Of the total, £221 billion was for childcare, £164 billion for nutrition and £156 billion for transport. By 2015, unremunerated care was estimated to be worth well over half the size of the money economy.[43] Similar exercises were conducted for other countries, including Australia, Canada, Finland (where housework was estimated to be 40 per cent of GDP), Germany, Hungary and Nepal.

In his book *The Growth Delusion* (2016), David Pilling claimed that 'counting home production lowers measured inequality' because if an activity is 'worth' something it should be added to other income.[44] This is fallacious. If someone providing unpaid childcare were actually paid, that would reduce inequality. But they are not paid, so it makes no sense to count the unpaid work as income. It is a cost, however much they might be prepared to do it.

These approaches did not cover one valuable form of household 'production' and time use. In 2013, a brilliant analysis by Julie Smith estimated the value of breastmilk and breastfeeding in Australia, Norway and the USA.[45] There is no intrinsic reason why milk from a cow, sheep or goat should be included in GDP and not women's milk. Such is the limitation of GDP that if a lactating mother changes to formula milk, national income goes up. It may go up doubly if, instead of using her time to breastfeed, she does a low-paying job instead. This is absurd.

Smith used the United Nations System of National Accounts guidelines to measure the economic value of human-milk production, using an imputed value based on donor milk-bank prices. In Australia, the imputed value exceeded $3 billion annually. In the USA, it was $72 billion, in Norway $907 million. This underestimated the true value, if one accepts that human milk is more valuable for the infant's development than other milk, and that breastfeeding lowers women's risk of breast cancer later. Other estimates put the public-health costs of suboptimal breastfeeding at $13 billion a year in the USA and over £40 million in the UK.[46]

In the USA, Smith estimated that nearly two-thirds of the $110 billion potential value of breastfeeding was lost due to premature weaning, taking an average of six months as the recommended norm for exclusive breastfeeding. In Norway, the loss was less, but still 40 per cent. In the first month, only 77 per cent of mothers were breastfeeding in the USA, compared with 99 per cent in Norway and 90 per cent in Australia. By the sixth month, only 47 per cent of American mothers were spending time breastfeeding, compared with 80 per cent in Norway.

Norwegian mothers were under less market pressure to allocate more time to labour market activity rather than to care work. Paid maternity leave was statutory in Norway, whereas in the USA it was up to employers to provide it. Pre-Covid, only 13 per cent of American women in private-sector jobs had paid maternity leave and 23 per cent were back to work after two weeks.[47] And the government subsidized formula milk for low-income families, encouraging substitution of a commodity for a healthier option. The GDP approach that gave women's milk no value led to less appreciation of schemes to support women spending time in breastfeeding.

Clearly, if unpaid care had been given a market value, the measured size of the economy would have been much greater. An Oxfam report in 2020 estimated that globally women and girls were doing over three-quarters of all unpaid care work, contributing $11 trillion to the global economy and accounting for 12.5 billion hours a day.[48] The United Nations was committed to measuring unwaged work in national accounts. But progress had been slow, so the Growth Transformation Commission was under pressure to deliver.

Integrating care in all its forms in a measure of economic progress was a central part of the commission's mandate. However, in this respect it was expected to draw on the second commission set up by the PAG in its first hundred days – the Independent National Care Commission (INCC).

The Independent National Care Commission

The commission's terms of reference included drawing lessons from the pandemic for all types of care and recommending how care could be incorporated in the new measure of economic progress to be proposed by the Growth Trans-formation Commission, taking into account earlier pro-posals for children's social care made in Independent Care Reviews for England and Scotland.[49] However, its core man-date was to assess all forms of care in the round: the aim was to enhance the capabilities and freedoms of all those with care needs, while protecting them and those providing care, as well as others – often overlooked –who act as care facili-tators. They include social workers charged with matching those in need with direct providers and also relatives often left responsible for making difficult decisions on type of care and how to pay for it.

The INCC was also asked to determine the most exped-ient way of phasing out private-equity capital in care provi-sion. It was an indictment of the whole social-care system that at the time of the Covid pandemic the three biggest care-home chains were owned by private equity – HC-One, Four Seasons and Care UK. The private-equity business model is based on debt-financed buyouts and cost cutting that enables them to pay generous dividends to their international investors before selling up. Their interest in care is to profit from the fees paid by local councils for residents and by residents themselves, a third of whom were 'self-funded' in 2022.[50] Thus, in the aus-terity decade that saw large budget cuts for local councils and reduced funding for social care, private-equity owners shut unprofitable care homes or sold out.

Other care homes raised charges way beyond costs for self-funded residents to make up for loss of income from local councils, while councils struggled with a shortage of care workers to help elderly people at home. In 2016, over a million older people in England were not getting the social care they needed, a 50 per cent increase from 2010.[51]

The INCC was expected to establish a constitutional right to receive care and identify rights of carers as well as of care recipients, including the right to provide care. It was expected to make care a core form of work, ensuring that all those involved in care relationships would have equal security and equal agency, or voice. All types of care recipient and all types of care providers are vulnerable to oppression and exploitation, including self-exploitation.

Because of its emotional nature and the trade-offs between quantity of time, quality and costs, a good social-care system cannot rely on statutory regulation alone and certainly not on market forces. Rather, a progressive system requires respect for a fundamental principle of guild socialism – having as many forms of representation as there are interests to represent. That has never existed. In all relevant forums at every level, carers need representation, if only to save them from self-exploitation and burnout; those connecting carers and care recipients need representation; and care recipients need representation, to protect them from everybody.

The Commons Capital Fund

The PAG recognized that the income-distribution system had broken down irretrievably and that the rentiers were taking the lion's share of income growth by exploiting the commons. They were depriving the citizenry of common resources (common property) or depleting the commons through the negative impact (externalities) of their activities. The PAG addressed three questions: how to charge for exploitation of the commons; how to manage and preserve the resultant revenue; and how to distribute the proceeds. They benefited from having studied several imagined and proposed variants.[52]

The signature reform was the Commons Capital Fund. This was aimed at confronting two existential threats: grotesque inequalities of wealth linked to rentier mechanisms; and accelerating ecological decay linked to pursuit of GDP growth, the underpricing of fossil fuels and the plunder of the commons.

Underpinning the fund was a transformational fiscal policy. The emphasis shifted from taxing income and consumption to raising revenue to compensate commoners for loss and degradation of the commons. The move to an eco-fiscal policy was all the more welcome because under previous governments the poor paid higher effective rates of tax than the rich, due to the relatively minimal taxation of wealth. Henceforth, conventional taxes were to fund expenditure by government, according to its priorities. The term 'levy' was used for sources of revenue raised for the commons, to be shared equally by all commoners.

As most land used to be commons, a progressive Land Value Levy was introduced and the proceeds paid into the fund. And a Seabed Value Levy returned part of the revenue gained by the Crown Estate from auctioning Britain's seabed for offshore windfarms and other purposes.[53]

Other levies included a Common Wealth Levy on the exploitation of common resources such as minerals, oil and gas, under the land or seabed. Firms permitted to mine or extract oil or gas were entitled to cover their costs and make a fair profit. But they were also required to pay a levy or royalty to the Commons Capital Fund. That contrasted with the policies of previous governments, which had given corporations large subsidies to cover risks and allowed them to make handsome profits that were only lightly taxed and increasingly diverted abroad.

The same principles guided the development of levies on use of water resources and exploitation of digital data, radio spectrum, intellectual property, and wind and wave power.[54] Particularly popular was the Superyacht Levy, a flat-rate charge on all private yachts longer than 78 feet (24 metres). The environmental platform EcoWatch, which analysed the carbon footprint of twenty billionaires, had shown that superyachts were their most environmentally damaging asset, pumping over 7,000 tonnes of carbon into the atmosphere, more than 1,500 times the emissions of a typical family car.[55] While most superyachts stayed out of British waters, the levy was symbolic, inducing other countries to follow suit.

Levies were also put on activities that deplete the commons through pollution of the air, water, land and sea. For example, a levy was imposed on the dirty diesel used by luxury cruise liners (and superyachts) that causes dangerous pollution of the surrounding air and water. While the polluters were the rich, the resulting ill-health was suffered mainly by the poor.

Most controversial was a high Carbon Levy, essential to combat climate change but vigorously resisted by multinational corporations and their political defenders. The uselessness of relying on the goodwill of businesses to reduce greenhouse gas emissions adequately had become abundantly clear. As *The Economist* had stated, 'putting a price on carbon sends a signal that reaches across the whole economy . . . and fully aligns the profit motive with the objective of cutting emissions'.[56] At the same time, fossil-fuel subsidies had to be phased out quickly. Since the Carbon Levy risked giving a price advantage to countries exporting to the UK, the PAG introduced a border-tax-adjustment mechanism at the same time as the levy.[57]

It was accompanied by a Frequent Flyer Levy, a charge on all those taking more than two flights a year. This had been proposed in a government report commissioned in 2021 but was erased from the published version under pressure from the airlines and in the unrealistic view that planes would soon become carbon-free.[58]

All the levies were justified on grounds of common justice. And the Commons Capital Fund gave people a sense of common ownership. By themselves, the levies would have been regressive, which made it crucial to promise that the revenue would be used to reduce inequalities. There was also a need to address the chronic economic uncertainty that was causing widespread stress. This twin need made it easy for the PAG to justify recycling the fund's net revenue as common dividends, in effect a basic income.

Common Dividends

> True freedom is to have complete power over one's own activities.
> — Michel de Montaigne, *Essays*, 1586

The dividends were presented as a common property right, an economic right to which every commoner was entitled.

Their level was to be determined by the size and structure of the fund, which was modelled on Norway's remarkably successful Government Pension Fund Global.

To respect commons principles, the fund's investment policy and the dividends had to adhere to two rules. First, they had to be consistent with the public trust doctrine – that is, common resources should be managed to preserve their value. Second, they had to respect the intergenerational equity principle, ensuring that future, as well as current, generations would benefit from the commons resources. It would be unfair to future generations to treat revenue from depleting an exhaustible asset, such as oil or minerals, as a windfall gain to pad current government spending or give to today's commoners.

So, the fund was required to maintain the capital value of non-renewable resources and could only distribute the net profit from investment of the revenue. In the case of the Norwegian fund, which derived its revenue entirely from non-renewable North Sea oil and gas, the net profit for distribution averaged 3.6 per cent between 1998 and 2022.

However, revenue from other levies was not so constraining. It could be recycled in its entirety, with modest deductions for management and investment costs. This applied to all eco-levies. For example, recycling a levy of £100 per cubic tonne of carbon emitted was enough to finance a rebate of £32 a week to every household, hardly adequate by itself but a start towards funding reasonable common dividends and redressing the levy's regressive effect.[59]

Although poorer households use less fossil fuel than richer ones, energy accounts for a higher proportion of their income. Recycling the revenue as equal dividends means poorer households gain more than the extra they pay in fuel costs, while richer households receive less. The PAG learned from moves to combine carbon tax and dividends in Canada, and the popularity of Switzerland's policy of recycling two-thirds of its carbon levy to households and firms.[60]

To minimize political opportunism, the fund's governance was made independent and democratic. The dividend level was to be determined by an independent Common Dividend Policy Committee, set up along the lines of the Monetary Policy Committee of the Bank of England. This meant that the government could not raise the level for political reasons before elections.

However, from the outset the dividends were high enough to constitute a basic income on which a person could survive in extremis. As the fund was being built up, the PAG topped it up with revenue saved by rolling back the enormous subsidy state that successive governments had constructed. Subsidies given to corporations, dubbed corporate welfare, came to £100 billion a year, while an incredible array of 1,190 tax reliefs went disproportionately to the wealthy, costing the Exchequer £400 billion a year in lost revenue. For example, some of the richest individuals were gaining hundreds of thousands of pounds a year in agricultural subsidies. They included Russian steel magnate Vladimir Lisin, an old associate of Vladimir Putin with a fortune of £20 billion, who owned a 1,210-hectare (3,300-acre) estate and castle in Scotland and Britain's most expensive residence, a sixteenth-century manor in Oxfordshire with 300 acres.[61] And all landlords were gifted full tax relief on gardening expenses.

Another unwarranted subsidy was the suspension of stamp duty on house purchases in 2020, a generous tax break worth up to £15,000. This was a something-for-nothing hand-out for the affluent when most people could barely dream of buying a home. Besides fuelling a record rise in property prices, about half the benefit went to people buying property costing over £500,000.[62]

As people became aware of the array of lavish handouts to the rich, they mocked as hypocrisy suggestions that modest common dividends for all were handouts. And phasing out subsidies saved revenue that could be used to top up the fund's base, without raising tax rates. It was supplemented by the revenue gained from eliminating the regressive personal tax allowance, which helped pay for the common dividends.

The PAG committed itself to an evidence-based approach to policymaking, trying out innovative, progressive policies in a few areas before applying them nationally. It took its cue from China's decades-old strategy of social-policy piloting, which had been shown to contribute to the country's development. Between 1980 and 2019, China initiated over 630 such pilot schemes, from business licensing to recyclable packaging.[63] About 46 per cent of local experiments were never rolled out nationally, but as Mao Zedong once said, failure is the mother of success – 'a fall into the pit, a gain in your wit'.

Fortunately, in the case of common dividends, there had already been dozens of pilot schemes and experiments around the world, with consistently positive results. And government efforts to help people through the pandemic had legitimized cash transfers, while the idea of basic income had become increasingly popular in many countries. The moral justification for dividends was easy to understand; they were a matter of common justice, compensating commoners for lost commons.[64]

They were also a matter of compassion justice. Granting everybody an equal economic right meant reduced emphasis on charity, which is discretionary, selective (aimed at target groups) and usually conditional (such as requiring claimants to spend time looking for jobs). Common dividends also strengthened 'work justice', implicitly rewarding forms of work that are not labour, most notably unpaid care. And by rewarding other forms of work, such as volunteering, they encouraged a shift of time towards what people want to do rather than are obliged to do.

Common dividends also fulfilled a need for basic security, vital in an era of chronic social and economic uncertainty combined with a high probability of pandemics and ecological shocks. They reduced insecurity by, in effect, giving *ex ante* protection from shocks rather than the *ex post* compensation provided by most post-1945 welfare policies. Moreover, if everybody has basic security, there is likely to be more social solidarity, altruism and tolerance. Psychologists had shown that people provided with basic security develop greater appreciation of reciprocity and the return of favours.[65]

Describing basic security as an economic right emphasized its emancipatory quality. A basic income as a right that stretches into the future tells people that they do have a future. It stretches the psychological horizon, a sign of good mental health. Living from day to day – or pay cheque to pay cheque – not only narrows the mental imagination but also shortens the mental horizon, restricting the imagination of personal change. Assured receipt of material resources raises the bar on an imagined future.

A third ethical rationale for common dividends was the enhancement of individual and community freedom. All politicians talk glibly of how they promote and support freedom. But you cannot be free if suffering from chronic insecurity; you must do whatever is necessary to survive. Freedom comes from having assured access to resources, which includes available time to pursue your aspirations and ambitions. Common dividends also offered greater republican freedom, freedom from potential domination by figures in positions of unaccountable power, whether family members, bureaucrats or employers.

Tellingly, experiments had shown that a basic income gave women a precious form of freedom – an improved ability to escape from abusive relationships. Evidence accumulated during the pandemic showed that economic insecurity led to a higher incidence of physical, sexual and mental abuse of women, with a rise in domestic abuse during the lockdowns.[66] The common dividends gave women some financial independence to go it alone if they wished. Partly as a result, it also improved the behaviour and attitudes of their partners.

Common dividends also increased the freedom to take risks with one's time. Some years earlier, James Dyson, then Britain's richest man, boastfully asserted the importance of failure:

I made 5,127 prototypes of my vacuum before I got it right. There were 5,126 failures. But I learned from each one. That's how I came up with a solution. So I don't mind failure. I've always thought that schoolchildren should be marked by the number of failures they've had. The child who tries strange things and experiences lots of failures to get there is probably more creative.[67]

Those thousands of failures must have taken up a lot of his time. And he could only try, try and try again because his wife earned enough to support him during that time. He was given, in effect, a basic income. Mark Zuckerberg, CEO of Meta, in advocating basic income, once told students at Harvard University that the 'greatest successes come from having the freedom to fail'.[68] Yet other would-be James Dysons and Mark Zuckerbergs will never have realized their potential for lack of basic security.

Despite all the arguments in favour of basic income, previous politicians – even those professing strong support in private – had prevaricated on grounds of affordability, fearing even to take the first steps on the road. The PAG broke with tradition by stating that reforms had to be assessed by whether or not they moved in the direction of a basic-income system. Universal Credit and the Department for Work and Pensions had moved far away from it. They had to go. By contrast, even if initially low, common dividends were moving in the desirable direction.

There were also practical reasons. Being an economic right and not targeted, the dividends moved away from means-tested social assistance, which created the poverty and precarity traps mentioned earlier. More people could take low-income jobs without losing most of what they would gain. This acted as an incentive for more people to take such jobs. The PAG pointed to US research suggesting that a basic income of $1,000 a month, if funded by a rise in federal debt, would boost economic growth by 13 per cent and employment by 2 per cent.[69]

Experiments with guaranteed income, targeting low-income individuals or households, backed up this picture. In the town of Hudson in New York State, the employment rate among individuals given $500 a month for five years jumped from 29 per cent to 63 per cent, with many recipients reporting better health, mended relationships and greater control of debt.[70] In Stockton, California, those given a guaranteed income of $500 a month were significantly more likely than those in the control group to move into full-time jobs.[71] Other experiments reported similar results.

Besides replicating this tendency, the common dividends introduced by the PAG also facilitated forms of work that were not labour, enabling people to develop their own sense of occupation. Basic income made it easier for people to adjust time uses, contrary to being in a job, where the activities are – quite properly, given who is paying for the time – determined by the employer. Paradoxically, being in a job can weaken occupational development. You must do what the boss wants, not what you want. That is the deal and, as long as the law is respected, fair enough.

A basic income unblocks people's time, allowing them to do more work that they would like to do, more commoning and less labour. It also lays the ground for a new

income-distribution system, recognizing that in rich countries the returns to labour will continue to decline. Real
wages will continue to stagnate and be more volatile, while
the financial returns to technology and property will continue to rise.

The PAG realized that the only way to overcome the
class-based inequalities accentuated by rentier capitalism was to build a tax structure and distribution system in
which rents from taking the commons were captured and
recycled as dividends on public wealth. This would encourage a work–commoning–leisure society rather than the jobholder society so feared by Hannah Arendt in *The Human
Condition*.

Basic-income experiments and opinion polls had indicated that when people had a basic income, or imagined having
one, they tended to become more creative or entrepreneurial
in the way Karl Polanyi approved of – that is, motivated by
a desire to be excellent, good at what they did, rather than
simply doing what was needed to obtain the wage. One poll
in November 2021 conducted by YouGov in France, Germany, Italy, Poland, Portugal and Spain found that two-thirds
of respondents were in favour of basic income, with a majority in every country. Asked what advantages they thought
it would provide, the most common answer was reduced
anxiety.[72] This tied in with experiments that consistently
showed that a basic or guaranteed income led to less anxiety
and mental ill-health.

Respondents also believed it would facilitate a better way
of living and working, granting more financial independence,
enhanced ability to pursue further education or training, and

time for work beyond jobs. Men and women of all ages said it would enable them to devote more time to their family. A significant proportion, especially among the young, said it would encourage them to launch a small-scale business, while many also said they would devote time to volunteering or social activism – over a quarter of young people in Germany and 13 per cent in France. Surely society wants more socially engaged and active youth?

Another survey, from 2020, covering over 72,000 registered users of a Berlin-based non-profit organization, Mein Grundeinkommen (My Basic Income), asked one group how they would like to change their time use, and another how they would change their time patterns if they had a basic income. The survey also asked about the likely effect with a monthly basic income of €500, €1,000 or €1,500. The effects were greater if the amount went from €500 to €1,000 but did not increase further with €1,500.[73]

The results suggested a basic income would result in small reductions in time doing labour, socializing and hobbies, and more time devoted to education, volunteering and care work. Gaining income paid for by the wider community appeared to strengthen feelings of social responsibility. And the effect was likely to be swift, occurring in the first year of receipt and remaining if the basic income continued.

A much-discussed experiment in Finland in 2017–18, in which 2,000 randomly selected unemployed aged between twenty-five and fifty-eight were given a basic income for two years, found that many recipients reported a decline in stress, an increase in wellbeing and a change in the way they used their time. There was a slight increase in seeking paid labour, showing there was no need to impose behavioural conditions on benefits. But many also started craft work or small-scale businesses that they could not have done had they been obliged to take the jobs they were likely to have been offered.[74]

Another experiment, launched by the Welsh government in 2022, sparked a sympathetic public conversation that proved influential. It provided young care leavers with a basic monthly income of £1,600 pre-tax for two years from their eighteenth birthday, previously the date when support was cut off. The scheme was operated by the devolved government of Wales against resistance from the DWP. As one supporter put it: 'In trusting people with access to a liveable amount of money, we're directly giving them control over their future. It's a radical way of improving the lives of vulnerable people.'[75]

As noted earlier, the PAG had realized that there could be no successful transformation without resolving the chronic debt crisis, but there were drawbacks in instituting a debt jubilee for household debt. However, experiments in various countries had shown that paying down debt was one of people's first priorities on receiving a basic income. This finding proved crucial in convincing some hitherto reluctant politicians.

Thus common dividends became a signature policy to match the Commons Capital Fund, serving a unique combination of ecological justice, time freedom and the route to a more sustainable form of economic progress.

Abolition of Universal Credit and the Department for Work and Pensions

While the dividends were being rolled out, the PAG took the morally courageous decision to abolish the cruel and hated Universal Credit system and the responsible state body, the Department for Work and Pensions.

The DWP had failed basic tests of accountability, both to those it claimed to serve and to the broader public. As a resolutely paternalistic edifice, its bureaucrats were shielded from the consequences of their own actions, as is typical of most bureaucracies.[76] Bureaucrats should follow what Taleb calls the Golden Rule and the Silver Rule.[77] First enunciated by Immanuel Kant, the Golden Rule is: 'Treat others the way you would like them to treat you.' The Silver Rule, regarded by Taleb as more robust, is: 'Do not treat others the way you would not like them to treat you.' On both counts, the DWP had failed.

Nor had the DWP succeeded in doing what it had originally been set up to do, matching job seekers to jobs. A survey in 2022 showed that fewer than one employer in six had made use of the DWP's Jobcentre Plus service to try to fill vacancies in the previous two years, while just one in five job seekers used it, only a third of whom thought it had helped them find a job.[78] The DWP's job-matching function had essentially been abandoned, subordinated to forcing benefit claimants into jobs, however unsuitable.

The PAG converted the DWP into a public employment and training service provider. Those DWP employees euphemistically called 'work coaches' were retrained to advise people seeking to improve their work and living standards. Meanwhile, provision of state benefits was turned over to the appropriate authority, His Majesty's Revenue and Customs (HMRC), renamed the Department for Revenue and Benefits.

With no state body driving people into jobs, it was easier to transform the imagery of work within a new eco-politics of time that encouraged and rewarded forms of work other than labour in jobs. And the PAG, reverting to principles of the 1217 Charter of the Forest, decided to recognize and encourage commoning, and to foster what the ancient Greeks and the Roman Stoics had taken as given – a wealth of quality time, without insecurity or stress, which was worth much more than wealth of goods and money stashed in banks or stock markets.

The DWP became the Department for Work, Care and Commoning (DWCC), with responsibility for extending and protecting care work, identifying and limiting work-for-labour, encouraging commoning and artisanal work, and nurturing vocational training. It also took over responsibility for occupational licensing and accreditation, charged with reversing the trend towards licensing and restricting it to occupations involving risk of harm to health or public safety. The modern poor law was slain.

The Withering of Jobs

Even before the pandemic, commentators were promoting a 'post-work' future.[79] But their target should have been labour and jobs, not all forms of work. What was needed were policies to liberate time from unwanted work-for-labour and work-for-the-state, so that more desirable forms of work could be undertaken.

As the pandemic faded, it became obvious that many more people, especially the young, had become part of the precariat. Young people returning to jobs were three times as likely to be on temporary, casual or zero-hours contracts as those who had stayed in jobs.[80] And mental ill-health was a heavy legacy. Yes, they could obtain jobs of a sort, for a while, at volatile uncertain pay. But the sense of precarity, feeling like wounded supplicants, further distanced many from the jobs fetish as they recognized that available jobs were unlikely to provide income security in the future.

The PAG argued that the problem was not a shortage of jobs but a surplus of them. Many commentators had claimed that robots and artificial intelligence (AI) represented an existential threat to human labour.[81] But as technology advanced, the number of jobs rose to the highest level ever. The main problem was one of distribution. Real wages had stagnated, while the flow of rental income to the owners of robots and AI technologies had grown.

In their book *Inventing the Future* (2015), Nick Srnicek and Alex Williams said that governments should push companies to invest in automation through higher minimum wages and capital-purchase tax incentives, stating that 'we should enthusiastically accelerate the replacement of human labour from the economy and keep creating wealth through machines'.[82] That objective was eminently sensible, although the gains would still go disproportionately to those owning the technology. The PAG's strategy was to recycle rental income to help pay for common dividends. Then people, if they wished, could take jobs at lower wages without being impoverished as a result.

In any case, the pandemic taught many to want what the Jeremiahs had falsely predicted. Let automation take over unpleasant or boring jobs. So the PAG adopted policies – and a rhetoric to go with them – to cut the number of jobs. This meant turning from a visceral fear of robots and AI to welcoming automation of routinized, draining labour, provided that income generated by job displacement was shared with everybody as commoners.

The Arrival of Time Rights

We have seen how much time people were obliged to use to enable them to labour in the tertiary time system. Successive governments took the time of the precariat for granted, considering it of little value. Thus they had no policies to reduce the amount of time spent doing work-for-labour. The PAG was committed to redress that injustice.

The first measure it introduced freed time for the vast number of people applying for jobs every year. In the tertiary labour market, job applications are mostly assessed by algorithms and may involve as many as six or more time-consuming and stressful rounds of tests and standardized interviews. The potential employer bears very little if any cost and expends no time until or unless there is an actual interview.

Under the PAG's new regulations, job applicants had to pay their own costs for the first round of assessment once the algorithm had approved their online application. But if recruitment involved more than one further round, the potential employer was required to make a modest payment to applicants, which increased for each subsequent round. Employers soon shortened their procedures, saving those being churned through the flexible labour market a great deal of time.

Another policy the PAG introduced in its first hundred days gave every jobholder 'the right to disconnect' – that is, a right not to receive or respond to emails, messages and labour requests outside contracted hours. This drew on precedents set by Ireland, where a code of conduct was introduced in 2022, and similar schemes in Belgium, France, Portugal and Spain.

However, the most valued gains in time were made by reducing work-for-the-state. Abolishing Universal Credit automatically reduced the onerous demands on time made on millions of claimants. No longer did low-income people have to waste time travelling to and attending long, pointless and degrading interviews by bureaucrats only too keen to punish any infringement. No longer did they have to endure the indignity of regular updating of stigmatizing resumés of lives testifying to market failure. It was a blow for time freedom.

The PAG also did something truly emancipatory. In reforming social policy, it introduced a rule that if statutory benefits or services were not delivered within defined periods, people would be compensated. This was the first time in history that the time of the disadvantaged and vulnerable in society was valued by the state. Time rights had arrived.

The Revival of Commoning

> England is not a free people, till the poor that have no land,
> have a free allowance to dig and labour the commons.
> — Gerrard Winstanley, 1649

Towards the end of the English Civil War, just after the execution of Charles I, the religious reformer Gerrard Winstanley (1609–76) was the most articulate voice among those calling for restoration of land taken from the commons. The quotation above continues: 'and so live as comfortably as the landlords that live in their enclosures'.[83] His True Levellers were soon to be known as the Diggers. And for planting and harvesting vegetables together, they were hastily and brutally persecuted. The ruling elite of the time wanted them in jobs instead.

Flash forward to 2021. One result of the pandemic and the associated lockdowns was a resurgence of interest in growing vegetables and fruit, in gardens and on allotments. In what amounted to a revival of agrarian time, people with gardens intensified their use of them while applications for allotments surged across Britain. Half the councils in England reported waiting times of eighteen months, with up to 400 people on waiting lists in some areas.[84]

As the National Allotment Society (NAS) pointed out: 'With one in eight of the UK population having no access to a garden – one in five in London – and a rise in awareness of the fragility of our food systems, perhaps now is the time for central government to reassess the potential for allotments to support public health and make a significant contribution to food security.' The NAS reminded the public that, in the 'Dig for Victory' campaign during the Second World War, 18 per cent of the country's fruit and vegetables were grown in gardens and allotments, compared with just 3 per cent before the pandemic.[85] Moreover, studies showed that urban allotments delivered substantial ecosystem benefits, helping to clean the air, regulate local climate, store more carbon, cut the risk of flooding and encourage biodiversity.[86]

The PAG announced a National Commons Investment Strategy, in which it committed to expanding allotments by at least 50,000 a year from the 330,000 that existed in 2020, restoring the loss of 65 per cent of allotments since the 1950s. Whereas, in the past, an expansion of allotments was mostly justified by the exigencies of war or economic hardship, the PAG saw allotments not solely as a means of subsistence but as a way to encourage commoning and reduced reliance on labour and GDP growth. It also recommended that produce from allotments, and the time devoted to allotment work, should be included in measures of national prosperity.

There was no shortage of land for potential allotments. In 2020, the founder of the Black Farmer food brand, Wilfred Emmanuel-Jones, called on the government, the Ministry of Defence and the Church of England, all owning vast swathes of land, to do more to encourage allotments. The issue was to take back for the commoners land that had been enclosed and privatized.

It was also recognized that loss of allotments was greater in deprived communities and was a form of inequality. So the PAG gave priority to such areas. The NAS was provided with extra funds to assist in the national effort, with a long-term target of raising the share of fruit and vegetables grown domestically closer to the Second World War level of 18 per cent. There was even talk of a 'right to grow' law, permitting people to bring unused land to life.

Nobody expected Hyde Park to become once again a jumble of allotments, but public spaces and land for common acquisition became potential food-growing sites all over the country. Research in Sheffield, for example, showed there were nearly 100 square metres per person that could be used for growing fruit and vegetables, more than enough to feed the whole population of the city.[87]

The PAG's plan drew on findings that tending allotments encouraged shared community activities and the sharing of food produce, knowledge and equipment, which helped to reduce loneliness and mental illness. One allotment holder made the point that this was not primarily about connecting with people similar to themselves as 'connecting with people you have nothing in common with apart from growing [things]'.[88]

There were similar developments in other countries. In the United States, the famous Victory Gardens of the Second World War had been abandoned in the post-war era, replaced by sterile suburban yards, in which many local authorities in the 'land of the free' forbade the growing of fruit and vegetables. But the fightback to establish a right to garden gathered pace until it figured in the legislation of every state. And community gardens flourished. New York served as a model. As of 2021, the city already sponsored the largest urban gardening programme in the USA, with 550 community gardens tended by 23,000 volunteers.[89]

Indicative of the new ethos of commoning, most community gardens were planted and harvested collectively. No longer were the self-serving attacks by food businesses on such activities deemed acceptable. They had mocked Michelle Obama's kitchen garden in the White House as elitist and anti-business. Now they kept their commercial mouths shut.

In the UK, the enthusiasm for a return to nature, and implicitly to commoning, recalled a similar period of recoil from the march of industrial time in the 1870s, when John Ruskin wrote *Fors Clavigera*, a series of public letters issued as pamphlets, addressed to British workmen urging them to return to cultivating the land. In his Letter 5 of 1871, for instance, he wrote: 'We will try to take some small piece of English ground, beautiful, peaceful and fruitful. We will have no steam-engines upon it, and no railroads; we will have no untended or unthought-of creatures on it; none wretched, but the sick; none idle, but the dead.'[90]

Ruskin, his mentor Thomas Carlyle and his contemporary William Morris were all prominent Victorian voices trying to arrest not just the relentless march of industrial time but the commodification of all life, which, in their view, severed a reciprocal respectful relationship of humanity with nature. In the twenty-first century, climate change and the existential threat of extinction give this perspective durable strength.

In the early 2020s, the momentum in this direction was shared between revived allotments, community gardens and rewilding schemes. Following the pandemic, more than 7 million people in the UK took up gardening for the first time.[91] One enthusiast described community gardens as revolutionary in a quiet way, reflecting a feeling that it was an unstoppable transformative development.[92]

The Royal Horticultural Society, a venerable charitable institution established in 1804, which passed the threshold of 600,000 members in 2021, latched on to the rising number of community gardens by launching an award scheme. Kay Clark, head of the society's community gardening programme, made the point: 'Where groups like this existed, communities seemed to be more resilient when it came to a crisis because they had a pre-established network of volunteers and people already knew each other so they could easily offer support.'[93]

Community gardens sprang up all over the country. One energetic group, CoFarm Cambridge, aimed to establish at least one in every local authority area in the UK by 2030, using a combination of their own money, local donations and corporate grants. A volunteer group launched the aptly named Hexham Fresh Food Bank in 2020, building a network of over 200 food growers to provide free food to hundreds of low-income households in west Northumberland.[94]

Another exemplary case was the Golden Hill Community Garden in Bristol, a 200-square-metre sanctuary between a prison and a primary school. Between 2011 and 2013, volunteers transformed a boggy area into a wheelchair-accessible green zone, with a big pond, raised vegetable beds and an 'edible forest' consisting of densely planted fruit and nut trees, fruit bushes and edible ground-cover plants.[95]

Community gardens are now found all over Britain. As one volunteer at a community garden on Clapham Common, in London, explained:

We grow vegetables and plants in a communal plot and sell them at the weekends for donations which are then invested back into the garden . . . The leftover produce gets turned into jams and chutneys that are also made communally. Sometimes we sit down for lunch together at the trestle table – eating the produce we ourselves have planted and grown. Recently, sitting between a Ph.D. student who's working on cell regeneration and a retired expert in international aid, I remember thinking this was better than any dinner party . . . We work together, and we talk about life, politics and food.[96]

One virtue of the increase in community gardens and allotments was that more people were eating the recommended five-a-day portions of fruit and vegetables. This had been a hidden form of inequality for generations. Before the pandemic, the richest 20 per cent ate on average one more portion than the poorest 20 per cent. This matters, since a diet lacking in fruit and vegetables increases the risk of stroke, heart disease and some cancers.[97]

At the end of the spectrum of activities was the anarchic practice of guerrilla gardening, an international mini movement encouraging groups to plant flowers and other ornamentals in unused or neglected public spaces. The movement began in the 1970s but was formalized in 2004 in London as a blog-cum-organization, GuerrillaGardening. org. Its main objective was to make spaces more aesthetically pleasing, green and healthy, but another aim had also been to protest about the shrinking commons. Being illegal, technically, the planting was for a long time carried out mainly at night, but this has now become more open and socially welcomed. The communal activity is done on common land as a form of commoning.

A related development was the PAG's promise of an independent national programme to create, recreate and enlarge common parks. This drew inspiration from the Camley Street Natural Park, a legacy of Ken Livingstone's time as leader of the Greater London Council. The GLC funded the conversion of a piece of wasteland the size of a football pitch next to Regent's Canal that had been used as a coal dump in the Victorian era, known as Coal Drops Yard. In 1985, Livingstone opened it as an outdoor classroom, declaring, 'A dead area has been transformed to bring a country setting to the inner city.'[98]

This gesture towards commoning came as the neoliberal ideology hostile to its ethics and to egalitarianism reached its zenith. The right-wing media attacked the park as wasteful spending, and symbolically Margaret Thatcher abolished the GLC less than a year later. But the park lived on, visited every year by 5,000 inner-city children to experience its seclusion, go 'pond-dipping', and enjoy the pondlife and birds. Refurbished during the pandemic, it became a beacon of a revived commons. A representative of the London Wildlife Trust, which manages the park, remarked that 'There should be at least five of these in every borough.'[99]

There was also a growth in communal farming in the form of 'hyperlocal food' – food grown close to where it is eaten. Some restaurants and shops started to use their premises or teamed up with locals, overlapping with farmers' markets and groups of gardeners putting produce together to sell by the roadside. And there was a burgeoning of hydroponic systems that grow food without soil, indoors or even underground, using nutrient-enhanced water and artificial lighting.

One feature of the societal response to the pandemic was an increase in 'green' or 'blue' social prescribing by doctors instead of using pharmaceuticals, in response to a growing body of research showing that spending time in nature – engaged in outdoor activities ('green') or participating in wetland programmes ('blue') – helped combat mental illness. Lord (Nigel) Crisp, a former chief executive of the NHS in England, adopted an old African adage, 'health is made at home, hospitals are for repairs', to champion such social prescribing.[100]

According to one Australian study, visits to green spaces of thirty minutes or more each week reduced rates of depression by 7 per cent.[101] A study in Britain found that a two-hour dose of nature a week significantly boosted well-being.[102] Woodland walks were conservatively estimated by Forest Research to save the UK £185 million a year in treatment for mental illness and labour days lost.[103] The Wildfowl and Wetland Trust (WWT) also reported that access to wetlands improved mental and physical health, as well as strengthening a sense of community by bringing people together. In addition, the report noted, wetlands helped to cool cities, reduce flooding and curb air pollution, all with clear benefits for health and the environment.[104]

A Blue Prescribing Project found that people diagnosed with anxiety or depression who participated in a six-week wetland course designed by the WWT and the Mental Health Foundation gained a clinical mental-health grade, going from below average to average.[105] This was time used communally to the advantage of both individuals and society. And having a basic income made it easier to do commoning, because people were less fearful of losing a job or all of their income. Common dividends also had a similar effect to the one shown by the two-year guaranteed-income experiment in Stockton, California, launched in 2019: people spent more in the local economy.[106]

PERMACULTURE

Permaculture became another popular form of commoning and work, without involving the contrived generation of jobs or labour. Its ethical principles, as articulated by its leading practitioners, are 'earth care, people care and fair share' (in distributing surplus food and other produce).[107] Permaculture emphasizes holistic approaches to growing food that echo natural systems, using organic, biodiverse and low-cost methods, natural materials, composting and recycling. But it also aims to support resilient local communities and cultures.

Its advocates, of which there are many across the world, notably in Australia where the movement began in the late 1970s, embrace commons principles for the provision of food, shelter, water, waste and energy systems, with deference to community governance. They repudiate neoliberal capitalism and its faith in infinite economic growth, depicting it as a linear system – producing, consuming, discarding, with a constant focus on speed – producing as much as possible in as little time as possible, discarding what is deemed obsolescent.

Permaculture enthusiasts believe everybody should try to apply its principles, to grow food for themselves, husband water and energy resources, and minimize waste. And there is an implication for public action. One advocate commented: 'When shown what we can do on a personal scale, our perspective changes from powerlessness to positivity.'[108] As this implies, the way we use our time influences how we think and the values that shape engagement with our community and society that Aristotle called *philia* or civic friendship.

The permaculture movement places a high value on time spent observing and understanding the natural world around us. Courses in permaculture introduce 'the key skill of observation – something our fast-paced society tells us we don't have time for'.[109] Stop to see, choose to watch, make the strange become familiar. Recovering our sense of observation is part of commoning. It keeps us grounded, close to nature, part of nature, protective of nature.

The idealism motivating the permaculture enthusiasts should not lead us to mock this way of responding to the global eco-social crisis. The tone for transformation is usually set by like-minded 'little platoons', to use Edmund Burke's description of the many associations that make up society. Permaculture goes hand in hand with the project-oriented lifestyle of artists in the precariat. Both nurture cooperative communities and commoning activities that, among other virtues, transcend discriminatory boundaries of race, age and gender.

Permaculture offers a feasible way for people to confront uncertainty and build societal robustness and resilience to shocks. In an economic system in which uncertainty is the core of insecurity, there is an added premium on cooperation and sharing based on a diversified range of time uses. The introduction of common dividends by the PAG helped, enabling people to have more control of their time and reducing anxiety about devoting time to observation, protection of biodiversity, conservation of resources, growing and enjoying local produce, and escaping from the restrictions of standardized tastes and the docile consumption of established brands.

Symbolizing the movement's ethos, during the pandemic a community permaculture farm in Northamptonshire delivered vegetable meals to homeless people put up in hotels in the area. It also assisted a Covid support group, delivering meals to key workers, people in safe houses due to domestic abuse, people with disabilities and the housebound elderly. In the words of the farm's co-founder, Sammuel Yisrael: 'Our aim is to connect homeless and vulnerable adults together with mother earth to improve people's mental and physical wellbeing, while also giving something back to nature.'[110]

All these forms of commoning became easier to do at scale as a result of the common dividends, which reduced pressure to do labour in jobs. Involvement in commoning means more than sharing activities; it also creates stronger connections and relationships between people, rather than the weak ties prevalent under neoliberalism. And it increases respect for nature.

If you spend time in the presence of a familiar old tree or a piece of land with familiar plants and shapes, you are more likely to respect it and want to preserve it. Old trees have great natural value that saplings cannot possess, and nurture diverse species in and around them. The old commoning activity of coppicing, periodically cutting trees to near their base but allowing them to regrow, so beneficial for biodiversity, allowed trees to live longer and recover their strength. And old trees have hollow cavities and areas of decay that shelter birds, insects and other creatures.[111]

Coppicing began to thrive again, as did pollarding, another commoning activity that dates back to at least ancient Rome. Regular cutting from higher up a tree was an activity linked to the right to *estover* enshrined in the Charter of the Forest of 1217, the right to take twigs and branches from the commons.

Other commoning practices sprang from little shoots during the pandemic into national movements. For example, city dwellers became agents for reviving ancient woodlands in their locality. As of 2021, ancient woodland, defined as woods that had existed since 1600, covered only about 2.5 per cent of England and Wales, having been chipped away by encroachment. There had been previous initiatives to revive some in and around London, the most promising being the Sydenham Hill Wood in Dulwich.[112] But now in cities and towns across the country, groups were being mobilized to save many more.

This was related to the rewilding movement that began in the early 2000s but was previously confined largely to small-scale, do-it-yourself efforts by private owners of woodlands.[113] Encouraged by the success of these efforts in restoring and increasing biodiverse ecosystems, the PAG urged all owners of woodland, which covers about 13 per cent of the country, to copy their example and to provide public access. Rewilding of woodlands has restored commoning practices, such as coppicing and gleaning. The work is driven by love of nature, not profit.

COMMUNITY SEA GARDENS

The PAG also promoted blue commoning in the form of community sea gardens. As an island nation, Britain has a huge coastline with numerous coves and estuaries. It also has 120 commercial cargo-handling ports and 400 smaller ports. Development of sea gardens in Denmark inspired a campaign to do the same in areas near British ports.

In 2011, a local association set about creating sea allotments in Denmark's Ebeltoft harbour, designating areas of sea where community members could grow shellfish and seaweed, in the process providing a cleaner marine environment and restoring life to an old fishing port. By 2022 there were fifteen sea-allotment societies, the largest being in Kerteminde Maritime Haver, and ten more were being set up. Initially, allotment holders focused on growing mussels in their individual plots. But they soon realized that skills and time availability varied to the point where closer cooperation would benefit the whole community.

All Denmark's sea allotments are now managed on the basis that the work is done in common. In Kerteminde, annual family membership cost 500 Danish kroner (£60) in 2022, which paid for use of the harbour, renting the sailing club's clubhouse, and removal of debris. The society bought an old fishing boat kitted with farming winches, and members began to grow sugar kelp and planned to attract lobsters.[114]

At around the same time, a movement emerged in the Pacific to revive and support ancestral sea gardens that had flourished in indigenous communities for thousands of years. Spearheaded by the Pacific Sea Garden Collective, a group describing themselves as 'indigenous knowledge holders, community practitioners, university researchers and artists', the movement spurred interest in indigenous maricultural practices and led to a range of initiatives to re-establish 'resilient, sustainable and equitable food systems'.[115] Communities across the Pacific region re-engaged in commoning practices that had faded under pressure from subsidized industrial fisheries.

The success of the Pacific sea-garden revival provided further encouragement for the PAG to emulate the Danish approach. Accordingly, it sought out prospective sites around the UK coastline. Sea commoning was reborn.

SHARING AND RECYCLING

The early twenty-first century saw the emergence of a sharing-economy movement, which was quickly hijacked by platform capital in the form of Uber, Deliveroo, Airbnb and other rent-seeking entities. However, there were also a growing number of sharing initiatives more akin to bartering that involved another type of commoning – work-for-consumption. Local groups sprang up to facilitate the sharing of consumer durables such as tools, appliances and means of transport, and to 'gift' items of all sorts that were no longer needed.

People overcame a threshold of reticence in rent-sharing their underused durables and even underused clothing. Women in particular had been led by the fashion industry to discard still wearable clothes or leave unfashionable outfits to moulder in their wardrobes. A much-cited finding was that 95 per cent of clothes Americans sent to landfill sites each year were in good enough condition for many years of use or for resale.[116] Why not share, rent out or recycle them for use?

Commercial platforms emerged during the pandemic to act as brokers for reselling and renting clothes, taking between 20 per cent and 60 per cent of the sale price. Firms such as The RealReal, By Rotation, Rotaro, ThredUp, Depop, Poshmark and Vestiaire turned the business into a new rentier asset class. Renting out clothes grew as fast as reselling. In the USA, wealthy women with lavish wardrobes were making up to £2,500 ($3,300) a month from rentier activity. Many other items, such as cameras, started to be traded in the same way. In 2022, the global value of all this renting amounted to many billions of dollars.

But it did not have to be commercial. The PAG wanted to encourage voluntary sharing, repairing and recycling, seeing these activities as essential for a healthy environment and as ways of strengthening community ties. Sharing as commoning was encouraged by an Anti-Obsolescence Drive, targeted initially at clothing.

People were encouraged to buy second-hand clothing, where possible, rather than new. This had been rekindled in the austerity years as charity shops selling second-hand clothes mushroomed. Community groups, encouraged by the PAG, also revived jumble sales, long used as church

fundraisers, which had almost died out with falling con-
gregations. These enabled people to pass on still useable or
mendable clothes for others to buy at negligible cost. The
fast-fashion industry, manufacturing cheap clothes to be
worn a few times and then discarded, fell out of favour as
people acknowledged the ecological cost. The ecological argument was persuasive, since clothing manufacturing and
distribution had been shown to account for anything between 2 per cent and 8 per cent of global carbon emissions,
more than aviation or shipping.[117]

For other shared items, the PAG's Anti-Obsolescence
Drive was able to build on two anti-commerce initiatives ori-
ginating in the USA. Launched in 2003 in Arizona, the Freecycle Network by 2022 had more than 5,000 town groups with
over 9 million members in 110 countries, including Britain,
which also had a similar national network, called Freegle.
Although Freecycle's founder and executive director Deron
Beal and his staff drew salaries, the network was operated
by thousands of self-motivated volunteers, working unpaid.

Anyone could join a local Freecycle group and post online
items they no longer wanted, to give away for free. The only
restrictions were that the items had to be legal and 'appropriate for all ages'. By 2022, the network claimed it was keeping over 1,000 tonnes a day of 'good stuff' out of landfill sites
and that 'by giving freely with no strings attached, members
of The Freecycle Network help instil a generosity of spirit as
they strengthen local community ties and promote environmental sustainability and reuse'.[118]

Another movement with US origins was the so-called
'right to repair', requiring manufacturers to design products

to be repairable and to allow consumers or third parties to do the repairs. This became an issue after angry users complained that Apple did not permit them to replace a worn battery in their iPhone, instead obliging them to buy a new phone. But it also applied to electronic controls in consumer durables such as vehicles, washing machines and dishwashers. In 2022, the US Congress passed the Fair Repair Act, requiring manufacturers to provide the tools and documentation necessary for people to repair their electronic devices and equipment or have them repaired.

The UK had acted earlier, with the Ecodesign for Energy-Related Products and Energy Information Regulations 2021. These obliged manufacturers of consumer durables – dishwashers, washing machines, dryers, refrigerators, freezers and televisions, though not smartphones or laptops – to make spare parts available to consumers and repair shops. In 2023, the European Union also introduced right-to-repair legislation. And more companies were obliged to match the trend, encouraging consumers to return superseded items, such as outdated mobile phones, for reconditioning, resale or recycling, to reduce electronic waste. The United Nations estimated that in 2021 every person on the planet produced on average 7.6 kilograms of e-waste (anything with a plug or battery), generating 57 million tonnes worldwide. Only a sixth was recycled. The remainder, containing valuable metals and rare earths that could be reused, as well as toxins such as mercury, was just dumped.[119]

Besides its Anti-Obsolescence Drive, the PAG introduced modest incentive payments for those volunteering to design websites and inform communities of sharing services. The business community lobbied intensively against this, saying it would slow economic growth. But the public were on the side of the PAG, which held its nerve.

THE MEDIA COMMONS

A very different form of commoning took place in the media. In 2022, a group known as the Media Reform Coalition released a 'Manifesto for a People's Media', reimagining the media as a commons. The largely private mainstream media were owned and dominated by the plutocracy. And social media, especially Meta and Twitter, had morphed into a means of amplifying political polarization and fomenting far-right populism by facilitating the spread of 'fake news' and misinformation. More than two-thirds of the UK public said they did not trust the media to be objective and non-partisan.[120]

The PAG took ideas from the manifesto in announcing a plan to mutualize the BBC and Channel 4, ending sole central government and bureaucratic control in favour of a devolved quasi-cooperative model, backed by public funding. The public would have a say in decisions, electing representatives to sit on governance boards, proposing programmes for commissioning, or sitting on panels to scrutinize coverage. This was a form of public work, for which compensation for those who allocated time to it was expected. The PAG also set aside funds to support local media, including over 300 community radio stations, that pursued a commons model. Readers or listeners could pay a small monthly fee to become direct owners as shareholders, with elected members serving on management boards.

CULTURAL COMMONING

The PAG realized, just in time, that capitalism had commodified time to such an extent that there had been a severe squeeze on two uses of time on which civilization, democracy and progressive politics depend, namely public participation in culture and active participation in political life.

Recall that, in ancient Greece, going to the amphitheatre to watch one of the great tragedies or comedies was more than entertainment; it was about learning empathy and compassion, about socializing the emotions and strengthening morality. By contrast, capitalism has always thrived on making the masses spend as much time as possible on labour and then on consumption and recuperation in preparation for more labour, not on mental enlargement, which leads the mind in potentially subversive directions.

Under capitalism, culture has tended to divide people along class lines, delivering dumbed-down entertainment for the masses while the elite and bourgeoisie were the main audiences for 'highbrow' culture. How could the PAG encourage people to use more of their time in cultural activities of all kinds? Governments had long subsidized museums, theatres, art galleries and orchestras, although successive Conservative governments had slashed funding for most cultural commons. However, people on low incomes, particularly youth, could not afford most ticketed events or were drawn by alternatives.

So, the PAG adapted a policy pioneered in Italy in 2016, France in 2021, and Spain and Germany in 2022. In France, the *pass Culture*, a youth culture pass, gave every eighteen-year-old €300 as an app-based voucher to spend on cinema, museum, theatre or concert tickets, as well as on books, art materials, arts courses, musical instruments or a subscription to a cultural digital platform. It was then extended to the over-fifteens. The Spanish government did something similar, worth €400. The German scheme gave a €200 *Kulturpass*.

However, the PAG recognized that this policy was paternalistic and recalled the ill-conceived subsidy given during the pandemic to reward people going to restaurants. The French scheme allowed too wide an array of items, defeating the social commoning objective. The PAG wanted to encourage public participation in interactive, reflective culture, to overcome what some called a culture deficit. With that in mind, it gave a £200 voucher to all school-leavers, to be used within three years of leaving school on museums, art galleries or theatres. It rejected criticism that this was elitist by asserting that the objective was to revive appreciation for the country's cultural traditions and the spirit of cultural commons.

The Slow Time Movement

> To see a World in a Grain of Sand
> And a Heaven in a Wild Flower
> Hold Infinity in the palm of your hand
> And Eternity in an hour.
> — William Blake, 'Auguries of Innocence', *c.* 1803

Commoning is usually slow, in respecting time shared. The Slow Time Movement in Britain, established after the PAG came to power, derived from a tradition that began with a flamboyant protest by Carlo Petrini against the opening of a McDonald's in central Rome in 1986. This sparked the creation of the Slow Food Movement which, renamed the Slow Movement, subsequently spread to about 150 countries. In 2004, Carl Honoré published a seminal book, *In Praise of Slow*, which the *Financial Times* described as 'to the Slow Movement what *Das Kapital* is to communism'. According to Honoré:

> It is a cultural revolution against the notion that faster is always better. The Slow philosophy is not about doing everything at a snail's pace. It's about seeking to do everything at the right speed. Savouring the hours and minutes rather than just counting them. Doing everything as well as possible, instead of as fast as possible. It's about quality over quantity in everything from work to food to parenting.[121]

The pandemic strengthened support for the ideas motivating the Slow Movement, which gelled into a national Slow Time Movement. This meshed with degrowth sentiments and the revival of commoning promoted by the PAG. It was supported by the common dividends, which gave people the economic security to slow down and spend more time on their own activities. In his book, Honoré argued that fear was the main obstacle to slowing down in a world geared to maximizing economic growth and productivity. Fear comes from insecurity, from uncertainty, from being a supplicant. By providing income security, common dividends helped reduce that fear, creating conditions in which slow time could flourish.

Lessons had been learned from the Slow Food Movement, one of which was the fast-food paradox. On average, particularly in rich countries, humans eat much more than previous generations, and foods from all over the world are available in most cities. But, paradoxically, humanity as a whole eats a much less diversified set of foods than existed in antiquity, among hunter-gatherers.[122]

Tastes have been homogenized by commodification. Arable land has been concentrated on a few cereals and other high-energy-yielding crops, while nearly three-quarters of agricultural land is devoted to domestic animals, to be slaughtered as quickly as feasible, then distributed and eaten as quickly as possible. Thousands of plant species that were harvested in the past have been jettisoned. A counter movement was needed, not only to produce a culture of slow food but also a recovery of local plants and other sources of nutrition.

An unanticipated finding from a large-scale basic-income pilot in Madhya Pradesh in India in 2011–12 was that payment of a monthly basic income was soon followed by revival of local crop varieties. These had previously been marginalized by the government's paternalistic public distribution system that provided subsidized food consisting of standardized varieties of rice and wheat.[123] With their basic income, locals started to regrow traditional local varieties and sell them in local markets.

Time in work and time in slow-food production and consumption were outcomes of a rollback of state paternalism. Shortly after the introduction of common dividends, the same was observed across the UK.

Deliberative Democracy:
The Revival of *Schole*

> He who knows only his own side of the case knows
> little of that. His reasons may be good, and no one
> may have been able to refute them. But if he is equally
> unable to refute the reasons on the opposite side, if
> he does not so much as know what they are, he has no
> ground for preferring either opinion . . . Nor is it enough
> that he should hear the opinions of adversaries from
> his own teachers, presented as they state them, and
> accompanied by what they offer as refutations. He must
> be able to hear them from persons who actually believe
> them . . . he must know them in their most plausible and
> persuasive form.
> — John Stuart Mill, *On Liberty*, 1859

The privatization of public discourse has been the dubious achievement of social media. Successful sustainable democracies require extensive social networks based on trust, strong civil-society institutions, shared stories and a robust commons. But social media weakened all of those elements. Jonathan Haidt, an American psychologist, depicted the leading American social-media platforms, Facebook and Twitter, as having built a new Tower of Babel. The key moment was when they offered users the ability to click 'like', retweet or share, encouraging them to treat connectivity as a superficial game in which the objective was to generate viral posts with provocative, unreflective messages designed to trigger outrage.[124]

Social media intensify communication-without-community, leading to silos of dialogues of the deaf. It is not free speech if only certain voices can be heard or are heard disproportionately loudly. And it is not free speech if people feel they have too little time to listen to the voices of those with whom they expect to disagree.

Democracy depends on widely held acceptance of the legitimacy of rules and norms, and a need to search for compromise. But social media have eroded trust in public institutions and polarized political and other opinion. They have become a conduit for bullying and intimidating people who speak up for unpopular causes or voice divergent opinions, inducing self-censorship and loss of diverse voices. Academics have become afraid to express views that might be controversial in case this leads to mob attacks online and loss of a job. Social media have become zones of anger and aggression.

They play on a weakness of democracy that was understood and articulated brilliantly by James Madison (1751–1836), a drafter of the US Constitution. In Federalist Paper No. 10, written in 1787, he recognized that because polarizing factions tend to rush to judgement, institutions had to be constructed to slow down action and favour compromise and the deliberative search for the truth.[125]

The ancient Romans worried about *imperium* – unaccountable power in the hands of the state – and *dominium*, unaccountable power in the hands of a few individuals, interests or corporations. In the modern era, aided by social media, both gained strength, but there was a relative shift to *dominium*. Both required institutions to combat them, for the same reason Madison highlighted.

Claims on social media can immediately go viral without contradiction, aided by the platform algorithms that feed users with messages they can be expected to 'like' and 'share' based on their posting history. And artificial intelligence programs are capable of spreading falsehoods without any constraint.[126] ChatGPT, for example – where GPT stands for 'generative pre-trained transformers' – can generate lengthy, entirely false articles that appear to be written by real people. This is in addition to digital alteration of photographs, which anyone with a modern smartphone can do, as well as 'deep fake' videos in which real people can be made to say things they have never said and would never say in reality.

The most frightening danger is political manipulation. As one well-qualified observer argued, 'Our information ecosystem is trending towards unreality.'[127] Russian misinformation campaigns on social media, for example, helped secure the election of Donald Trump in 2016 and the Brexit vote in Britain the same year.

And the intention of much political misinformation is not necessarily to support a particular candidate or cause but to sow doubt and confusion, much like the tactics of the tobacco industry on the health effects of smoking or those of Big Oil in seeking to discredit climate science. The intention is to create weary resignation with the political system, leading to disengagement that leaves the field open to extremists. If you believe that all politicians tell lies, what does it matter if a Trump or a Johnson does this?

So, what was to be done? The PAG launched a two-pronged

initiative. First, it required social-media platforms to ensure posts were made by identifiable real people and not bots, and to make it harder to share posts beyond a restricted number of contacts, obliging people to use more time if they wished to do so. These strengthened policies that were being grudgingly adopted by some social media platforms in the early 2020s.

The second prong was to counter fake news and misinformation, and manipulation by powerful interests, by going back to the foundational principles of democracy and respecting John Stuart Mill's argument. This required a twenty-first-century reinvention of deliberative democracy, a participatory kind epitomized by ancient Greece. The PAG aimed to resurrect *schole* as quality time preserved for public participation in the life of society, in the *polis*, in the *agora*, or, in modern parlance, in the village hall or town square.

In his famous tour of the United States in the 1830s, Alexis de Tocqueville was struck by the active involvement of citizens in clubs, societies and politics. Earlier, Tom Paine's 1776 pamphlet *Common Sense*, said to be in every cabin in North America, drew on Aristotle's idea of *philia*, civic friendship, in lauding the idea of deliberative democracy taking place between friends. It required time set aside for real work.

Deliberative democracy can combat misinformation because it obliges us to hear and assess all shades of opinion, on a common factual basis, instead of being prisoners of confirmation bias, listening only to those ideas that reinforce our existing beliefs. It can thereby weaken wedge politics in which politicians and political parties deliberately emphasize a divisive issue (such as immigration) intended to split off part of the support base of other parties by appealing to their prejudices.

Deliberative democracy can also foster egalitarianism by discussing issues based on the veil-of-ignorance principle, consideration of policies not knowing where you yourself would be in the distribution of outcomes. When people are required or encouraged to think in this way, they tend to favour more egalitarian policies.

In this respect, the common dividends played a dual role. Experiments in the 1980s had shown that people with basic security were more likely to be altruistic and tolerant of others.[128] Other experiments showed that deliberative democracy increases support for altruism and the idea that no one should fall below a given social-protection floor, embodied in the concept of common dividends.

One problem was that many felt they did not have the time to participate in politics. And it is true that, in the tertiary time era, the time for leisure in the ancient Greek sense was squeezed by commercial pressures to labour, work and consume ever more. So the PAG applied mild moral pressure to help change attitudes. Everybody entitled to common dividends was asked to sign a statement committing themselves to register to vote if they had not already done so, to voting in general elections and to participating in at least one political meeting a year in their community.

At these meetings, all political movements with 10 per cent or more support according to recent opinion polls – that is, indicating current support – had representatives to state their views on topical issues. And to ensure people had the time to attend and participate, the PAG created a new public holiday, Deliberation Day.

Commoning as Transformation

How do all the old and novel forms of commoning relate to the transformation away from rentier capitalism and dour labourism? Quite simply, they reflect a change in lifestyle. During the pandemic, many people experienced what psychologists call 'languishing', an emotional state of being in limbo, with feelings of aimlessness and low mood, all of which leads to depression. It affected about one in ten adults in many countries, including Britain.[129]

Community involvement and commoning are positive ways of overcoming this sense of apathy. Commoning is conducive to societal conviviality, which is known to improve the mental health of individuals and communities. In turn, good mental health improves connectivity with others, through commoning and the sharing of resources.[130]

The PAG understood that instead of promoting endless GDP growth and endless consumption of commodities, the state had to foster Slow Time, deliberative democracy as *schole*, and commoning as future-oriented, decommodifying work. We have to live in the Now, while also thinking of guarding and reviving a sense of the Future. This way of thinking is quite different from living just for the day, believing that there is no Tomorrow.

The perspective is a form of singularity, a concept associated with Silicon Valley and artificial intelligence, but here symbolizing a time when the collective mind focuses equally on the Present and the Future. What we do today must be shaped by what we want, or could expect, to do in the fore-seeable future. We cannot ignore the future today. We must strengthen respect for the precautionary principle, the ecological imperative of the twenty-first century. This amounts to a restoration of human humility, a reversal of René Descartes' hubristic seventeenth-century assertion of the supremacy of humans in the cosmos that was harnessed to the dictates of industrial capitalism and that shaped industrial time.

Green and blue commoning is a form of work that is not labour but whose enormous value has been disregarded in mainstream economic accounting. The Land Trust conducted a survey in 2016 that indicated that every £1 invested in green-space activities contributed up to £30 to public health and wellbeing, a finding that not only strengthened the momentum towards community gardening, allotmenteering, woodland revival, rewilding and even guerrilla gardening, but also strengthened the urgency of revising what is meant by economic growth. The PAG could not miss the chance to do something transformative there too.

Commoning is a form of activity in which everybody has skin in the game – that is, they are all potentially affected by its improvement or degradation. For Nassim Nicholas Taleb, the commons adheres to the Golden Rule in being 'a space in which you are treated by others the way you treat them'.[131] He cited the Nobel Prize winner Elinor Ostrom as having shown that groups below a certain size usually act in the collective interest, beyond that size much less so. For the PAG, reviving social solidarity required a particular form of devolution and of governance, which is why commoning was central to the transformation.

Postscript

The famous adage that small is beautiful, associated with the economist E. F. Schumacher, has been rephrased as 'local is beautiful'. However, commoning can only thrive by recognizing that *work* as a form of time use is not frightening or alienating; it is liberating. The human condition is to want to work, alongside spending time on leisure and commoning. Karl Marx memorably remarked when celebrating the masterpiece of the great Puritan poet John Milton: 'Milton produced *Paradise Lost* in the way that a silkworm produces silk, as the expression of his own nature.'[1] An underlying theme of that epic poetic work is that, in the Garden of Eden, the boundary between work and pleasure doesn't exist.

The politics of time has crystallized slowly, with elements of all earlier time regimes figuring in today's repositioning of the collective imagination. The rigidities of industrial time have gone but Taylorism has remained, backed by the panopticon apparatus driven by information technology. Progressive policies intended to combat the worst excesses of industrial time have continued but with diminished relevance in the tertiary time era. Tertiary time has been chaotic. But it is worse than that. Reliance on old policies suited to industrial time has hindered the evolution of a progressive politics for the challenge that has existed since the beginning of time – how to achieve time freedom and time equality.

The politics and the economics hinge on finding the appropriate way of apportioning time use. The ancient Greeks offered a model. But the historical error of most critics of capitalism, and certainly of the political parties ostensibly opposed to it, has been to allow advocates for capitalism to frame the discussion of time use as little more than a dualism between time for labour and time for consumption.

Why, the critics of capitalism should ask themselves, did we allow real leisure to disappear? Why did we not rescue commoning when apologists for capitalism were dismissing it as idling and parasitic? Why did feminists not succeed in having care legitimized as work? Perhaps it took the excesses of rentier capitalism and the growth of the precariat to erode, finally, the legitimacy of the labourism of the twentieth century. Perhaps it took the Covid pandemic to clarify what should have been obvious all along, that care and commoning were 'essential services'.

Whatever the reasons, the Future is back, and time is surely being emancipated and, better still, being shared more equitably – in the mind of social reformers, if not yet in reality. A politics of time can only improve from there. Bring it on.

Notes

In the following notes, page numbers have been provided in references to *The Economist* and other periodicals only when the source consulted was the printed, rather than the online, version.

PREFACE

1. S. Moore, 'The way we once lived is now redundant. We need to reinvent ourselves', *Guardian*, 20 April 2020.
2. G. J. Whitrow, *What is Time?* (Oxford: Oxford University Press, 2003), p. 1.
3. O. Burkeman, *Four Thousand Weeks: Time Management for Mortals* (London: Vintage, 2021).
4. A. Einstein, 'Relativity and the problem of space', in idem, *Ideas and Opinions*, trans. Carl Seelig (New York: Crown, 2010), p. 363.

CHAPTER 1: TIME IN ANCIENT TIMES

1. J. Kamrin, 'Telling time in ancient Egypt', Heilbrunn Timeline of Art History, Metropolitan Museum of Art (website), February 2017.
2. Christmas Day was set on 25 December because it was around the time of the winter solstice, not because there was reason to believe that Christ was born on that day. The date for Easter has remained variable because it was linked to the time of a full moon, rather than to knowledge of when the crucifixion took place.
3. W. Shakespeare, *Julius Caesar*, Act 4, Scene 3, ll. 218–24.

4. E. C. White, *Kaironomia: On the Will-to-Invent* (Ithaca, NY, and London: Cornell University Press, 1987), p. 13.

5. O. O'Neill, 'The age of the cyber romantics is coming to an end', *Noema Magazine*, 4 October 2017.

6. H. Arendt, *The Human Condition* (Chicago: Chicago University Press, 1958), p. 82.

7. Quoted in ibid., p. 325.

8. Noted in J. Suzman, *Work: A History of How We Spend Our Time* (London: Bloomsbury, 2020), p. 80.

9. F. Nietzsche, *The Gay Science: With a Prelude in Rhymes and an Appendix of Songs*, trans. Walter Kaufmann (New York: Knopf Doubleday, 2010), p. 108.

10. S. Mann and R. Cadman, 'Does being bored make us more creative?', *Creativity Research Journal* 16:2 (2014), pp. 165–73; F. Kets de Vries, 'Doing nothing and nothing to do: the hidden value of empty time and boredom', Faculty and Research Working Paper, INSEAD, Fontainebleau, 2014; J. D. Eastwood et al., 'A desire for desires: boredom and its relation to alexithymia', *Personality and Individual Differences* 42 (2007), pp. 1035–45.

11. Seneca, *On the Shortness of Life*, trans. C. D. N. Costa (London: Penguin, 2004), p. 14.

12. Ibid., p. 23.

13. Quoted in B. Hughes, *The Hemlock Cup: Socrates, Athens and the Search for the Good Life* (London: Jonathan Cape, 2010), p. 59.

14. J. Lucassen, *The Story of Work* (New Haven, CT: Yale University Press, 2021).

15. Suzman, *Work*, pp. 110–14.

16. Ibid., p. 114.

17. M. Hudson, . . . *And Forgive Them Their Debts: Lending, Foreclosures and Redemption from Bronze Age Finance to the Jubilee Year* (Dresden: Islet, 2018); see also D. Graeber, *Debt: The First 5,000 Years* (Brooklyn: Melville House, 2014).

18. Quoted by Michael Hudson in B. Marcetic, 'When debts become unpayable, they should be forgiven', *Jacobin*, 23 December 2021.

19. J. Cruddas, *The Dignity of Labour* (Oxford: Polity Press, 2021). This book by a Labour MP was enthusiastically endorsed on publication by the leader of the Labour Party, Sir Keir Starmer.

20. For an extended discussion of the Charter of the Forest, see G. Standing, *Plunder of the Commons: A Manifesto for Sharing Public Wealth* (London: Pelican, 2019), Chapter 1.

21. A. Smith, *The Wealth of Nations* (Harmondsworth: Penguin, 1979), Book 2, p. 431.

22. K. Marx, *The Economic and Philosophical Manuscripts of 1844*, in *Marx/Engels Collected Works*, Vol. 3 (New York: International Publishers, 1976), p. 274.

23. M. Maxey, *Occupations of the Lower Classes in Roman Society* (Chicago: University of Chicago Press, 1975).

24. P. Mason, 'Time for postcapitalism', *Social Europe*, 1 July 2019.

25. J. Habermas, *Legitimation Crisis* (London: Heinemann, 1976).

CHAPTER 2: THE AGRARIAN TIME ERA

1. For related analyses, see W. Heydebrand, 'The time dimension in Marxian social theory', *Time and Society* 12:2/3 (2003), pp. 147–88; D. Harvey, *The Limits to Capital*, 2nd edn (London: Verso, 2006); N. Castree, 'The spatio-temporality of capitalism', *Time and Society* 18:1, pp. 26–61; P. Bourdieu, *Pascalian Meditations* (Palo Alto, CA: Stanford University Press, 2000).

2. Suzman, *Work*.

3. C. D. Liddy, 'Urban enclosure riots: risings of the commons in English towns, 1480–1525', *Past and Present* 226:1 (2015), pp. 41–77.

4. G. J. Whitrow, 'Introduction', in F. Greenaway (ed.), *Time and the Sciences* (Paris: United Nations Educational, Scientific and Cultural Organization, 1979), pp. 1–2.

5. Standing, *Plunder of the Commons*.

6. L. Lohmann, 'Forestry, politics and violent conflict', in M. Suliman (ed.), *Ecology and Violent Conflict* (London: Zed Books, 1999).

7. See S. Harper et al., 'Women and fisheries: contribution to food security and local economies', *Marine Policy* 39:1 (May 2013), pp. 56–63; S. Harper, 'Contributions by women to fisheries economies', *Coastal Management* 45:2 (February 2017), pp. 91–106; M. D. Chapman, 'Women's fishing in Oceania', *Human Ecology* 15 (1987), pp. 267–88; N. Weeratunge et al., 'Gleaner, fisher, trader, processor: understanding gendered employment in fisheries and aquaculture', *Fish and Fisheries* 11 (2010), pp. 405–20.

8. D. McGregor, 'Coming full circle: indigenous knowledge, environment, and our future', *American Indian Quarterly* 28:3 (2004), pp. 385–410.

9. K.-L. Thompson et al., 'A review of indigenous knowledge and participation in environmental monitoring', *Ecology and Society* 25:2 (2020).

10.   Quoted in P. A. J. Pettit, *The Royal Forests of Northamptonshire: A Study in Their Economy, 1558–1714*, Vol. 23 (Northampton: Northamptonshire Record Society, 1968), p. 163.

11.   J. Watt, 'Public or plebs: the changing meaning of "The Commons", 1381–1549', in H. Pryce and J. Watts (eds), *Power and Identity in the Middle Ages: Essays in Memory of Rees Davies* (Oxford: Oxford University Press, 2007), pp. 242–60.

12.   A. Young, *The Farmer's Tour Through the East of England*, Vol. 4 (London: Strahan & Nicoll, 1771), p. 361.

13.   S. Nagyszalanczy, *The Art of Fine Tools* (Newtown, CT: Taunton Press, 2000), p. 131.

14.   The discussion of Franklin draws on Suzman, *Work*, pp. 167–8.

15.   B. Franklin, *Wit and Wisdom from Poor Richard's Almanack* (Chelmsford, MA: Courier Corporation, 1999), p. 8.

16.   B. Franklin, letter to Benjamin Vaughan, 26 July 1784, Founders Online, National Archives (website).

17.   B. Franklin, *The Autobiography of Benjamin Franklin, 1706–1757* (Carlisle, MA: Applewood Books, 2008), p. 126.

18.   Ibid., pp. 182–3.

19.   R. A. Church, 'Nineteenth-century clock technology in Britain, the United States, and Switzerland', *Economic History Review* 28:4 (1975), pp. 616–30.

20.   E. Sbaraini, 'What 18th-century suicide inquests tell us about growing old in Georgian England', The Conversation, 26 August 2021.

CHAPTER 3: INDUSTRIAL TIME: TRIUMPH OF LABOURISM

1.   Suzman, *Work*, p. 231.

2.   J. Uglow, *The Lunar Men: The Friends Who Made the Future* (2003). The book has appeared in several editions, each with a different subtitle.

3.   G. Standing, *The Corruption of Capitalism: Why Rentiers Thrive and Work Does Not Pay*, 2nd edn (London: Biteback, 2021), pp. 17–18.

4.   Note that the factory system essentially pre-dated the emergence of dominant capitalists with just one owner in charge of a factory, so that a few owners of machines might be operating alongside each other in the factory.

5.   R. Williams, *Keywords: A Vocabulary of Culture and Society* (New York: Oxford University Press, 1985), p. 161.

6. K. Polanyi, *The Great Transformation: The Political and Economic Origins of Our Times* (Boston, MA: Beacon Press, 2001), pp. 35, 37.

7. Ibid., pp. 41, 191.

8. A. Malm, *Fossil Capital: The Rise of Steam Power and the Roots of Global Warming* (London and Brooklyn, NY: Verso, 2016), p. 192.

9. D. Sobel, *Longitude: The True Story of a Lone Genius Who Solved the Greatest Scientific Problem of His Time* (London: Fourth Estate, 1995).

10. E. P. Thompson, 'Time, work discipline and industrial capitalism', *Past and Present* 38:1 (1967), pp. 58–97; see also idem, *The Making of the English Working Class* (Harmondsworth: Penguin, 1968).

11. Thompson, 'Time, work discipline and industrial capitalism', p. 70.

12. I. Pinchbeck, *Women Workers and the Industrial Revolution, 1750–1850* (London: Routledge & Sons, 1930).

13. A. Douglas, *The Feminization of American Culture* (New York: Farrar, Straus & Giroux, 1998).

14. K. Marx, *Capital*, Vol. 1: *A Critical Analysis of Capitalist Production*, trans. S. Moore and E. Aveling (New York: International Publishers, 1967), p. 167.

15. J. S. Mill, *Principles of Political Economy* (London: Longmans, Green & Co., 1848), Book II, Chapter VII, p. 286.

16. J. Ruskin, *The Stones of Venice*, Vol. 2: *The Sea Stories* (London: Smith Elder, 1853), pp. 161–2.

17. K. Mannheim, *Ideology and Utopia: An Introduction to the Sociology of Knowledge*, trans. L. Wirth and E. Shils (London: Routledge & Kegan Paul, 1936).

18. Quoted in F. MacCarthy, *William Morris: A Life for Our Time* (New York: Knopf, 1995), p. v.

19. E. Hobsbawm, 'Birth of a holiday: the First of May', in idem, *Uncommon People: Resistance, Rebellion and Jazz* (London: Abacus, 1998), pp. 150–70.

20. P. Kropotkin, *The Conquest of Bread* (London: Elephant Editions, 1985), p. 33.

21. Quoted in 'The growth of the asylum – a parallel world', Historic England (website).

22. For a moving analysis, see E. R. Sigurdarddóttir, 'Women and madness in the 19th century: the effect of oppression on women's mental health', Háskóli Íslands (Iceland), Hugvísindasvið, Department of English, September 2013.

23. J. Rose, 'The workers in the Workers' Educational Association, 1903–1950', *Albion* 21:4 (Winter 1989), pp. 591–608.

24. Suzman, *Work*, p. 241.

25. 'Testimony of Frederick W. Taylor at hearings before the Special Committee of the House of Representatives, January 1912', reprinted in *Bulletin of the Taylor Society*, 11:3–4 (June–August 1926), p. 135.

26. S. Crowther, 'Henry Ford: why I favor five days' work with six days' pay', *The World's Work* 52 (May–October 1926), p. 513.

27. H. Braverman, *Labour and Monopoly Capital: The Degradation of Work in the Twentieth Century* (New York: Monthly Review Press, 1974).

28. R. Dore, *British Factory, Japanese Factory: The Origins of National Diversity in Industrial Relations* (London: George Allen & Unwin, 1973).

29. P. Bischoff, 'Surveillance camera statistics: which cities have the most CCTV cameras?', Comparitech, 11 July 2022.

30. C. Fourier, 'Accusation of the uncertain sciences', in J. Beecher and R. Bienvenu (eds), *The Utopian Vision of Charles Fourier: Selected Texts on Work, Love, and Passionate Attraction*, trans. J. Beecher and R. Bienvenu (London: Jonathan Cape, 1972).

31. Alexis de Tocqueville, *Discours de M. de Tocqueville sur le droit au travail* (Paris: Librairie L. Curmer, 1848), pp. 7–9.

32. K. Marx, *The Class Struggles in France 1848–1850*, trans. F. Engels (Moscow: Progress Publishers, 1968), p. 62.

33. W. E. Forbath, 'The ambiguities of free labor: labor and the law in the gilded age', *Wisconsin Law Review* 4 (1985), pp. 767–817.

34. Ibid.; see also C. L. Estlund, 'An American perspective on fundamental labour rights', in B. Hepple (ed.), *Social and Labour Rights in a Global Context* (Cambridge: Cambridge University Press, 2002), pp. 192–214.

35. T. H. Marshall, *Citizenship and Social Class* (Cambridge: Cambridge University Press, 1950), p. 80.

36. G. Standing, 'The ILO: an agency for globalization?', *Development and Change* 39:3 (2008), pp. 355–84.

37. R. Hirshon, 'Law and the billable hour', *ABA Journal*, February 2002.

38. G. B. Shaw, *The Doctor's Dilemma: Preface on Doctors* (Project Gutenberg ebook, 2012).

39. Marx, *Capital*, Vol. 1, p. 410.

40. B. Costea and P. Watt, 'How a Soviet miner from the 1930s helped create today's intense corporate workplace culture', The Conversation, 29 June 2021.

41. S. H. Slichter, 'The current labor policies of American industries', *Quarterly Journal of Economics* 43:3 (May 1929), pp. 393–435.

42. Suzman, *Work*, pp. 127–30.
43. Standing, 'The ILO: an agency for globalization?'
44. M. A. Bienefeld, 'The normal week under collective bargaining', *Economica* 36:142 (May 1969), pp. 172–92.
45. J. Passey, 'How the Victorians invented the "staycation"', The Conversation, 13 August 2021.

CHAPTER 4: TERTIARY TIME: LABOURISM'S LAST LEGS

1. G. Standing, *The Corruption of Capitalism: Why Rentiers Thrive and Work Does Not Pay*, 3rd edn (London: Biteback, 2021).
2. For an elaboration, see G. Standing, *The Precariat: The New Dangerous Class*, 4th edn (London: Bloomsbury, 2021); idem, *A Precariat Charter: From Denizens to Citizens* (London: Bloomsbury, 2014).
3. C. Burlina and A. Rodríguez-Pose, 'Alone and lonely: the economic cost of solitude for regions in Europe', CEPR Discussion Paper DP16674, Centre for Economic Policy Research, October 2021.
4. N. Hertz, *The Lonely Century: A Call to Reconnect* (Strongsville, OH: Scepter, 2021).
5. D. Schawbel, 'How technology created a lonely workplace', MarketWatch, 2 December 2018.
6. S. Storm, 'Why the rich get richer and interest rates go down', Institute for New Economic Thinking, 13 September 2021.
7. G. Crocker, *Basic Income and Sovereign Money: The Alternative to Economic Crisis and Austerity Policy* (London: Palgrave Macmillan, 2020).
8. B.-C. Han, 'Why revolution is no longer possible', Our World, 3 November 2015.
9. F. Hirsch, *The Social Limits to Growth* (London: Routledge & Kegan Paul, 1977), p. 5.
10. 'Free exchange: assume the positional', *The Economist*, 21 August 2021, p. 54.
11. T. Mitchell and T. Hale, 'China's nanny state: why Xi is cracking down on gaming and private tutors', *Financial Times*, 6 August 2021.
12. J. Preston, 'Facebook, the metaverse and the monetisation of higher education', The Conversation, 9 November 2021.
13. E. Houghtaling, 'I sold my eggs for an Ivy League education – but was it worth it?', *Guardian*, 7 November 2021.

14. A. Berg and C. Moore, 'Charles Koch gave $25m to our university. Has it become a rightwing mouthpiece?', *Guardian*, 2 May 2019.

15. G. Standing, *The Blue Commons: Rescuing the Economy of the Sea* (London: Pelican, 2022), p. 368.

16. M. Foucault, *The Birth of Bio-Politics: Lectures at the Collège de France, 1978–1979*, ed. F. Ewald and A. Fontana (Basingstoke: Palgrave Macmillan, 2010), p. 226.

17. L. Boltanski and E. Chiapello, *The New Spirit of Capitalism* (London: Verso, 2005), p. 312.

18. 'A special report on mobility: nomads at last', *The Economist*, 12 April 2008.

19. S. O'Connor, 'We are creeping towards a continuous working week', *Financial Times*, 14 September 2021.

20. Eurofound (European Foundation for the Improvement of Living and Working Conditions), *Sixth European Working Conditions Survey – Overview Report (2017 Update)* (Luxembourg: Publications Office of the European Union, 2017).

21. E. Zimmermann, 'More than 7 million people in Germany in precarious employment', World Socialist Web Site, 4 October 2021.

22. G. Standing, 'Global feminization through flexible labour', *Development and Change* 17:7 (1989), pp. 1077–95.

23. R. Partington, 'Almost 40% of UK workers get less than a week's notice of shift patterns', *Guardian*, 15 April 2021.

24. Cited in S. O'Connor, 'Look to the US for "workweek" laws that work', *Financial Times*, 11 May 2021.

25. Smith, *The Wealth of Nations*, Book I, Chapter 1, pp. 6–7.

26. G. Standing, 'Taskers in the precariat: confronting an emerging dystopia', in E. Paus (ed.), *Confronting Dystopia: The New Technological Revolution and the Future of Work* (Ithaca, NY: Cornell University Press, 2018), pp. 115–33.

27. C. Hernanz-Lizarraga, 'Dancers, podcasts and OnlyFans: how Covid popularised the side hustle', *Guardian*, 15 April 2021.

28. 'In numbers: Britain's precarious workforce', *Prospect*, 28 September 2021.

29. K. Wiggers, 'Google employs machine learning to boost translation capabilities to near-human level', Digital Trends, 30 September 2016.

30. J. Ashworth, 'Labour analysis reveals NHS staff were working more than 1.1 million hours of unpaid overtime every week even before Covid-19', Labour, 30 December 2020.

31. HESA (Higher Education Statistics Agency), 'Higher education staff statistics: UK, 2021–22', 17 January 2023.

32. National Tertiary Education Union, 'Issues paper: the growth of insecure employment in higher education', August 2020.

33. A. McKeen, 'With rising numbers of precarious appointments, more university teachers than ever face "invisible" barriers to doing their jobs and moving up', *Toronto Star*, 17 October 2018.

34. M. O'Hara, 'University lecturers on the breadline: is the UK following in America's footsteps?', *Guardian*, 17 November 2015.

35. P. Butler, 'Andy Haldane: "We have allowed the voluntary sector to wither"', *Guardian*, 22 May 2019.

36. A. Petrosyan, 'Time spent online per week per person in the United Kingdom (UK) 2005–2020', statista.com, 29 August 2022.

37. A. Perrin and S. Atske, 'About three-in-ten U.S. adults say they are "almost constantly" online', Pew Research Center, 26 March 2021.

38. Quoted in R. Foroohar, 'Automation exacts its toll on inequality', *Financial Times*, 30 January 2022.

39. K. Szreder, *The ABC of the Projectariat: Living and Working in a Precarious Art World* (Manchester: Manchester University Press, 2021), p. 41.

40. G. Deleuze, 'Postscript on the societies of control', *October* 59 (Winter 1992), pp. 3–7.

41. A. R. Hochschild, *The Managed Heart: Commercialisation of Human Feeling* (Berkeley, CA: University of California Press, 1983).

42. J. Bariso, 'Want to hire people with high emotional intelligence? Look for these 5 things', *Inc.*, 30 November 2020.

43. M. Foucault, *Discipline and Punish: The Birth of the Prison*, trans. A. Sheridan (New York: Vintage, 1995).

44. P. Tough, 'Dad's performance review', *New York Times Magazine*, 15 December 2002, p. 65.

45. A. R. Hochschild, 'When work becomes home and home becomes work', *California Management Review* 39:4 (1997), pp. 79–97.

46. Cited in G. Standing, 'Tertiary time: the precariat's dilemma', *Public Culture* 25:1 (2013), pp. 5–23, at p. 12.

47. J. Grant, 'Budget 2015 – what have the Tories got against young people?', Kilburn Unemployed Workers Group, 13 July 2015.

48. Private communication.

49. C. Cavendish, 'Better management, not endless training, will solve our corporate ills', *Financial Times*, 24 June 2022.

50. Cited in L. V. Anderson, 'Ethics trainings are even dumber than you think', *Slate*, 19 May 2016.

51. 'Workforce diversity programmes often fail, or backfire', *The Economist*, 25 August 2022.

52. S. Corbridge, 'Waiting in line, or the moral and material geographies of queue-jumping', in R. Lee and D. M. Smith (eds), *Geographies and Moralities* (Oxford: Blackwell, 2004), pp. 183–98.

53. S. Bean, 'Over three-quarters of UK workers reluctant to ask for time off for a health-related issue', Insight, 5 February 2019.

54. Editorial Team, '3 out of 4 people are forcing themselves into work despite being ill', HR News, 26 May 2022.

55. A. Shahvisi, 'British employers have long discouraged staff from taking sick days. Will coronavirus change that?', *Prospect*, 30 March 2020.

56. CIPD (Chartered Institute of Personnel and Development)/Simplyhealth, *Health and Well-being at Work Survey*, 2018.

57. P. Rubinstein, 'Why do ill people still come in to work?', BBC Worklife, 28 February 2019.

58. S. Kumar et al., 'Policies to reduce influenza in the workplace', *American Journal of Public Health* 103:8 (August 2013), pp. 1406–11.

59. B. Liversedge, '15.4 million days lost to work-related stress in 2017/18', British Safety Council, 1 November 2018.

60. R. Paulsen, *Empty Labour: Idleness and Workplace Resistance* (Cambridge: Cambridge University Press, 2014), p. 5.

61. G. Brown, *Sabotage: A Study in Industrial Conflict* (Nottingham: Spokesman, 1977).

62. J. C. Scott, *Two Cheers for Anarchism: Six Easy Pieces on Autonomy, Dignity and Meaningful Work and Play* (Princeton, NJ: Princeton University Press, 2012).

63. F. Campagna, *The Last Night: Anti-Work, Atheism, Adventure* (Winchester: Zero Books, 2013), p. 44.

64. A. McCain, 'Wasting time at work statistics [2022]', Zippia, 23 May 2022.

65. Paulsen, *Empty Labour*, p. 92.

66. H. Görg et al., 'Trust-based work-time and product improvements: evidence from firm level data', IZA Discussion Paper 8097, Institute of the Study of Labor, Bonn, April 2014.

67. B. Waterfield, 'German civil servant says he "did nothing for 14 years"', *Telegraph*, 12 April 2012.

68. D. Bolchover, *The Living Dead: Switched Off, Zoned Out: The Shocking Truth About Office Life* (Chichester: Capstone, 2005), p. 22.

69. K. Morris, 'Here's how many hours workers are actually productive (and what they're doing instead)', Zippia, 12 May 2022.

70. P. Rothlin and P. R. Werder, *Boreout! Overcoming Workplace Demotivation* (London: Kogan Page, 2007).

71. M. Power, *The Audit Society: Rituals of Verification* (London and New York: Oxford University Press, 1997).

72. C. Edwards, 'Occupational licensing', Cato Institute, 15 December 2022.

73. See G. Standing, *Work After Globalization: Building Occupational Citizenship* (Cheltenham: Elgar, 2009).

74. P. McLaughlin, M. D. Mitchell and A. Philpot, 'The effects of occupational licensure on competition, consumers and the workforce', Mercatus Center, George Mason University, Arlington, VA, November 2017, p. 2.

75. T. Boland, 'Job seeking is the religious pilgrimage of the 21st century', The Conversation, 19 August 2021.

76. Quoted in Boland, 'Job seeking is the religious pilgrimage of the 21st century'.

77. C. Kolmar, 'How many applications does it take to get a job [2022]', Zippia, 15 August 2022.

78. P. Capelli, *Why Good People Can't Get Jobs: The Skills Gap and What Companies Can Do About It* (Philadelphia, PA: Wharton Digital Press, 2012), p. 10.

79. D. Wessel, 'Software raises the bar for hiring', *Wall Street Journal*, 31 May 2012.

80. A. Fennell, 'Job search statistics in the UK', StandOut CV, June 2022.

81. Kolmar, 'How many applications does it take to get a job [2022]'.

82. Cited in Standing, *A Precariat Charter*, p. 158.

83. C. Fernandez-Araioz, B. Groysberg and N. Nohria, 'The definitive guide to recruiting in good times and bad', *Harvard Business Review*, May 2009.

84. Szreder, *The ABC of the Projectariat*, p. 12.

85. 'Were you rejected in one of the University of California job searches utilizing the unlawful "diversity statements"?', Leiter Reports: A Philosophy Blog, 28 January 2020.

86. Quoted in A. Chakelian, 'People work for weeks unpaid in "abhorrent practice" hidden by a gap in DWP data', *New Statesman*, 28 October 2020.

87. D. Webster, 'Benefit sanctions: Britain's secret penal system', Centre for Crime and Justice Studies, London, 26 January 2015.

88. Standing, *Plunder of the Commons*, pp. 150–1.

89. N. Folbre, 'Accounting for care in the United States', in M. Daly (ed.), *Care Work: The Quest for Security* (Geneva: International Labour Organization,

2001), pp. 175–91; see also J. Robinson and G. Godbey, *Time for Life: The Surprising Ways Americans Use Their Time* (University Park, PA: Penn State University Press, 1997).

90. D. Hallberg and A. Klevmarken, 'Time for children: a study of parents' time allocation', *Journal of Population Economics* 16:2 (May 2003), pp. 205–26.

91. C. Bean, *Independent Review of UK Economic Statistics: Final Report*, Cabinet Office, HM Treasury, March 2016, p. 84.

CHAPTER 5: REACTIONS TO TERTIARY TIME

1. A. Sen, *Development as Freedom* (New York: Alfred A. Knopf, 1999).

2. 'Dirty work', *The Economist*, 26 February 2022, p. 55.

3. J. Derrida, 'Remarks on deconstruction and pragmatism', in S. Critchley et al. (eds), *Deconstruction and Pragmatism* (London: Routledge, 1996), p. 96.

4. Y. Varoufakis, *Another Now: Dispatches from an Alternative Present* (London: Bodley Head, 2020).

5. M. Johnson, '"We need people to know the ABC of finance": facing up to the financial literacy crisis', *Financial Times*, 4 October 2021.

6. US Bureau of Labor Statistics, 'Characteristics of minimum wage workers, 2021', BLS Report 1098, April 2022.

7. A. Johnson Hess, 'Here's how many paid vacation days the typical American worker gets', CNBC, 6 July 2018.

8. A. McCulloch, 'UK employees fail to use holiday entitlement', *Personnel Today*, 25 May 2018.

9. E. D. Eaker, J. Pinsky and W. P. Castelli, 'Myocardial infarction and coronary death among women: psychosocial predictors from a 20-year follow-up of women in the Framingham study', *American Journal of Epidemiology* 135:8 (15 April 1992), pp. 854–64.

10. B. B. Gump and K. A. Matthews, 'Are vacations good for your health? The 9-year mortality experience after the multiple risk factor intervention trial', *Psychosomatic Medicine* 62:5 (September–October 2000), pp. 608–12.

11. J. Partridge, 'Behold London's "landscraper"! Google's new UK HQ – as long as the Shard is tall', *Guardian*, 1 July 2022.

12. L. Biggerstaff et al., 'Is your firm underperforming? Your CEO might be golfing too much', *Harvard Business Review*, 30 November 2016.

13. W. Beveridge, *Social Insurance and Allied Services* (London: HMSO, November 1942), p. 7.

14. Storm, 'Why the rich get richer and interest rates go down'.

15. N. N. Taleb, *The Black Swan: The Impact of the Highly Improbable* (London: Allen Lane, 2007).

16. N. N. Taleb, *Antifragile: How to Live in a World We Don't Understand* (London: Allen Lane, 2012).

17. A. Kessel, 'The (awareness of) uncertainty pandemic', *The Author* (Winter 2020), pp. 27–8.

18. Intergovernmental Panel on Climate Change, *Climate Change 2021: The Physical Science Basis*, Sixth Assessment Report (Geneva: IPCC, 2021).

19. R. Thaler and C. Sunstein, *Nudge: Improving Decisions about Health, Wealth and Happiness* (New Haven, CT: Yale University Press, 2008).

20. 'Nudge factor', *The Economist*, 30 July 2022, pp. 58–9.

21. J. Kantor and D. Streitfeld, 'Inside Amazon: wrestling big ideas in a bruising workplace', *New York Times*, 15 August 2015.

22. B.-C. Han, *Burnout Society* (Palo Alto, CA: Stanford University Press, 2015).

23. M. Hardt and A. Negri, *Empire* (Cambridge, MA: Harvard University Press, 2000).

24. N. N. Taleb, *Skin in the Game: Hidden Asymmetries in Daily Life* (London: Penguin, 2018), p. 107.

25. Z. Corbyn, '"Bossware is coming for almost every worker": the software you might not realize is watching you', *Guardian*, 27 April 2022.

26. A. Bernhardt, L. Kresge and R. Suleiman, *Data and Algorithms at Work: The Case for Worker Technology Rights* (Berkeley, CA: UC Berkeley Labor Center, 2021).

27. There have been several treatments of the difficulty of dealing with unstructured 'free' time. See, for instance, S. B. Linder, *The Harried Leisure Class* (New York: Columbia University Press, 1970); W. Leff and M. Haft, *Time Without Work* (Boston: South End Press, 1983).

28. I. Illich, *Shadow Work* (London: Marion Boyars, 1981).

29. A. Gorlick, 'Media multitaskers pay mental price, Stanford study shows', *Stanford News*, 24 August 2009.

30. M. Wainwright, 'Emails pose threat to IQ', *Guardian*, 22 April 2005.

31. E. Beddington, 'Multitasking is a menace – it should come with a health warning', *Guardian*, 5 July 2021.

32. P. Hirsch, I. Koch and J. Karbach, 'Putting a stereotype to the test: the case of gender differences in multitasking costs in task-switching and dual-task situations', *PLOS ONE* 14:8 (14 August 2019).

33. T. Roethke, 'Infirmity', in *Collected Poems of Theodore Roethke* (New York: Doubleday, 1966).

34. H. Simon, 'Designing organizations for an information-rich world', in M. Greenberger (ed.), *Computers, Communications, and the Public Interest* (Baltimore, MD: Johns Hopkins Press, 1971), p. 40.

35. M. Granovetter, 'The strength of weak ties', *American Journal of Sociology* 78:6 (1973), pp. 1360–80.

36. C. Young and C. Lim, 'Time as a network good: evidence from unemployment and the standard workweek', *Sociological Science* 1 (2014), pp. 10–27.

37. A. Gabbatt, '"A five-day wait for $5,000": the man who queues for the super-rich', *Guardian*, 5 May 2022.

38. K. Szreder, *The ABC of the Projectariat*, p. 15.

39. Han, *Burnout Society*, p. 8.

40. D. Foster, *Lean Out* (London: Repeater, 2016), p. 39.

41. J. Moeller et al., 'Highly engaged but burned out: intra-individual profiles in the US workforce', *Career Development International* 23:1 (2018), pp. 86–105.

42. A. McRobbie, 'Rethinking creative economy as radical social enterprise', *Variant* (Spring 2011), p. 32.

43. L. Parramore, 'America, Land of the Dying? Alarming study shows US killing its own population', *INET*, 8 August 2022.

44. J. Davies, *Sedated: How Modern Capitalism Created Our Mental Health Crisis* (London: Atlantic Books, 2021).

45. S. Taylor et al., 'Dependence and withdrawal associated with some prescribed medicines: an evidence review', Public Health England, 2019; 'Mental health prescriptions on the rise', *Insurance Journal*, 22 April 2021.

46. J. Davies, 'The new opium of the people', *IAI News* 95 (4 June 2021).

47. V. Mousteri, M. Daly and L. Delaney, 'Underemployment and psychological distress: propensity score and fixed effects estimate from two large UK samples', *Social Science and Medicine* 244, Article 112641 (January 2020).

48. A. Aubrey, 'Childhood stress may prime pump for chronic disease later', Shots (National Public Radio), 29 September 2015.

49. Y.-L. Liu, 'China's "involuted" generation', *New Yorker*, 14 May 2021.

50. Quoted in J. Kynge, 'China's young "lie flat" instead of accepting stress', *Financial Times*, 2 August 2021.

51. A. Yan, 'Young employees rebel against Chinese work ethic by being lazy, refusing overtime and hiding in the toilets', *South China Morning Post*, 3 January 2021.

52. K. Harknett, D. Schneider and R. Wolfe, 'Losing sleep over work scheduling? The relationship between work schedules and sleep quality for service sector workers', *SSM-Population Health* 12:100681 (21 October 2020).

53. D. Schneider and K. Harknett, 'Consequences of routine work-schedule instability for worker health and well-being', *American Sociological Review* 84:1 (2019), pp. 82–114.

54. J. Lalljee, 'Service workers have less stable work schedules – and it impacts their kids' health, sleep, and behavior', Business Insider, 2 February 2022.

55. K. Harknett and D. Schneider, 'Precarious work schedules and population health', *Health Affairs*, 13 February 2020; see also A. Irvine and N. Rose, 'How does precarious employment affect mental health? A scoping review and thematic synthesis of qualitative evidence from western economies', *Work, Employment and Society*, 6 December 2022.

56. 'Hail to the "chiefs"', *The Economist*, 30 January 2021, p. 53.

57. S. Ratnayake, 'CBT is wrong in how it understands mental illness', The Conversation, 3 March 2022.

58. T. J. Johnsen and O. Friborg, 'The effects of cognitive behavioral therapy as an anti-depressive treatment is falling: a meta-analysis', *Psychological Bulletin* 141:4, pp. 747–68.

59. Cited in R. Kelley, 'Being well: I've got a feeling', *The Idler*, March–April 2022, pp. 142–4.

60. W. Shakespeare, *Macbeth*, Act 5, Scene 5, ll. 23–7.

61. S. O'Connor, 'Why are we all working so hard?', *Financial Times*, 7 June 2022.

62. In the USA, it can take those with disabilities up to three years to obtain benefits. And a growing number of states now insist on urine tests for illegal drugs, to determine whether claimants are 'deserving poor'. To add insult to injury, they must pay to be tested.

63. S. Wickham, L. Bentley, T. Rose and M. Whitehead, 'Effects on mental health of a UK welfare reform, Universal Credit: a longitudinal study', *Lancet* 5:3 (March 2020), pp. 157–64.

64. S. Arie, 'Doctors' concerns over universal credit are mounting', *BMJ* 363 (5 December 2018).

65. R. Adams, 'Free childcare policy "damages life chances" of poor children in England', *Guardian*, 19 August 2021.

66. P. Foster, 'Charities underpin the UK's social safety net as cost of living crisis bites', *Financial Times*, 7 August 2022.

67. A. Haldane, 'Charity: reweaving the social fabric after the crisis', *The Economist*, 24 April 2020.

68. F. Ryan, 'Millions of destitute Britons rely on charity handouts, yet ministers feel no shame', *Guardian*, 29 July 2021.

69. J. Goldblum and C. Shaddox, 'America's unspoken hygiene crisis', Century Foundation, 16 July 2021.

CHAPTER 6: TIME IN THE EYE OF COVID

1. D. Furceri et al., 'Covid-19 will raise inequality if past pandemics are any guide', VoxEU, 8 May 2020; see also J. P. Cuesta and S. A. Hannan, 'Recoveries after pandemics: the role of policies and structural features', IMF Working Paper Series WP/21/181, International Monetary Fund, Washington, DC, 9 July 2021.

2. D. Strauss and C. Smith, 'Runaway house prices: the "winners and losers" from the pandemic', *Financial Times*, 25 June 2021.

3. Office for National Statistics, 'Prevalence of ongoing symptoms following coronavirus (COVID- 19) infection in the UK', 2 February 2023.

4. I. Blake, 'Extreme heart care disruption linked to 30,000 excess deaths involving heart disease', British Heart Foundation, 2 November 2022.

5. P. Linde, 'James Davies: "Cutting down on work and spending the time on meaningful pursuits would be to the advantage of our mental health"', *El País*, 17 March 2022.

6. M. L. Pathirathna et al., 'Impact of the Covid-19 pandemic on suicidal attempts and death rates: a systematic review', *BMC Psychiatry* 22, Article 506 (28 July 2022).

7. Cited in S. O'Connor, 'There is a deepening mental health recession', *Financial Times*, 22 November 2022.

8. Quoted in 'Will the economic and psychological costs of covid-19 increase suicides?', *The Economist*, 5 October 2020.

9. Pathirathna et al., 'Impact of the Covid-19 pandemic on suicidal attempts and death rates'.

10. J. Twenge, 'How much is social media to blame for teens' declining mental health', Institute for Family Studies, 11 April 2022.

11. J. Burn-Murdoch, 'Smartphones and social media are destroying children's mental health', *Financial Times*, 9 March 2023.

12. E. Holt-White et al., *Wave 1 Initial Findings – Mental Health and Wellbeing*, COVID Social Mobility & Opportunities (COSMO) study, Briefing No. 4 (London: UCL Centre for Education Policy and Equalising Opportunities and the Sutton Trust, 2022).

13. NHS Digital, 'Mental health of children and young people in England 2022 – wave 3 follow up to the 2017 survey', 29 November 2022.

14. O'Connor, 'There is a deepening mental health recession'.

15. A. Raval, 'When your boss becomes your banker', *Financial Times*, 20 November 2022.

16. C. Jansson-Boyd, 'Covid-19 is giving us a new appreciation for physical shops', The Conversation, 12 February 2021.

17. R. Bowlby, *Back to the Shops: The High Street in History and the Future* (Oxford: Oxford University Press, 2022).

18. C. Ibbetson, 'Could Covid-19 save the high street', YouGov, 10 July 2020.

19. 'Take your child to work (every) day', *The Economist*, 22 May 2021, pp. 54–6. Statistics cited in the rest of this section are from the same source.

20. 'Update in progress', *The Economist*, 22 January 2022, p. 69.

21. Quoted in 'Free exchange: stay of execution', *The Economist*, 19 June 2021, p. 68.

22. See, for instance, D. Susskind, *A World Without Work: Technology, Automation and How We Should Respond* (London: Allen Lane, 2021).

23. R. Neate, 'End of the checkout queue? Stores rush to deploy till-free technology', *Guardian*, 23 October 2021.

24. 'Triumph of the Luddites', *The Economist*, 24 December 2022, p. 51.

25. P. Aghion et al., 'What are the labor and product market effects of automation? New evidence from France', CEPR Discussion Paper DP14443, Centre for Economic Policy Research, March 2020; idem, 'The effects of automation on labour demand: a survey of the literature', CEPR Discussion Paper DP16868, Centre for Economic Policy Research, February 2022.

26. D. Adachi, D. Kawaguchi and Y. Saito, 'Robots and employment: evidence from Japan, 1978–2017', VoxEU, 9 February 2021; J. Hirvonen, A. Stenhammar and J. Tuhkuri, 'New evidence on the effect of technology

on employment and skill demand', ETLA Working Papers 93, Research Institute of the Finnish Economy, Helsinki, 2022.

27. D. Autor, D. A. Mindell and E. B. Reynolds, *The Work of the Future: Building Better Jobs in an Age of Intelligent Machines* (Cambridge, MA: MIT Press, 2022).

28. OECD, *Job Retention Schemes During the COVID-19 Lockdown and Beyond* (Paris: OECD, October 2020).

29. L. Elliott, 'UK needs mini-furlough if Omicron hits economy, IMF says', *Guardian*, 14 December 2021; O. Jones, 'With Tories in revolt, Labour can push them to better protect the public from Covid', *Guardian*, 15 December 2021.

30. A. Lockey, 'Work shift: the pandemic kick-started new ways of thinking around employment', *RSA Journal* 1 (2022), p. 24.

31. S. O'Connor, 'Rot festers in the lower depths of the British labour market', *Financial Times*, 3 May 2022.

32. A. Hern, '"Eat out to help out" may have caused sixth of Covid clusters over summer', *Guardian*, 30 October 2020.

33. S. O'Connor, 'Donald Trump golf resorts claimed at least £3.3 million in UK furlough support', *Financial Times*, 27 December 2021.

34. M. Sweney, 'Fraudsters likely to target furlough scheme', *Guardian*, 8 April 2020.

35. G. Standing, 'Why the UK's job retention scheme makes no sense', Alphaville (*Financial Times*), 17 April 2020; idem, 'UK's erupting fraud scandal confirms furlough was a nonsensical mistake', *Daily Telegraph*, 18 June 2020.

36. A. McCulloch, 'Third of employees asked to commit furlough fraud', *Personnel Today*, 18 June 2020.

37. HMRC, 'Tackling error and fraud in the Covid-19 support schemes', HMRC Policy Paper, 18 July 2022; for previous estimates, see R. Neate, 'Over £5.5bn of Covid support funds lost to fraud or error', *Guardian*, 4 November 2021.

38. M. McDougall, 'Closure of HMRC unit puts £5bn of taxpayers' money at risk, warn MPs', *Financial Times*, 7 March 2023.

39. D. Thomas and S. Morris, 'Scale of Covid loan fraud leaves UK struggling to reclaim billions lost', *Financial Times*, 7 April 2022.

40. House of Commons Committee of Public Accounts, *Bounce Back Loan Scheme: Follow-up*, Fiftieth Report of Session 2021–22, HC 951, 27 April 2022.

41. 'Ill-gotten gains', *The Economist*, 30 April 2022, p. 61.

42. Ibid.

43. S. Barnes and D. MacDonald, 'How businesses are surviving Covid-19: the resilience of firms and the role of government support', VoxEU, 16 July 2021.

44. V. Romei, 'Corporate insolvencies jump in England and Wales after withdrawal of Covid support', *Financial Times*, 2 August 2022.

45. S. Copland, 'Belittling the Canberra convoy protesters will just push ostracised people further into their bunkers', *Guardian*, 16 February 2022.

46. United States Census Bureau, 'The number of people primarily working from home tripled between 2019 and 2021', press release, 15 September 2022; source for UK figure is the Office for National Statistics, cited in 'The shape of things to come', *The Economist*, 9 May 2020, p. 21.

47. J. Berg, F. Bonnet and S. Soares, 'Working from home: estimating the worldwide potential', VoxEU, 11 May 2020.

48. J. M. Barrero, N. Bloom and S. J. Davis, 'Covid-19 is also a reallocation shock', Brookings Papers on Economic Activity, Summer 2020, pp. 329–71.

49. S. Nauta, 'How to ensure that the future of work is fair for all', *The Economist: The World Ahead 2022*, 8 November 2021.

50. O. Vargas Llarve, 'Covid-19 unleashed the potential for telework – how are workers coping?', Eurofound, 9 June 2020.

51. 'Homeworking and spending during the coronavirus (COVID-19) pandemic, Great Britain: April 2020 to January 2022', Office for National Statistics, 14 February 2022.

52. 'The spread of the shed', *The Economist*, 23 January 2021, p. 24.

53. J. M. Barrero, N. Bloom and S. J. Davis, 'Why working from home will stick?', NBER Working Paper 28731, National Bureau of Economic Research, Cambridge, MA, April 2021; see also D. Strauss, 'Nick Bloom: "It is becoming pretty clear now that hybrid working is here to stay"', *Financial Times*, 22 December 2021.

54. Quoted in 'Office politics', *The Economist*, 12 September 2020, p. 11.

55. J. Partridge, 'How the pandemic transformed the world of work in 2021', *Guardian*, 30 December 2021.

56. K. Makortoff, 'PWC's UK staff to split office and homeworking after Covid crisis', *Guardian*, 31 March 2021.

57. J. Partridge, 'How the pandemic transformed the world of work in 2021', *Guardian*, 30 December 2021.

58. G. Hammond, 'Office space shrinks by millions of square feet in England', *Financial Times*, 3 January 2022.

59. Quoted in 'The shape of things to come', *The Economist*.

60. C. G. Aksoy et al., 'Commute time savings when working from home', VoxEU, 24 January 2023.

61. Microsoft, 2021 *Work Trend Index: The Next Great Disruption is Hybrid Work – Are We Ready?*, 22 March 2021.

62. P. Clark, 'Don't make me go back to hard pants five days a week', *Financial Times*, 6 June 2021.

63. S. Taneja et al., 'Working from home is revolutionising the UK labour market', VoxEU, 15 March 2021.

64. C. Williams, 'The fight over the hybrid future of work', *The Economist: The World Ahead 2022*, 8 November 2021.

65. P. Adrjan et al., 'Teleworking is here to stay and may raise productivity if implemented appropriately', VoxEU, 10 February 2022.

66. S. Forbes et al., 'Flexible working and the future of work: managing employees since COVID-19', Equal Parenting Project, United Kingdom, University of Birmingham and University of York, 2022.

67. 'People are working longer hours during the pandemic', *The Economist*, 24 November 2020.

68. Cited in H. Osborne, 'Home workers putting in more hours since Covid, research shows', *Guardian*, 4 February 2021.

69. Cited in 'The great divide', *The Economist*, 27 March 2021, p. 51.

70. T. Weber and O. Vargas Llave, *Right to Disconnect: Exploring Company Practices* (Luxembourg: Eurofound, September 2021), p. 5.

71. Royal Society for Public Health, *Disparity Begins at Home: How Home Working is Impacting the Public's Health* (London: RSPH, February 2021), p. 12.

72. Emma Stewart, quoted in Osborne, 'Home workers putting in more hours since Covid, research shows'.

73. 'The missing pandemic boom', *The Economist*, 3 September 2022.

74. PwC, 'It's time to re-imagine where and how work will get done: PwC's US remote work survey', 12 January 2021.

75. S. Bevan, 'Remote working: why some people are less productive at home than others – new research', The Conversation, 30 April 2021.

76. Cited in C. Cavendish, 'It's time to admit that hybrid is not working', *Financial Times*, 7 January 2022.

77. C. Warzel and A. H. Petersen, *Out of Office: The big problem and bigger promise of working from home* (London: Knopf, 2021).

78. J. Conaghan, 'Why flexibility fails precarious workers', Frontiers of Socio-Legal Studies, 22 February 2023.

79. D. Strauss, 'UK employees to be given more flexible working rights', *Financial Times*, 5 December 2022.

80. Cited in R. Partington, 'Britons working at home spend more time on job in Covid crisis, ONS finds', *Guardian*, 19 April 2021.

81. Quoted in P. Yeung, '"If you switch off, people think you're lazy": demands grow for a right to disconnect from work', *Guardian*, 10 February 2021.

82. Cited in J. Dingle and B. Neiman, 'How many jobs can be done at home', VoxEU, 7 April 2020.

83. J. Dingel and B. Neiman, 'Making a good job of remote work', *Financial Times*, 7 February 2021.

84. Office for National Statistics, 'Characteristics of home workers, Great Britain: September 2022 to January 2023', 13 February 2023.

85. Forbes et al., 'Flexible working and the future of work'.

86. D. Lee, 'Apple's return-to-office order sparks anxiety among tech workers', *Financial Times*, 24 August 2022.

87. Cited in D. Britto et al., 'Anywhere jobs and the future of work', VoxEU, 10 July 2021.

88. See, for example, T. Makimoto and D. Manners, *Digital Nomad* (Hoboken, NJ: Wiley, 1997).

89. J. Curtis, 'PBS "Future of Work" series features the new "precariat" – people moving from gig to gig – digital nomads and other rapidly growing professional trends', No Censor, 22 August 2021.

90. Deloitte, *2022 Deloitte Travel Outlook: The Winding Path to Recovery* (2022).

91. 'Roam work', *The Economist*, 2 October 2021, p. 24.

92. A. Keen, *The Internet is Not the Answer* (London: Atlantic Books, 2015).

93. D. Cook, 'Digital nomads have rejected the office and now want to replace the nation state', The Conversation, 7 September 2022.

94. C. Middlehurst, 'Get ready for the new perk culture', *Financial Times*, 5 May 2021.

95. For assessments, see S. Norgate and C. Cooper (eds), *Flexible Work: Designing Our Healthier Future Lives* (London: Routledge, 2020); A. Auerbach, *Flex: Reinventing Work for a Smarter, Happier Life* (New York: HarperOne, 2021).

96. Quoted in E. Jacobs, 'Why our work trips are starting to look like holidays', *Financial Times*, 9 May 2022.

97. Cited in D. Strauss, 'Pandemic leaves 22 million people out of work in advanced economies, OECD finds', *Financial Times*, 7 July 2021.

98. Quoted in L. Frias, 'Mark Zuckerberg said Facebook employees who move out of Silicon Valley may face pay cuts', Business Insider, 22 May 2020.

99. 'English housing survey 2021 to 2022: headline report', Department for Levelling Up, Housing and Communities, 15 December 2022.

100. Joint ILO–Eurofound Report, *Working Anytime, Anywhere: The Effect on the World of Work* (Dublin and Geneva: Eurofound and International Labour Organization, 2017).

101. J. Partridge, 'Flexible working: a system set up for women to fail', *Guardian*, 20 November 2021.

102. R. Faroohar, 'Forget the "she-cession" – women will redefine the labour market', *Financial Times*, 19 September 2021.

103. G. Standing, 'Global feminization through flexible labor', *World Development* 17:7 (1989), pp. 1077–95; idem, 'Global feminization through flexible labor: a theme revisited', *World Development* 27:3 (1999), pp. 583–602.

104. Partington, 'Britons working at home spend more time on job in Covid crisis'.

105. A. Collins, 'Why you should call in sick more often than you think – even if working from home', The Conversation, 28 September 2020.

106. Partington, 'Britons working at home spend more time on job in Covid crisis'.

107. J. Cribb, I. Delestre and P. Johnson, 'Who is excluded from the government's Self-Employment Income Support Scheme and what could the government do about it?', Institute of Fiscal Studies Briefing Note, 27 January 2021.

108. Trades Union Congress, '647,000 festive workers get no statutory sick pay – TUC analysis', 6 December 2021.

109. H. Janssens, 'The relation between presenteeism and different types of future sickness absence', *Journal of Occupational Health*, 4 October 2013.

110. E. Jacobs, 'Arup's seven-day week: is this the future of work?', *Financial Times*, 10 October 2021.

111. D. Schofield, '"It's the biggest open secret out there": the double lives of white-collar workers with two jobs', *Guardian*, 16 November 2021.

112. R. Mason et al., 'Geoffrey Cox accrued at least £6m from second job while a parliamentarian', *Guardian*, 10 November 2021.

113. Quoted in Schofield, '"It's the biggest open secret out there"'.

114. M. Murphy, 'Working from home? You are probably being spied on by your boss', *Telegraph*, 30 March 2020.

115. A. Gilbert and A. Thomas, 'The Amazonian Era: how algorithmic systems are eroding good work', Institute for the Future of Work, 2021.

116. 'One-third of firms deploying home-working surveillance', Consultancy. UK, 16 May 2022.

117. Quoted in Corbyn, '"Bossware is coming for almost every worker"'.

118. 'Webcam monitoring', RemoteDesk.com (accessed 22 March 2023).

119. J. R. Carlson et al., 'Applying the job demands resources model to understand technology as a predictor of turnover intentions', *Computers in Human Behavior* 77 (December 2017), pp. 317–25.

120. Trades Union Congress, 'I'll be watching you: a report on workplace monitoring', 17 August 2018.

121. *The New Frontier: Artificial Intelligence at Work*, a final report produced by the All-Party Parliamentary Group on the Future of Work, Institute for the Future of Work, November 2021.

122. Quoted in P. Walker, 'Call centre staff to be monitored via webcam for home-working "infractions"', *Guardian*, 26 March 2021.

123. P. Clark, 'The looming legal minefield of working from home', *Financial Times*, 27 September 2020.

124. 'The right kind of recovery', *The Economist*, 10 October 2020, p. 14.

125. Quoted in S. O'Connor, 'Benefit cuts focus debate on shape of post-Covid safety net', *Financial Times*, 13 July 2021.

126. 'Flattened', *The Economist*, 9 October 2021, p. 29.

127. S. O'Connor, 'UK plan shows how not to deal with labour shortages', *Financial Times*, 31 January 2022.

128. Royal Society of Arts, *Key Workers in the Pandemic: Security Traps Among Britain's Essential Workers* (London: RSA, 2021).

129. U. Aminjonov, O. Bargain and T. Bernard, 'Gimme shelter: social distancing and income support in times of pandemic', Bordeaux Economics Working Papers 2021-12, Bordeaux School of Economics, 2021.

130. R. Tribe, 'Giving people cash rather than food parcels would empower them', *Guardian*, 22 November 2021.

131. 'Backlog Britain: How public sector delays spiralled to record levels', *Financial Times*, 28 November 2022.

132. O'Connor, 'UK plan shows how not to deal with labour shortages'.

133. National Audit Office, *Benefit Sanctions*, HC 628, Session 2016–17, House of Commons, 30 November 2016.

134. G. J. van den Berg and J. Vikström, 'Monitoring job offer decisions, punishments, exit to work, and job quality', *Scandinavian Journal of Economics* 116:2 (April 2014), pp. 284–334.

135. J. Ingold, 'Employers' perspectives on benefit conditionality in the UK and Denmark', *Social Policy Administration* 54:2 (March 2020), pp. 236–49.

136. J. Pring, 'DWP is forcing distressed claimants to attend weekly meetings, says whistleblower', Disability News Service, 10 March 2022.

137. P. Butler, 'Hunt's disability plans put 1 million people at risk of losing £350 a month, IFS says', *Guardian*, 15 March 2023.

138. F. Ryan, 'Good riddance to the work capability assessment, the cruellest social policy of modern times', *Guardian*, 22 March 2023.

139. C. Gray et al., 'Evidence on the net effects of work requirements in safety net programmes', VoxEU, 4 October 2021.

140. A. M. Larson et al., 'Sanctions and education outcomes for children in TANF [Temporary Assistance for Needy Families] families', *Child and Youth Services* 32:3 (2011), pp. 180–99.

141. D. Strauss, 'End of Covid job schemes still leaves US, EU and UK short of workers', *Financial Times*, 27 September 2021.

142. 'Blue-collar burnout', *The Economist*, 8 January 2022, pp. 51–2.

143. Microsoft, 2021 *Work Trend Index: The Next Great Disruption is Hybrid Work*.

144. EY Global, 'More than half of employees globally would quit their jobs if not provided post-pandemic flexibility, EY survey finds', press release, 12 May 2021.

145. M. Brignall, '"The Great Resignation": almost one in four UK workers planning job change', *Guardian*, 1 November 2021.

146. I. Williamson, 'The great resignation is a trend that began before the pandemic – and bosses need to get used to it', The Conversation, 12 November 2021.

147. T. N. Rogers, 'The switching generation: US workers quit jobs in record numbers', *Financial Times*, 23 November 2021.

148. C. Carrillo-Tudela et al., 'The truth about the "great resignation" – who changed jobs, where they went and why', The Conversation, 28 March 2022.

149. S. O'Connor, 'Covid retirees show work-from-home revolution has not benefited everyone', *Financial Times*, 9 November 2021.

150. D. Strauss and D. Mosolova, 'UK labour shortages are "shape of things to come", lords warn', *Financial Times*, 19 December 2022.

151. R. Joyce, S. Ray-Chaudhuri and T. Waters, 'The number of new disability benefit claimants has doubled in a year', Institute for Fiscal Studies, London, 7 December 2022.

152. Cited in 'Where have all the workers gone', *The Economist*, 28 January 2023, p. 81.

153. Quoted in D. Strauss, 'Where did all the workers go?', *Financial Times*, 22 November 2021.

154. 'Get up and go', *The Economist*, 23 April 2022, p. 69.

155. Statistics here and in the previous paragraph are cited in 'America's entrepreneurial boom continued apace in 2021', *The Economist*, 13 January 2022.

156. S. O'Connor, 'Where have all the self-employed gone?', *Financial Times*, 9 August 2022.

157. L. Cernik, '"I've always thrown myself into work – now it keeps me alive": the over-65s forced to join the "great unretirement"', *Guardian*, 14 September 2022.

158. J. Hobsbawm, *The Nowhere Office: Reinventing Work and the Workplace of the Future* (London: Public Affairs, 2022).

159. T. Bell, 'Forget all you've heard about working life in modern Britain. It's wrong', *Observer*, 20 February 2022.

160. J. Faberman et al., 'Has the willingness to work fallen during the Covid pandemic?', Working Paper 29784, National Bureau of Economic Research, Cambridge, MA, February 2022.

161. T. N. Rogers, 'Reddit "antiwork" forum booms as millions of Americans quit jobs', *Financial Times*, 9 January 2022.

162. D. Price, *Laziness Does Not Exist: A Defense of the Exhausted, Exploited and Overworked* (New York: Atria Books, 2021).

163. S. Kale, 'Time millionaires: meet the people pursuing the pleasure of leisure', *Guardian*, 12 October 2021.

164. J. Odell, *How To Do Nothing: Resisting the Attention Economy* (Brooklyn, NY: Melville House Publishing, 2019).

CHAPTER 7: JOB OPTIONS: LABOURIST ENDGAMES

1. G. Hinsliff, 'The next wave of coronavirus disruption? Automation', *Guardian*, 30 April 2020.

2. National Audit Office, *Employment Support: The Kickstart Scheme*, HC 801, House of Commons, Session 2021–22, 26 November 2021.

3. Department for Work and Pensions, *Universal Credit at Work*, DWP, February 2015.

4. House of Lords Select Committee on Economic Affairs and House of Commons Select Committee on Work and Pensions, Corrected Oral Evidence: Reports: *Universal Credit Isn't Working: Proposals for Reform* and *Universal Credit: The Wait for the First Payment*, 9 March 2021.

5. R. Skidelsky, 'Britain's benefit madness', Project Syndicate, 16 April 2021.

6. P. Gregg and R. Layard, 'A job guarantee', London School of Economics, mimeo, 2009.

7. S. McElwee, C. McAuliffe and J. Green, 'Why democrats should embrace a federal jobs guarantee', *The Nation*, 20 March 2018.

8. R. Skidelsky and S. Gasperin, 'Reinstating fiscal policy for normal times: public investment and public jobs programmes', *PSL Quarterly Review* 74:296 (March 2021), pp. 3–24, at p. 16 (italics in the original).

9. Ibid.

10. R. Skidelsky and R. Kay, *How to Achieve Shorter Working Hours* (London: Progressive Economy Forum, 2019), p. 11.

11. E. Loomis, 'The case for a federal jobs guarantee', *New York Times*, 25 April 2018.

12. Quoted in A. Peters, 'What is a job guarantee – and how could it help us recover from the coronavirus?', *Fast Company*, 7 May 2020.

13. G. Standing, *Unemployment and Labour Market Flexibility: Sweden* (Geneva: International Labour Organization, 1988).

14. Skidelsky and Gasperin, 'Reinstating fiscal policy for normal times', p. 16.

15. P. Tcherneva, *The Case for a Job Guarantee* (Cambridge: Polity Press, 2020).

16. 'The *Guardian* view on a job guarantee: a policy whose time has come', *Guardian*, 3 May 2018.

17. Quoted in S. O'Connor, 'Not all green jobs are safe and clean', *Financial Times*, 26 October 2021.

18. London Plus, *London Good Work Commission Investigation into Poverty and Bad Work: Interim Findings* (London: London Plus, 2019), p. 7.

19. N. Cominetti et al., *Low Pay Britain 2022: Low Pay and Insecurity in the UK Labour Market* (London: Resolution Foundation and Centre for Economic Performance, London School of Economics, 2022), pp. 21, 8, 9.

20. K. Henderson, *The Crisis of Low Wages in the US: Who Makes Less than $15 an Hour in 2022* (Washington, DC: Oxfam America, 2022).

21. Skidelsky and Kay, *How to Achieve Shorter Working Hours*, p. 47.

22. G. Abebe et al., 'Urban public works in spatial equilibrium: experimental evidence from Ethiopia', CEPR Discussion Paper DP16691, Centre for Economic Policy Research, November 2021. Albeit in a developing country, this showed that private labour supply decreased and private-sector wages rose by over 18 per cent.

23. Skidelsky and Gasperin, 'Reinstating fiscal policy for normal times', p. 17.

24. Skidelsky and Kay, *How to Achieve Shorter Working Hours*, p. 45.

25. O. Kangas et al., *Experimenting with Unconditional Basic Income* (Cheltenham: Edward Elgar, 2021).

26. H. P. Minsky, *Ending Poverty: Jobs not Welfare* (New York: Levy Economics Institute, 2013).

27. G. Standing, *A Precariat Charter*.

28. D. Thomas and E. Jacobs, 'Most companies in UK four-day week trial to continue with flexible working', *Financial Times*, 21 February 2023.

29. S. Kuper, 'A four-day work week would help save the planet', *Financial Times*, 28 October 2021.

30. Autonomy, *The Shorter Working Week: A Radical and Pragmatic Proposal* (London: Autonomy, 2019).

31. P. Inman and J. Jolly, 'Productivity woes? Why giving staff an extra day off can be the answer', *Observer*, 17 November 2018; 'Do more with less: New Zealand firm's four-day week', Reuters, 5 November 2019.

32. Thomas and Jacobs, 'Most companies in UK four-day week trial to continue with flexible working'.

33. H. Delaney and C. Casey, 'The promise of a four-day week? A critical appraisal of a management-led initiative', *Employer Relations* 44:1 (2022), pp. 176–90.

34. C. Harrington, 'The 4-day week is flawed. Workers still want it', *Wired*, 3 February 2022.

35. E. Russell, C. Murphy and E. Terry, 'What leaders need to know before trying a 4-day work week', *Harvard Business Review*, 27 May 2022.

36. D. A. Spencer, 'A four-day working week: its role in a politics of work', *Political Quarterly* 93:3 (July–September 2022), pp. 401–7.

37. Thomas and Jacobs, 'Most companies in UK four-day week trial to continue with flexible working'.

38. Skidelsky and Kay, *How to Achieve Shorter Working Hours*, p. 10.

39. E. Jacobs, 'The 4-day week: does it actually work', *Financial Times*, 3 December 2022.

40. TUC, *A Future That Works for Working People* (London: Trades Union Congress, 2018).

41. D. Méda, 'The French experience', in A. Coote and J. Franklin (eds), *Time on Our Side: Why We All Need a Shorter Working Week* (London: New Economics Foundation, 2013); Skidelsky and Kay, *How to Achieve Shorter Working Hours*, pp. 31–4.

42. C. Foss, 'Stalin's topsy-turvy work week', *History Today* 54:9 (September 2004), pp. 46–7.

43. These calculations are taken from C. Young and C. Lim, 'Time as a network good: evidence from unemployment and the standard workweek', *Sociological Science* 1 (2014), pp. 10–27.

44. Cited in 'Arguing about laziness', *The Economist*, 11 February 2023, p. 23.

45. TUC, *A Future That Works for Working People*.

46. M. Busby, 'UK's growing army of night workers "need rest centres" for sanctuary', *Observer*, 5 December 2021.

47. 'Why governments are paying people to go on holiday', *The Economist*, 27 July 2020.

48. I. Ferrares et al., 'Life after Covid-19: decommodify work, democratise the workplace', *The Wire*, 15 May 2020. The manifesto was published in media across the world.

49. D. Graeber, *Bullshit Jobs: A Theory* (London: Penguin, 2019).

50. Quoted in A. L. Morton, 'Introduction', in William Morris, *Three Works by William Morris* (London: Lawrence & Wishart, 1977), p. 25.

CHAPTER 8: THE EMANCIPATION OF TIME

1. M. Wolf, *The Crisis of Democratic Capitalism* (London: Allen Lane, 2023).

2. B. Dawson, 'Many in the UK face a grim choice this winter between eating and heating as a cost-of-living crisis grips the nation', *Business Insider*, 9 October 2022.

3. J. Bivens, 'Corporate profits have contributed disproportionately to inflation', Working Economics Blog, Economic Policy Institute, April 2022.

4. H. Stewart, 'Work-life balance as important as pay, says university staff union', *Guardian*, 10 February 2023.

5. K. Schofield, 'Rishi Sunak has earned more than £4.7 million in the last three years', HuffPost, 22 March 2023.

6. R. E. Lucas Jr, 'The Industrial Revolution: past and future', *The Region* (2003 Annual Report of the Federal Reserve Bank of Minneapolis), pp. 5–20.

7. 'Fleshing out the olive', *The Economist*, 28 August 2021, p. 60.

8. 'Establishing the cause of death', *The Economist*, 31 July 2021, p. 55.

9. 'Nasty, British and short', *The Economist*, 11 March 2023, p. 25.

10. Office for National Statistics, 'Prevalence of ongoing symptoms following coronavirus (COVID-19) infection in the UK', 2 February 2023.

11. British Medical Association, 'NHS backlog data analysis', BMA, March 2023.

12. E. Mahase, 'Government must get a "firmer grip" on mental health crisis, says watchdog', *BMJ* 380 (9 February 2023), p. 324.

13. R. G. Tedeshi and L. G. Calhoun, *Posttraumatic Growth: Conceptual Foundation and Empirical Evidence* (Philadelphia, PA: Lawrence Erlbaum Associates, 2004).

14. It was reckoned that consumers gained only 70 per cent of the benefit, the rest going to energy companies incentivized to raise prices and thus increase profits. 'When duty falls', *The Economist*, 26 March 2022, pp. 9–10.

15. R. Partington, 'UK households suffer biggest fall in available cash in eight years', *Guardian*, 12 January 2022.

16. Beveridge, *Social Insurance and Allied Services*, p. 6.

17. S. Lewandowsky, K. Facer and U. K. H. Ecker, 'Losses, hopes, and expectations for sustainable futures after Covid', *Humanities and Social Sciences Communications* 8, Article 296 (25 November 2021).

18. G. Tett, 'Don't deride the Davos prophets of doom', *Financial Times*, 13 January 2022.

19. Labour, '5 missions for a better Britain: a "mission-driven" government to end "sticking plaster" politics', 5 February 2023.

20. P. Kellner, 'Can a progressive alliance ever win in the UK?', *Prospect*, 4 January 2022.

21. B. Disraeli, 'Speech to the Conservatives of Manchester (3 April 1872)', quoted in T. E. Kebbel (ed.), *Selected Speeches of the Late Right Honourable the Earl of Beaconsfield*, Vol. 2 (London: Longmans, Green & Co., 1882), p. 516.

22. A. Haldane, 'How to remake Britain: why we need community capitalism', *New Statesman*, 17 March 2021.

23. See G. Standing, *The Corruption of Capitalism: Why Rentiers Thrive and Work Does Not Pay*, 3rd edn (London: Biteback, 2021), Chapter 4; L. Boone et al., *Debt: The Eye of the Storm: The 24th Geneva Report on the World Economy* (Geneva: International Centre for Monetary and Banking Studies; and London: the Centre for Economic Policy Research, 2022). The latter was overly sanguine about household debt.

24. L. Bauluz, F. Novokmet and M. Schularick, 'The anatomy of the global saving glut', CEPR Discussion Paper 17215, Centre for Economic Policy Research, London, April 2022.

25. V. Romei, 'UK credit card debt hits record high as inflation and cost of living bite', *Financial Times*, 29 March 2022.

26. C. Giles, 'Brexit and the economy: the hit has been "substantially negative"', *Financial Times*, 30 November 2022.

27. D. Bailey and P. Tomlinson, 'April will be cruel to UK households, but the economy's problems are much longer-term', The Conversation, 31 March 2022; Giles, 'Brexit and the economy'.

28. 'A mean feat', *The Economist*, 9 January 2016.

29. J. Kay and M. King, *Radical Uncertainty: Decision-Making beyond the Numbers* (New York: W.W. Norton, 2020).

30. L. Guiso et al., 'The financial drivers of populism in Europe', CEPR Discussion Paper DP17332, Centre for Economic Policy Research, London, May 2022.

31. 'The new normal is already here. Get used to it', *The Economist*, 18 December 2021.

32. Taleb, *Antifragile*, p. 106.

33. E. J. Mishan, *The Costs of Economic Growth* (London: Pelican, 1967).

34. J. Stiglitz, A. Sen and J.-P. Fitoussi, *Mis-Measuring Our Lives: Why GDP Doesn't Add Up* (New York and London: New Press, 2010).

35. J. Runge and N. Hudson-Sharp, 'Public understanding of economics and economic statistics', ESCoE Occasional Paper 03, Economic Statistics Centre of Excellence, London, November 2020.

36. W. Dahlgreen, '37% of British workers think their jobs are meaningless', YouGov, 12 August 2015.

37. D. Carrington, 'McKinsey: Fundamental transformation of global economy needed for net zero', *Guardian*, 25 January 2022.

38. P. Allin, D. Coyle and T. Jackson, 'Beyond GDP: changing how we measure progress is key to tackling a world in crisis', The Conversation, 18 August 2022.

39. H. Daly and J. Cobb, *For the Common Good: Redirecting the Economy toward Community, the Environment and a Sustainable Future* (Boston: Beacon Press, 1989).

40. R. Floud, *An Economic History of the English Garden* (London: Penguin, 2020), p. 19.

41. B. Bridgman et al., 'Accounting for household production in the national accounts 1965–2010', *Survey of Current Business* 92 (May 2012), pp. 23–36.

42. Office for National Statistics, *Household Satellite Account (Experimental) Methodology* (London: HMSO, 2002).

43. Office for National Statistics, 'Changes in the value and division of unpaid care work in the UK: 2000 to 2015', 10 November 2016.

44. D. Pilling, *The Growth Delusion: The Wealth and Well-Being of Nations* (London: Bloomsbury, 2016), p. 71.

45. J. P. Smith, '"Lost milk?": counting the economic value of breast milk in Gross Domestic Product', *Journal of Human Lactation* 29:4 (November 2013), pp. 537–46. A more recent study showed the economic cost of not breastfeeding but ignored the value of women's time in the process. D. D. Walters, L. T. H. Phan and R. Mathisen, 'The cost of not breastfeeding: global results from a new tool', *Health Policy and Planning* 34:6 (July 2019), pp. 407–17.

46. S. Radzyminski and L. C. Callister, 'Health professionals' attitudes and beliefs about breastfeeding', *Journal of Perinatal Education* 24:2 (2015), pp. 102–9; Unicef UK, 'Preventing disease and saving resources: the potential contribution of increasing breastfeeding rates in the UK', October 2012.

47. '30+ maternity leave statistics in 2022', myshortlister.com, 2022.

48. C. Coffey et al., *Time to Care: Unpaid and Underpaid Care Work and the Global Inequality Crisis* (Oxford: Oxfam International, January 2020).

49. Independent Care Review Scotland, *The Promise*, 2020; J. MacAlister, *The Independent Care Review of Children's Social Care: Final Report*, May 2022.

50. Office for National Statistics, 'Care homes and estimating the self-funding population, England: 2021 to 2022', 30 May 2022.

51. Age UK, '1.2m older people don't get the social care they need', 17 November 2016.

52. Among them, see Y. Varoufakis, *Another Now: Dispatches from an Alternative Present* (London: Bodley Head, 2020), pp. 54–6; P. Barnes, *OURS: The Case for Universal Property* (London: Wiley, 2021); Standing, *Plunder of the Commons*.

53. See Standing, *The Blue Commons*, pp. 377–85.

54. Standing, *Plunder of the Commons*.

55. I. Ungoed-Thomas, 'Superyacht sales surge prompts fresh calls for curbs on their emissions', *Guardian*, 29 January 2022.

56. 'The meaning of green', *The Economist*, 8 January 2022, p. 10.

57. For more on carbon levies, see F. Caselli, A. Ludwig and R. van der Ploeg (eds), *No Brainers and Low-Hanging Fruit in National Climate Policy* (London: CEPR Press, 2021).

58. S. Laville, 'UK meat tax and frequent-flyer levy proposals briefly published then deleted', *Guardian*, 20 October 2021.

59. M. Paoli and R. van der Ploeg, 'Recycling revenue to improve political feasibility of carbon pricing in the UK', VoxEU, 4 October 2021.

60. *Taxe sur le CO2* (Bern: Office fédéral de l'environnement, Confédération suisse, 2020).

61. R. Amery, 'Nicola Sturgeon to review payments to Perthshire estate owned by Kremlin associate', The Courier, 3 March 2022.

62. G. Hammond, 'UK homeowners secure £800bn windfall with house price rise', *Financial Times*, 30 January 2022.

63. 'China has a celebrated history of policy experiments', *The Economist*, 9 April 2022.

64. The points in this section are developed at length elsewhere. See G. Standing, *Basic Income: And How We Can Make It Happen* (London: Pelican, 2017).

65. R. Cialdini, *Influence: The Psychology of Persuasion* (New York: William Morrow, 1984).

66. T. Shepherd, 'Women three times more likely to be abused if in pandemic-induced financial stress', *Guardian*, 30 January 2022.

67. Quoted in C. Salter, 'Failure doesn't suck', *Fast Company*, 1 May 2007.

68. Quoted in C. Clifford, 'Mark Zuckerberg: success comes from "the freedom to fail," so billionaires like me should pay you to do that', CNBC, 25 May 2017.

69. D. Matthews, 'Study: a universal basic income would grow the economy', Vox, 30 August 2017.

70. T. Visram, 'What happened when people in this upstate New York town started getting monthly $500 checks', *Fast Company*, 17 December 2021.

71. D. Baker et al., *Preliminary Analysis: SEED's First Year* (Stockton Economic Empowerment Demonstration, 2021).

72. 'Results of the YouGov poll about UBI', WeMove Europe, December 2021.

73. M. Linek, 'Time use with basic income: evidence from a large-scale survey experiment', Hertie School Working Paper, Berlin, 29 September 2020.

74. O. Kangas et al. (eds), *Experimenting with Unconditional Basic Income: Lessons from the Finnish BI Experiment 2017–2018* (Cheltenham: Edward Elgar, 2021).

75. K. Murray, 'Those of us who grew up in care will know how dire the need is for extra financial support', *Big Issue*, 18 February 2022.

76. Taleb, *Skin in the Game*, p. 12.

77. Ibid., p. 19.

78. T. Wilson et al., *Working for the Future: Launch Report for the Commission on the Future of Employment Support* (London: Institute for Employment Studies, 2022).

79. A. Beckett, 'Post-work: the radical idea of a world without jobs', *Guardian*, 19 January 2018.

80. L. Murphy, 'Leaving lockdown: young people's employment in 2021', Resolution Foundation, London, 31 January 2022.

81. See, for instance, M. Ford, *Rule of the Robots: How Artificial Intelligence Will Transform Everything* (New York: Basic Books, 2021); M. Ford, *Rise of the Robots: Technology and the Threat of a Jobless Future* (New York: Basic Books, 2015).

82. N. Srnicek and A. Williams, *Inventing the Future: Postcapitalism and a World without Work* (London: Verso, 2015), p. 12.

83. G. Winstanley, 'A declaration from the poor oppressed people of England' (1649).

84. R. Smithers, 'Interest in allotments soars in England during coronavirus pandemic', *Guardian*, 10 August 2021.

85. National Allotment Society, 'National Allotments Week 2020, 10 to 16 August', 31 July 2020.

86. D. L. Evans et al., 'Ecosystem service delivery by urban agriculture and green infrastructure – a systematic review', *Ecosystem Services* 54 (April 2022).

87. J. Edmondson and S. Caton, 'Urban health, wellbeing and food supplies are all under threat: growing more food in cities could change that', The Conversation, 18 January 2022.

88. Quoted in E. V. Bramley, 'It's official: allotments are good for you – and for your mental health', *Observer*, 8 November 2020.

89. 'The Green Apple', *The Economist*, 10 April 2021, p. 34; 'A shovel-ready project', *The Economist*, 20 June 2020, p. 36.

90. J. Ruskin, *Fors Clavigera*, Vol. 1, Letter 5, in E. T. Cook and K. Wedderburn (eds), *The Works of John Ruskin*, Vol. 27 (London: George Allen, 1905–12), p. 96.

91. Mind, 'Over 7 million have taken up gardening since the pandemic: new research shows spending more time in nature has boosted nation's wellbeing', 23 May 2022.

92. A. Turns, '"Revolutionary in a quiet way": The rise of community gardens in the UK', *Guardian*, 21 September 2021.

93. Quoted in ibid.

94. M. Busby, 'How coronavirus has led to a UK boom in community food growing', *Guardian*, 24 August 2020.

95. Turns, '"Revolutionary in a quiet way"'.

96. Quoted in M. France, 'The wonder of the community garden', *Prospect*, 11 August 2021.

97. Edmonson and Caton, 'Urban health, wellbeing and food supplies are all under threat'.

98. Quoted in P. Barkham, 'How Camley Street brought nature to the heart of the capital', *Observer*, 8 August 2021.

99. Quoted in ibid.

100. N. Crisp, *Health is Made at Home, Hospitals are for Repairs: Building a Healthy and Health-Creating Society* (London: Salus, 2021).

101. D. F. Shanahan et al., 'Health benefits from nature experiences depend on dose', *Scientific Reports* 6, Article 28551 (June 2016).

102. M. P. White et al., 'Spending at least 120 minutes a week in nature is associated with good health and wellbeing', *Scientific Reports* 9, Article 7730 (June 2019).

103. D. Carrington, 'Woodland walks save UK £185m a year in mental health costs, report finds', *Guardian*, 4 December 2021.

104. Wildfowl and Wetland Trust, *Creating Urban Wetlands for Wellbeing: A Route Map* (Slimbridge, UK: WWT, 2022).

105. Mental Health Foundation, 'A new project has been announced today to improve people's mental health through connecting to "watery" nature', 12 May 2021.

106. A. Lowrey, 'Stockton's basic income experiment pays off', *The Atlantic*, 3 March 2021.

107. 'Permaculture ethics', at https://permacultureprinciples.com/ethics/.

108. Quoted in M. Martinez, 'How permaculture can build resilience and meet basic needs during a pandemic', *Waging Nonviolence*, 4 May 2020.

109. Ibid.

110. Quoted in Busby, 'How coronavirus has led to a UK boom in community food growing'.

111. G. Monbiot, 'The gift we should give to the living world? Time and lots of it', *Guardian*, 8 August 2021.

112. C. J. Schuler, 'What happened to London's lost woods?', *Financial Times*, 15 January 2022.

113. P. Greenfield and P. Weston, '"It's good for the soul": The mini rewilders restoring UK woodland', *Guardian*, 23 May 2020.

114. R. Orange, 'Grow your own mussels: the new phenomenon of sea allotments', *Guardian*, 25 June 2022.

115. Pacific Sea Garden Collective, 'Sea gardens across the Pacific: reawakening ancestral mariculture innovations', 2022.

116. 'One woman's fashion', *The Economist*, 18 December 2021, p. 43.

117. Ibid.

118. 'About Freecycle', freecycle.org (accessed 26 March 2023).

119. 'The growing environmental risks of e-waste', Geneva Environment Network, 14 October 2022.

120. D. Grayson, *Manifesto for a People's Media: Creating a Media Commons* (London: Media Reform Coalition, 2021); see also A. Toomer-McAlpine, 'Co-ops and the commons: imagining a "People's Media"', *Coop News*, 31 January 2022.

121. C. Honoré, *In Praise of Slow: How the Worldwide Movement is Challenging the Cult of Speed* (Toronto: Vintage Canada, 2004).

122. Suzman, *Work*, pp. 156–7.

123. S. Davala et al., *Basic Income: A Transformative Policy for India* (London and New Delhi: Bloomsbury, 2015).

124. J. Haidt, 'Why the past 10 years of American life have been uniquely stupid', *The Atlantic*, 11 April 2022.

125. Quoted in ibid.

126. R. DiResta, 'The supply of disinformation will soon be infinite', *The Atlantic*, 20 September 2020.

127. Ibid.

128. N. Frohlich and J. A. Oppenheimer, *Choosing Justice: An Experimental Approach to Ethical Theory* (Berkeley, CA: University of California Press, 1992).

129. J. Burke, 'Languishing: what to do if you're feeling restless, apathetic or empty', The Conversation, 17 January 2022.

130. I. Kavedzija, 'Wellbeing: how living well together works for the common good', The Conversation, 16 February 2022.

131. Taleb, *Skin in the Game*, p. 61.

POSTSCRIPT

1. K. Marx, 'Theories of productive and unproductive labour', in idem, *Theories of Surplus-Value* (Moscow: Foreign Languages Publishing House, 1956), p. 389.

Index

F

M ————————————————

U